THE LOCATION OF ECONOMIC ACTIVITY
discusses the economics of industry location,
land utilization, urban structure, and regional
development. Primarily, Dr. Hoover's approach
is analytical rather than descriptive, devotes
particular attention to problems of locational
change and adjustment, and emphasizes the
objectives, methods, and implications of
policies of public control.

Dr. Edgar M. Hoover has served with the
National Resources Planning Board, the
Office of Price Administration, the War
Production Board, the Office of Strategic
Services. Much of his teaching and gov-
ernment work has been concerned with
location problems. He has also served as
Senior Staff Economist on the Council of
Economic Advisors.

The Location of Economic Activity

Edgar M. Hoover

McGRAW-HILL BOOK COMPANY, INC.
New York   Toronto   London

Preface

THIS BOOK is a lineal descendant of a manuscript completed at the end of 1941 and published in Spanish in 1943.[1] Other commitments during the war period delayed preparation of an English version. In the interim the author has had the benefit of more mature reflection, some nonacademic experience, and an opportunity to inflict various drafts of the manuscript on students and professional associates. The result is a thoroughgoing revision, with nearly all new illustrative material.

The author has drawn much enlightenment and inspiration from the work of the late August Lösch, which will soon become available in English translation.[2]

With particular gratitude the author wishes to acknowledge three major contributions. His wife's unfailing encouragement and patience have been indispensable. His former students in the economics of location at the University of Michigan will recognize here many ideas that they helped to form and clarify. His former colleagues in the interdepartmental research seminar in metropolitan community problems at the University of Michigan, especially Prof. Amos Hawley of the Department of Sociology, have broadened his views and directed his attention to much relevant material in less familiar fields.

Others who have been helpful at various stages include Prof. Richard Hartshorne of the Department of Geography, University of Wisconsin; Prof. Kenneth May of the Department of Mathematics, Carleton College; Marion Hayes of the U. S. Department of Commerce; Dr. Glenn E. McLaughlin of the National Security Resources Board; Dr. Walter Isard of Massachusetts Institute of Technology; Michael Daly of Foote Cone & Belding, New York

---

[1] "Economía geográfica," Fondo de Cultura Económica, Mexico City, 1943.

[2] August Lösch, "Die räumliche Ordnung der Wirtschaft," Gustav Fischer Verlag, Jena, 1940 (2d ed., 1944). The English translation mentioned was published in 1954 by the Yale University Press under the title "The Economics of Location." In the present reprint, page references to Lösch's book have been revised so as to apply to the English translation.

v

City; Prof. A. P. Usher of the Department of Economics, Harvard University; Profs. C. F. Remer, Z. C. Dickinson, Daniel Suits of the Department of Economics, University of Michigan; and Grace Potter, Associate Editor of Scholarly Publications of the University of Michigan Press. The author is also grateful to the many authors and publishers who have generously given permission for quotations and reproduction of maps.

This book was written prior to the author's connection with the President's Council of Economic Advisers and is not to be taken as reflecting in any way the views of that agency.

EDGAR M. HOOVER

WASHINGTON, D. C.
May, 1948

Contents

PART FOUR. LOCATIONAL OBJECTIVES AND PUBLIC POLICY

Editor's Introduction

FOR YEARS many teachers of economics and other professional economists have felt the need of a series of books on economic subjects that is not filled by the usual textbook or by the highly technical treatise.

This present series, published under the general title "The Economics Handbook Series," was planned with these needs in mind. Designed first of all for students, the volumes are useful in the ever-growing field of adult education and also are of interest to the informed general reader.

The volumes are not long—they give the essentials of the subject matter within the limits of a few hundred pages; they present a distillate of accepted theory and practice, without the detailed approach of the technical treatise. Each volume is a unit, standing on its own.

The authors are scholars, each writing on an economic subject of which he is an authority. In this series the author's first task was not to make important contributions to knowledge—although many of them do—but so to present his subject matter that his work as a scholar will carry its maximum influence outside as well as inside the classroom. The time has come to redress the balance between the energies spent on the creation of new ideas and on their dissemination. Economic ideas are unproductive if they do not spread beyond the world of scholars. Popularizers without technical competence, unqualified textbook writers, and sometimes even charlatans control too large a part of the market for economic ideas.

In the classroom the Economics Handbook Series will serve, it is hoped, for brief surveys in one-semester courses, as supplementary reading in introductory courses and in other courses to which the subject is related.

In this volume Professor Hoover writes on "The Location of Economic Activity." In it he presents the essential problems of location and in so doing makes important contributions. This book is indispensable in courses dealing with location. Teachers of courses in economic theory, economic history, international trade, market organization, agriculture, and planning will also find this volume most useful, since it deals with problems of significance for each of these fields. Businessmen interested in the problem of location, as most of them are, would do well to examine this book.

Professor Hoover is well qualified to write this volume. After receiving his A.B. at Harvard with highest honors, he taught at Harvard and received a Ph.D. there. For the last eleven years, with interruptions for government service and active service in the Navy, Professor Hoover has been at the University of Michigan. Recently he resigned his post as Professor of Economics at the latter institution to join the staff of the Council of Economic Advisers in Washington. At various times, he has served with the National Resources Planning Board, the Office of Price Administration, the War Production Board, and the Office of Strategic Services. Much of his teaching and government work was concerned with location problems. Among his books are the following: "Location Theory and the Shoe and Leather Industries," "The Economic Effects of the St. Lawrence Power Project" (U. S. Department of Commerce), "Industrial Location and National Resources" (with others, for the National Resources Planning Board), "Economía geográfica." In addition, he has written numerous articles dealing with the range of problems treated in this book.

His present volume organizes a body of principles relating to the spatial relations of economic activities. It develops ideas on the selection of locations for private and public facilities, land utilization, metropolitan and regional planning, and programs of industrial development and stabilization at local, state, regional, and national levels.

Attention is focused first on factors determining the relative advantages of different types of location from the standpoint of the individual producing enterprise. These advantages are discussed under two heads: access to suppliers of and to markets for the product, and production cost. Features of transport- and communication-rate structures are explained and discussed as they bear on locational choice and on the formation of patterns of market areas and supply areas in various types of production. In connection with production cost, special attention is given to the economies and dis-economies of concentration, the causes and significance of labor-cost differentials, and differentials in the cost of land.

The role of accessibility and of other features of urban sites is given special attention in a section explaining the principal characteristics of the internal geography of cities.

In the second part of the book a dynamic approach is used, analyzing the causes of locational change, the ways in which such change occurs, and the stresses and the maladjustments that may accompany it. A theory of the process of regional economic development and industrialization is set forth. The locational effects of technological changes, especially improvements in transportation and the use of energy, are evaluated. Factual material in this part includes a statement of the principal over-all trends of industrial and population shift in the United States and identification of some leading "problem areas."

The third part of the book advances further toward realism by taking account of the effects of political boundaries as barriers to trade, hindrances to the mobility of labor and capital, and factors complicating the coordinated administration and development of natural economic areas such as river basins.

The fourth and last part of the book examines the aims and methods of public locational policy. Policies appropriate to economic stabilization, local industrial promotion, flexible adjustment to change, fuller utilization of resources, and national security are analyzed in some detail both as to their interrelations and implications and as to the methods of implementation.

SEYMOUR E. HARRIS

CHAPTER 1

Introduction

THIS BOOK represents an attempt to bring more unified and systematic thought to bear on a range of issues that, in English-speaking countries at least, have been considered piecemeal by specialists in many fields but too often ignored by economists. These issues all involve the question of where people earn and consume their incomes. Our main concern here is not description or analysis of specific actual distributions of resources, industries, or populations but the formulation of principles governing the interrelation of individual locations, the significance of locational changes, and the legitimate scope of public planning and control.

1·1 *Some Current Applications*

Some of our subject matter comes under the head of "the economics of plant location" and involves questions with which business executives and engineers constantly wrestle. The choice of a suitable location may spell the difference between business success and failure. But the businessman himself is not the only one interested in knowing what constitutes a good location for an enterprise of the type he operates. Banks, utility companies, transportation companies, and community leaders also have a stake in plant location and can make good use of an understanding of the site requirements of different types of industries.

From a social standpoint, accurate weighing of comparative costs and returns is especially necessary in the cases of private monopoly and public enterprises, where bad location may spell an indefinitely continued waste of resources rather than the prompt elimination of a private venture by competition.

The economics of "land utilization" involves similar questions seen from another angle. Any producer may in the long run choose both *what* he shall produce and *where*. At any one time,

1

however, he is likely to be found concentrating on one or the other of these decisions. The farmer or urban land developer who is already committed to a particular location is concerned with what to do with it, *i.e.*, the problem of land utilization. All those directly concerned with the returns from a given area have a stake in its most economic utilization, and those responsible for the decision need a basis for appraisal of the relative advantages of the location in various alternative types of use.

Land-utilization problems in practice fall under the following main heads:

a. Farm management (choice of products and methods of production)

b. Urban planning and zoning

c. Land-use planning (stressing rural uses) by counties, special districts, states, regional authorities, and national governments

The most important and difficult problems are those involving adjustment to change. Not only does the availability of new methods of production, transportation, communication, and distribution require constant reconsideration of decisions regarding land use and the location of production, but people themselves multiply, outgrow economic opportunities in some areas, and migrate in response to motives still imperfectly understood. Questions of regional and national economic development and the problems raised by migration of industries and people (or by their failure to migrate) will occupy a large share of our attention in chapters to follow.

The need for a better ordered analytical approach to location problems as a whole is evidenced by the strong emotional connotations of certain distressingly vague terms. What are "balanced regional economies" and "fair competition among regions," and what do they imply in regard to the practical issues of regional freight-rate differentials, subsidized industrialization of the South and West, national minimum-wage standards, and antitrust policy? What is "industrialization," and why is it assumed to be a panacea for the backward regions of the world? Does "migration of industry" really imply migration in the sense in which people migrate? Does "decentralization" mean (a) a shift of industry to small towns, (b) a proliferation of branch plants by large concerns, (c) greater equalization of the distribution of industry among regions, or (d) movement of industry from large cities to their suburbs? All these meanings are in current use.

We shall need firmer footing on such controversial ground. The first step is to reach some understanding of the fundamental forces affecting location.

1·2 Interdependence of Locations

The most obvious basis for the distribution of industries and people is the disposition of natural resources. Clearly it is better to grow oranges in Florida and wheat in Kansas than the other way round; it is almost equally clear that New York's harbor and its "water-level" route to the interior predestined the growth of a great seaport.

Simple and direct relations to natural resources, however, do not take us far in accounting for most locations. They give no convincing explanation for the concentration of automobile manufacturing in Michigan or of woolen manufacturing in Massachusetts. The reason is that economic interrelations between different industries and firms play such an important part in shaping the pattern of location as a whole. Even in the absence of any initial differentiation at all, i.e., if natural resources were distributed uniformly over the globe, patterns of specialization and concentration of activities would inevitably appear in response to economic, social, and political principles.[1]

Interdependence of units of production is illustrated by the economies of concentration, which will be examined in Chap. 5. Up to certain limits, there are advantages in concentrating a given kind of business in relatively few locations. Thus a locality with

[1] To take a familiar analogy, frost crystals build up on a cold windowpane in patterns that depend not upon irregularities in the glass but upon the laws of crystal structure for water molecules. One may say they are the result of the forces of "locational interdependence" among molecules. Analogous principles of pattern formation, based on locational interdependence among economic units. are what concern us here.

an early start in some industry has thereby a competitive advantage that it may retain and increase even though the early start was due to pure chance or whim. Economic history is full of examples.

Interdependence is also involved in the advantages of proximity of related processes, discussed in Chap. 8. A location where one of these activities is established becomes thereby a good location for the related activity.

Finally, production and consumption are locationally interdependent. Ultimate consumer market patterns are determined by the geographic distribution of consumer income, which in turn depends primarily on the location of production. To the extent that production seeks to locate near its markets and at the same time creates market demand, locational change may be cumulative. It is evident that actual locational patterns cannot be explained merely in terms of the distribution of natural resources or population at any given time.

To arrive at an understanding of this complex system of economic interrelations one must proceed by easy stages. The forces of mutual attraction and repulsion that shape the whole geographic structure will be examined severally as they affect the individual units of the structure. We must begin by putting ourselves into the shoes of the individual consumer or producer to see what makes him prefer one location to another. His "environment" (including the location of everything else) is for that stage regarded as fixed. At the next stage we can try to see how the economic interrelations of numerous producers and consumers create locational patterns of industries, communities, and regions.

1·3 Locational Preferences of Consumers and Producers

Everyone has some preference as to "consumer location," *i.e.*, where he would like to live and spend his income. For all but an envied minority there is also the question of "producer location," *i.e.*, the best place to earn an income. Acting as consumers, people seek to settle where living is secure, cheap, and agreeable. As producers, they seek to locate where earnings will be large and assured and the working conditions pleasant. These consumer and producer motives often exert conflicting pulls on the individual, who then has to work out some compromise location giving due weight to both points of view.[2]

Producers' motives are much more significant than consumers' motives in shaping the over-all distribution of activities. Geographic differentials in wage rates or the profit prospects of particular occupations are larger and better known than are differentials in living costs or conditions. Producer motives are more compelling: he who ignores them risks unemployment or bankruptcy rather than a mere diminution of the joy of life. Moreover, the less tangible consumer motives are strongly shaped by habit and past association. Most people come to prefer the kind of environment in which they have been living rather than some other social, racial, or institutional atmosphere; unfamiliar climate and landscape; or change from urban to rural living or vice versa. Finally, there seems to be less frequent and fundamental change in the geographic patterns that determine consumer preferences than in the patterns determining producer preferences. Differences in climate, for instance, are well-nigh permanent, whereas the optimum location for a specific line of production is subject to sudden and frequent shifts. This is an important point, since most practical problems involving location arise in connection with adjustment to such changes.

All this justifies approaching the problem of location by investigating the factors that determine the location of individuals and firms as *producers*. Consumer motives will, however, be admitted through the back door. In the discussion of labor costs and their effect on producer location (Chap. 7) it will be explicitly recognized that these costs are determined in part by consumer considerations such as cost-of-living differentials. Some account will also be taken of the criteria by which people judge the desirability of residential neighborhoods in cities (Chap. 8).

[2] Some can resolve the conflict by producing in one place and consuming in another. Thus executives who locate a plant do not always have to live near it. Some workers leave their families for considerable periods to work elsewhere, sending remittances home. Daily commutation to and from work is, of course, limited at present to relatively short distances.

1·4   The Producer's Choice of Locations

Incomes are earned from the services of wage and salaried workers (who may be lumped together as "employees"), investors, self-employed proprietors, and firms that hire employees. In all cases, however, the ultimate basis of producer preference for locations is the rate of earnings (wages, profits, or interest) obtainable at different places.

Regularity and security of earnings are important. Other things being equal, a community with a stable economy is a better place to get a job or to establish a grocery store or a bank, say, than a community whose main livelihood depends on the mercurial behavior of seasonal or cyclically vulnerable industries.

The expected trend of earnings is likewise relevant. In choosing a job or a business location, the sensible producer takes into account not only the initial rate of returns but also the prospects for improvement. Pioneer settlers ordinarily go through a period of extra hard work and subnormal returns in the hope of eventual reward. Their industrial counterparts—enterprisers who pioneer in establishing industries in new areas—often face the same situation.

Proper evaluation of these factors of stability, security, and future prospects calls for more information and foresight than the average person possesses. These factors are rather consistently underrated. One of the objectives of locational guidance is a fuller and more accurate evaluation of the importance of stable, secure, and expanding opportunity for the individual.

For each of the various classes of producers that have been mentioned, the relative earning prospects of a location depend on a different range of considerations. The employee has only his labor to sell, and for him locational advantage runs in terms of the demand for that kind of labor. For the *rentier* or inactive investor, locational advantage depends on the relative demand for new capital at various locations. Business enterprisers get a residual return depending directly on the success of the business as a whole after payment for any capital or labor that is hired. The self-employed enterpriser must weigh the relative advantages of different locations in terms of the facilities offered for cheap assembly of the necessary materials and supplies, efficient processing, and easy sale of the product. The firm with a pay roll has all these factors to consider, plus labor cost.

The most comprehensive approach to an understanding of producers' location, then, is an examination of the typical location problems of the *business firm with a pay roll*. Since the relative advantages of location for a firm depend partly on labor costs and interest rates, the locational preferences of employees and investors are also indirectly involved.

1·5 *Procurement, Processing, and Distribution Costs and Locational Advantages*

The activities of a productive enterprise can be divided for our purposes into three stages:

a. *Procurement:* purchasing and bringing the necessary materials and supplies to the site of processing
b. *Processing:* transforming the materials into more valuable forms (products)
c. *Distribution:* selling and delivering the products

These three stages are always present, though sometimes one or another may be unimportant. In some extractive activities such as mining or farming, the procurement of materials and supplies usually has little locational significance.[3] In purely commercial establishments, "processing" may involve merely holding goods and dividing them into smaller lots or different assortments and is thus difficult to separate neatly from the distribution stage.

From the standpoint of distribution, what the producer wants to know about a proposed location is the schedule of demand for his output at that point, *i.e.*, how much he could expect to sell at various levels of realized price per unit after deduction of selling and delivery expenses. Ordinarily a larger volume of sales will entail a lower net realized price. To sell more, the producer

---

[3] An exception to "prove the rule" may be cited. In 1945 the output of French, Belgian, and German coal mines was effectively limited by lack of transportation to bring the necessary pit props from the forests to the mines.

will have to cut his price, pay freight to more distant markets, give better service, or spend more on sales promotion. Any of these steps reduces his net realized price.

Similarly, the advantages of a location from the standpoint of procurement are measured by the prices at which various quantities of the required materials (in their proper relative proportions) can be bought there. Shipment of some materials from other places is generally involved, and greater distance from sources of materials usually means higher procurement costs.

It is clear that distribution and procurement costs have one feature in common. They nearly always depend on the transportation of products or materials (or, in the special case of such consumer services as haircuts, a journey by the customer himself). For this reason and also because the negotiations involved in purchasing and selling are less conveniently carried on at a distance, we find the distribution and procurement advantages of sites varying rather systematically according to distance from customers and suppliers. It will be convenient at some points in our exposition to throw distribution and procurement together, referring to both simply as *transfer* operations involving transfer costs.[4]

The advantages of sites for processing are measured by "production costs" in the usual sense. These in turn depend on two things: the prices of factors of production and the amounts of those factors needed per unit of output. Both prices and amounts may depend on the scale of production. To determine the location for most efficient processing, then, a firm would have to know first of all the wage rates, interest rates, and rents prevailing at various places and whether or not an adequate supply of labor, capital, and land would be available without raising those prices. It would have to investigate also the relative amounts of labor, capital, and land needed per unit of output at different locations. In some places, processing costs would be much higher than elsewhere even if the prices of factors were the same. A dairy needs

---

[4] Professor Bertil Ohlin introduced the term "costs of transfer," defining them as including "transportation costs as well as the costs of overcoming other obstacles [to commodity movements], such as tariff walls." "Interregional and International Trade," p. 142. Harvard University Press, Cambridge, Mass., 1933.

more cooling equipment in a warm climate than in a cool climate, and textile mills in dry climates have to use more artificial humidification than in damp climates. Efficient labor can reduce both the man-hours and the capital investment needed per unit of output.

1·6 *Relation of Individual Location Preferences to the Evolution of Locational Patterns*

The fact that some new location may have greater income potentialities than the one now occupied does not mean that the person or firm concerned will immediately move to the new location or even that he ought to. There are many obstacles to the mobility of persons and productive equipment.

One important obstacle, of course, is that our producer may be unaware of the superior prospects of the other location. He may not have time, means, or inclination to inquire about such opportunities. He may be under some artificial restraint, such as immigration restrictions or zoning laws, which makes any comparison of earnings irrelevant for him. The move in any event would involve expense, extra effort, and usually some disruption of established trade contacts. The greater economy of the new site may be realizable only in the long run, in the form of a lower level of total costs of production, including upkeep and amortization of facilities. In that case the proper timing of a move will be based on a comparison of out-of-pocket costs at his present location with total costs at the new location, less whatever might be realized by disposing of the fixed investment at the present location. Both private and social interests are often best served by continued operation at a location that is "obsolete" on a total-cost basis as long as no extensive renewal of capital facilities is needed.

It is not surprising, then, that locational adjustments by actual migration of producers are normally sluggish. Producers who happen to have selected a poor location or a location that loses its original advantages may remain there as long as they can stay in business at all.

But the location patterns of industries are by no means so

haphazard or so sluggish in adjustment to differential advantage as the locations of individual firms. Competition, in so far as it prevails, will reward and encourage well-located enterprises and shorten the lives of poorly located ones. Even if new establishments were to be located purely by guesswork or whim or by sticking pins into a map at random, and if they were never relocated, some semblance of a reasonable pattern would still emerge as the result of competition.

A good analogy is the scattering of certain types of seeds by the wind. These seeds may be carried for miles before finally coming to rest, and nothing makes them select spots particularly favorable for germination. Some fall in good places and get a quick and vigorous start; others fall in sterile or overcrowded spots and die. Because of the survival of those which happen to be well located, the resulting distribution of such plants from generation to generation follows closely the distribution of favorable growing conditions. So in the location of economic activities it is not strictly necessary to have both competition and wise business planning in order to have a somewhat rational locational pattern emerge; either alone will work in that direction. But since each method has its shortcomings, some judicious combination seems desirable. Competition among ignorant or stupid producers means that many new ventures are started only to fail, entailing a large waste of resources. On the other hand an attempt to plan and administer the whole geography of the economy without the stimulus and purge of competition shows little promise in the absence of a degree of information and foresight far beyond our present experience.

1·7 The Plan of Subsequent Chapters

The reader will have by now some appreciation of (a) the crucial role of the locational decisions of business enterprisers; (b) the essential difference between transfer-cost and processing-cost considerations in location; (c) the parts played respectively by planning, trial and error, and competitive survival in the shaping of location patterns; and (d) the variety of problems of private and public policy to which an understanding of locational economics is relevant. We are ready to build on this foundation. First, however, a quick sketch of the sequence of development in the rest of the book is in order.

The next three chapters are devoted to an examination of the influence of transfer costs on location. Chapter 2 discusses some features of the "structure" of transfer costs, *i.e.*, how they vary with distance, direction, size of shipment, and other traffic characteristics. In Chap. 3 we see why the producer's best location from the standpoint of transfer costs is sometimes near the market, sometimes near his source of materials, and under certain conditions at an intermediate point. Chapter 4 discusses the locational patterns arising from the competition of producers within an industry and from the industry's transfer relations with its suppliers and customers.

Chapter 5 introduces processing-cost differentials, with emphasis on the significance of site rents, overhead costs in general, and the advantages and disadvantages of concentrated organization of production. Chapters 6 and 7 explore the reasons for development of systematic geographic patterns in the cost of land and labor respectively.

Chapter 8 is concerned with the degree of conformity among the locational patterns of different activities and the way in which urban communities arise from a conjunction of various activities at the same location. The characteristic patterns of land uses within urban areas are also discussed.

At that point the static approach is dropped, and Part Two is devoted to various aspects of locational change and adjustment. Chapter 9 outlines the principal kinds of locational shift, the ways in which they are consummated, and their repercussions on activities other than those directly involved. A brief statistical summary of locational trends in the United States is included for background purposes. Chapter 10 analyzes the locational effects of technological change, including developments in transport and communication, processing, and the conversion and transmission of energy. Chapter 11 takes us for the first time into the field of locational pathology as we investigate arrested regional development, urban blight, and the problems of adjustment to locational change in general.

Part Three proceeds toward realism by introducing the consideration of political boundaries. Locational effects of boundaries as trade barriers are examined in Chap. 12, while Chap. 13 takes up the effects of boundaries on the mobility of labor and capital and on the development and control of land use in areas where coordination is needed.

Part Four comprises five chapters on the ends and means of public policy in regard to location. Certain general objectives and guiding principles are laid down in Chap. 14. Chapter 15 follows with a survey of the various means by which policies can be put into effect. The three final chapters discuss and evaluate three themes of locational policy: flexibility of adjustment to change (Chap. 16), stability and the related concept of diversification (Chap. 17), and national security (Chap. 18).

Part One

Locational Preferences
and Patterns

CHAPTER 2

The Structure of Transfer Costs

THE EXPENSE and inconvenience of distributing to distant customers and procuring materials from a distance invite producers to locate nearer their markets and their sources of materials. The incentive to reduce transfer costs is thus the basis of *mutual attraction between successive stages of production.*

In this chapter and the next, we shall try to see (a) what determines the effect of this attraction on the location of any given kind of production, (b) under what conditions an industry is drawn toward its material sources rather than toward its markets or vice versa, and (c) what types of location offer general advantages in transfer cost. The present chapter opens the inquiry by exploring the dependence of transfer cost on distance, type of commodity, volume of traffic, and other factors.

2·1 Variety of Transfer Mediums

The transfer of goods or services is often a complex operation involving shipment by one or more kinds of goods carriers and also the effecting of necessary commercial contacts via one or more means of communication. The following list of transfer mediums is suggestive rather than exhaustive.

Railroads (all classes of traffic)
Water carriers (all classes of traffic)
Highway vehicles (all classes of traffic)
Pipe lines (bulk liquids and gases)
Aircraft (where speed is essential and where access by surface agencies is especially difficult)
Pack animals (in difficult terrain)
Belt, cable, or rail conveyors of various types (short distances)
Human carriers (short distances and small quantities, *e.g.,* pur-

chases of compact finished consumer goods and delivery of letter mail to final destination)

Self-delivery (livestock and self-propelled vehicles)

Electric cables (electric energy)

Telecommunications (information, commercial negotiation)

Most of the above agencies offer a choice of different classes of service according to the speed desired. There is often the further option of using a common carrier, a contract carrier, or carrier equipment belonging to the seller or to the buyer.

A rough idea of the relative importance of the principal agencies of medium- and long-distance freight transport in the United States is given by Table 2·1.

Table 2·1 *Estimated Volume of Intercity Commodity Traffic, by Transport Agencies, 1940, 1945, 1946*

Transport agency	Millions of ton-miles			Percentage of total ton-miles		
	1940	1945	1946	1940	1945	1946
Railways, steam and electric, including mail and express.....	376,218	691,116	602,185	61.3	68.2	68.1
Inland waterways (including Great Lakes as largest category)..	117,296	142,756	123,113	19.1	14.1	13.9
Pipe lines (oil).........	71,279	123,293	92,490	11.6	12.2	10.5
Motor carriers of property...............	48,500	56,155	66,061	7.9	5.5	7.5
Airways (domestic revenue service including mail and express)....	14	92	78	0.002	0.01	0.01
Total..............	613,307	1,013,412	883,927	100.0	100.0	100.0

SOURCES: Interstate Commerce Commission, *55th Annual Report*, 1941, p. 9; *61st Annual Report*, 1947, p. 7.

Commercial contact, as distinct from the actual delivery of the goods or services sold, uses communication agencies (mail and telecommunication) and also passenger transport for the buyer's or seller's agents.[1] In some cases it may involve a significant amount of transport of goods as well (chiefly samples and sales-promotion material).

Transfer mediums, despite their diversity, have certain economic characteristics in common. These common characteristics are conveniently illustrated by reference to the familiar case of freight transport, but it should be kept in mind that other transfer mediums, *e.g.*, telephone communication, behave generally in similar fashion.

2·2   Costs vs. Rates on Specific Shipments

The costs of performing a transfer service are one thing, and the charges that a shipper or consignee has to pay to have those services performed are another. A transfer agency as an independent enterprise seeks to maximize its returns through its system of pricing. The existence of a large proportion of overhead costs in such agencies, not easily assignable to any single shipment or category of shipments, gives considerable leeway in apportioning charges among shipments so as to cover those overheads. At the same time, the extensive nature of transfer operations and the economies of large-scale unified operations limit competition. It is not surprising that wide variations exist between the rates charged and any reasonably assignable costs. Some kinds of shipments are charged barely the out-of-pocket costs they occasion, while others pay a disproportionate share of the general overhead.

The rates charged by transfer agencies are themselves not always a good measure of the disadvantages entailed in dealing with suppliers or customers at a distance. These disadvantages include such items as the added costs of sales promotion and customer servicing at longer distances. Maintenance of larger inventories and the necessity of earlier ordering are costly in trades where styles and demand change quickly; under these circumstances fast service may mean a great deal more than low haulage rates. The

---

[1] It is hardly possible or necessary to distinguish sharply between such commercial contact and the delivery of the product itself in cases where the use of the product by the buyer requires instruction and servicing by agents of the seller.

rapidly growing freight and express business of American air-
lines is based on traffic for which the disadvantage of distance is
measured in hours and minutes.

2·3 Dependence of Transfer Costs on Type of Route

In general, a longer distance involves a greater transportation
and transfer expense. However, certain important qualifications
must be noted.

The "distance" in question is not measured air line but is along
the most economical route. Topography and climate, which determine what routes are easiest to institute and maintain, evidently have much to do with the variation of transfer costs. Thus,
in one direction from a town there may be dry level land with
occasional gravel supplies, ideal for the construction of roads and
railroads; in another direction, swamps; in another, mountains
and deserts; in another, broad rivers requiring expensive bridg-
ing or long detours; in another, a natural waterway affording the
cheapest transportation of all. Even airways still require flat land-
ing areas and some climatic stability. The economic significance
of distance thus differs according to direction and physical features.

2·4 Network Density and Circuity

A denser network of routes permits less roundabout transfer
and increases the number of points to be considered as possible
production locations. Thus, the relatively coarse network of American railroads, with about 250,000 miles of line, has been filled
in by the much finer network of intercity truck transport, with
nearly 1,400,000 miles of surfaced roads and over 1,600,000 miles
of unsurfaced roads available.[2] Route network density depends

² Board of Investigation and Research, "The National Traffic Pattern," 79th
Congress, 1st Session, Senate Document No. 83, Table 3a, pp. 3–4. Intercity busses
operate on about 350,000 miles of routes, according to W. F. Ogburn, "The Social
Effects of Aviation," p. 225, Houghton Mifflin Company, Boston, 1946. As of July,
1946, air routes totaling 59,110 miles had American Railway Express service.
Domestic Transportation, Department of Commerce Industry Report, December,
1946–January, 1947, p. 15. Ogburn, op. cit., also cites the estimates of E. P. Warner

on the volume of traffic offered and on the economic characteristics of the transfer agency—in particular, the extent to which costs are reduced by large-volume terminals and large-unit traffic.

2·5 Relation of Transfer Costs to Length of Haul

On any given type of transfer agency, costs of transfer generally increase less rapidly than in proportion to distance. This is primarily because terminal costs and some other expenses are independent of the length of haul.

This tendency of transfer costs to "taper off" with increasing distance is characteristic of all agencies, but naturally much more marked in those which need a heavy investment in terminal facilities and have their terminals so located that pickup and delivery are costly. In water shipment long-haul economies are more important than in railroad transport and on the highways less important. Agencies with relatively low terminal cost and high line-haul cost have an advantage for shorter hauls, whereas agencies involving high terminal, pickup, and delivery expenses and low line-haul costs are in a position to compete more effectively for the longer haul business.

For short distances the cheapest way to ship freight is usually by truck, which has, however, a comparatively rapid rate of increase of cost with distance. Beyond a certain distance rail transport (with lower line-haul costs) becomes the cheapest. For still longer hauls the very low line-haul costs of water transport give it the advantage if a water route is available.

The typical relation of highway, rail, and waterway cost progressions according to distance is shown in Fig. 2·1. The line representing costs of highway shipment is the lowest of the three for the shortest distances but rises rapidly on account of the relatively high line-haul costs of this mode of transport. The progression of railroad freight costs starts off higher but rises more grad-

(Requirements of Local Air Transport Service, *Aeronautical Engineering Review*, February, 1944, pp. 45–47) on "100 per cent" air service for the United States. To put an air-line stop within 10 miles of 75 per cent of the population and within 25 miles of 99 per cent of the population would require 3,400 stops and about 200,000 miles of route.

ually, so that for an intermediate range of distances (approximately 35 to 380 miles, in the particular case in hand) the railroad

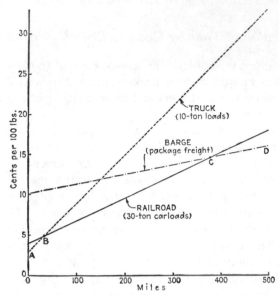

FIG. 2·1   Mileage-cost scales development for movements of commodities in carloads or equivalent in the lower Mississippi Valley area, 1939 to 1940. These costs include return on investment. (*Board of Investigation and Research, Comparisons of Rail, Motor, and Water Carrier Costs, 79th Congress, 1st Session, Senate Document No. 84, Table 5, p. 9, Washington, 1945.*)

appears as the most efficient carrier. At about 380 miles the still lower line-haul costs of water transport come into play, making the barge the most efficient long-distance carrier.[3]

In so far as transfer agencies compete for business outside their

[3] Figure 2·1 is inserted for illustrative purposes only. Its indications as to relative efficiency of the three carriers over different distances are based on conditions in one area at one period, and under other conditions the slopes and heights of the cost lines would differ considerably from those shown. For less-than-carload and less-than-truckload shipments the same survey showed truck costs lower than rail costs even on the longest hauls. This comparison appears in Table 2·2.

It should be noted that the progressions of cost by all three modes of transport shown in Fig. 2·1 are linear. Average line-haul costs per mile, in other words, do not respond significantly to distance. The "economies of the long haul" involve primarily a spreading of the terminal costs over a greater number of miles.

respective spheres of greatest advantage, they have to set rates to meet competition from other agencies. Railroad rates for the shortest distances are kept down by truck competition, while on many of the longer hauls they are kept down by water competition.[4]

The unequal apportionment of overhead costs to rates for various distances in response to interagency competition helps to

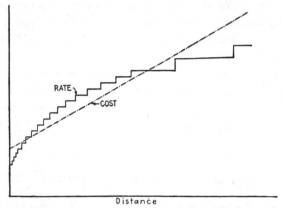

Distance

FIG. 2·2 Characteristic relationship of transport cost and rate progressions. This sketch is drawn up on the assumption that the competition of alternative means of transport requires rates to be low in relation to costs for the shortest and the longest haul, as seems to be the case with carload rail traffic. The "cost" gradient is of the type illustrated in Fig. 2·1. The progression of rates is patterned after those shown in the Interstate Commerce Commission's Statement No. 4031, "Progression in Freight Rate Mileage Scales" (revised), Washington, 1940 (processed). For the sake of clarity, the curvature and regularity of the rate curve have been somewhat exaggerated.

explain why cost progressions and rate progressions are commonly related in the way shown in Fig. 2·2. The progression of rates does not have a uniform upward slope but rises more and more gradually with increasing length of haul.

[4] Or even, in the case of passenger and express traffic, by airway competition. Air passenger miles in 1946 totaled 40 per cent of Pullman passenger miles in the United States (Department of Commerce news release, Feb. 21, 1947). Air-express ton-miles in 1946 totaled nearly 24 million, which is of the order of 1 per cent of rail-express ton-miles. (Based on data in Domestic Transportation, Department of Commerce Industry Report, December, 1946–January, 1947.)

2·6   Relation of Costs and Rates to Direction of Haul

Not infrequently there is a differential in transfer costs and rates according to the direction of travel over a given route. In the direction of lighter traffic flow, a relatively low rate may be quoted, since it costs little more to run with a load than empty. Such low back-haul rates have been important, for instance, in the development of iron and steel works at upper Great Lakes ports and more recently in Brazil. In both instances fuel is shipped in by water at low back-haul or "ballast" rates and used with near-by ores.[5]

It is worth noting that such back-haul economies apply systematically only to freight rates proper. There is no corresponding advantage in either speed or contact. In communication mediums, the direction of traffic has no significant relation to line capacity or cost.

2·7   Other Characteristics of Rate Structures

Rate schedules are commonly simplified by grouping the points of origin or destination in blocks or zones so that a uniform rate applies over a considerable range of distance. Thus the progression of rates from any one point to successive points along a route resembles a flight of steps rather than a smooth ramp but is somewhat irregular and becomes less and less steep as it ascends. Figure 2·2 above indicates a typical form of rate progression.

If two routes compete in serving the same major point or two competing major points, the rates are likely to be equalized for those particular hauls even though the distances are unequal and

---

[5] The lake carrier rate on coal from lower Lake Erie ports to Duluth is about half the rate on iron ore for the reverse haul. The Brazilian steelworks location is mentioned again in Section 3·9.

A new development of the theory of social costs of transportation in relation to location, involving the principle here cited, is being prepared by Prof. Tjalling Koopmans of the University of Chicago. This analysis proceeds from a determination of optimum routing to a rate scheme for a transfer network on which individual vehicles make triangular or other circuitous journeys before returning to their starting points.

though this policy may disturb the proportionality of these rates with those for intermediate distance along the same lines.[6] In general, rates to or from points served by alternate routes and rates over heavily traveled routes are lower. Since these are precisely the points that in any event have more frequent and varied service, the transfer advantage of such points is twofold.

A vast variety of special rates is made to cover particular types of traffic or special competitive situations. An illustration is the "fabrication-in-transit" rate:

> The special privilege of milling in transit, or in more common terms a stopover privilege for processing, is a very important element of the grain rate structure. Competition between railroads to get flour mills on their roads so that grain and flour would move over their rails has forced railroads to provide this privilege at almost every point. This "in-transit" privilege has also been established for other commodities, such as structural steel, so that manufacturing plants have been located on the railroads first granting such privileges under their rates.[7]

2·8   Size and Volume of Shipments

All elements of transfer cost per pound are reduced when shipments are larger. Terminal handling costs and administrative and sales overhead are hardly any greater for a large shipment than for a small one, and larger consignments may even reduce line-haul costs per ton by permitting fuller stowage or speedier and more direct routing. Especially important is the saving of time and trouble when a whole vehicle can be loaded at one point and unloaded at a single destination.

The great variations in cost according to size of shipment on American railroads, truck lines, and water routes are shown in Table 2·2. This table also indicates the relative economy of the small-unit carrier (trucks) for small shipments and the relative

---

[6] Numerous examples are cited in Kent Healy, "The Economics of Transportation," Chaps. 12–13, The Ronald Press Company, New York, 1940.

[7] Ibid., p. 25.

Table 2·2   Average Cost of Rail, Truck, and Barge Transport
(Including Return on Investment) in the Lower Mississippi
Valley, 1939–1940

(Cents per 100 lb.)

Size of shipment	60-mile haul			500-mile haul		
	Rail	Truck	Barge *	Rail	Truck	Barge *
Under 100 lb....................	301	138	†	366	173	†
501–2,000 lb.....................	54	30	†	120	65	55
Carload (30 tons), truckload (10 tons), or equivalent quantity of package freight by barge........	5.5	6.2	11	18	33	16

* Barge transport costs are adjusted to allow for 50 per cent additional circuity, and include pickup and delivery.

† Data not available.

SOURCE: Board of Investigation and Research, "Comparison of Rail, Motor, and Water Carrier Costs," 79th Congress, 1st Session, Senate Document No. 84, Table 3, p. 6, and Table 5, p. 9, Government Printing Office, Washington, 1945.

economy of the larger-unit carriers (freight cars and ships) for larger loads.

Part of the economy of large shipments accrues directly to the seller or buyer in terms of diminished handling and overhead expense in connection with sales and delivery. The freight bill itself generally reflects such economies too, since rate concessions are made for shipments above certain size limits.

A different but related factor is the saving in transfer costs when the *total volume of shipment or receipts by a single shipper or consignee is large,* irrespective of the size of the individual shipments. Even where no actual concession in freight rates is made, the carrier is naturally more ready to adjust schedules and service to the needs of the large shipper than the small. The shipper himself sometimes has the alternative of doing his own transporting. In any event, he is likely to be able to operate his shipping, traffic, and sales departments more efficiently than a small shipper could.

2·9 *Relative Transportability of Goods*

The various features of transfer cost and rate structure thus far described relate to the pattern of transfer costs for a specific kind of goods. Most transfer agencies, however, can use the same facilities alternatively for many kinds of traffic. The relative rates charged have to be determined by considerations of relative cost and competitive opportunity (as measured by the elasticity of demand for the transfer service).

Perishable, dangerous, fragile, or offensive cargoes require special handling and thus entail extra cost. Bulky goods cost more per ton to carry than compact or easily stowed goods. Cargo in certain easily handled forms, *e.g.,* liquids in bulk, goes more cheaply than the same material in small containers. All these genuine cost differentials are normally reflected in freight rates, as well as in the shipper's additional outlay for packing, insurance, and replacement of damaged goods.

When goods of high value per pound are shipped, the transfer charge constitutes a smaller relative addition to the total cost of the delivered article, and such goods are said to be "more transportable" or to be "capable of bearing" a higher transfer charge. In more technical terms, the *elasticity of demand for the transfer service* is less in such cases than with goods of lower unit value. Consequently, transfer agencies find it profitable to make such traffic bear a higher proportion of the overhead costs.[8]

---

[8] This proposition is by no means so simple as is often supposed, and space does not permit a full analysis here. However, it can be shown that when transfer rates are passed on to the consignees, the elasticity of sales in a given market with respect to transport rates into that market will always be numerically smaller than the elasticity of those sales with respect to the total (delivered) price. The smaller the transfer costs in relation to the delivered price the greater the disparity in elasticities. It is well known that when a vendor is in a position to discriminate between two markets, he will gain by discriminating against the market with the lower price elasticity for his goods. Therefore as between two classes of traffic alike in all respects save that transfer costs are a smaller part of the delivered price of one than of the other, the transfer agency will be led to discriminate in its rates against the class of traffic for which transfer costs are a smaller part of the price. Analogous reasoning applies if the freight is paid or "absorbed" by shippers.

SUMMARY

Producers have an incentive to locate as near as possible to their suppliers and markets in order to reduce transfer costs. Transfer costs, however, do not vary simply and directly with distance. Transfer is canalized along organized routes forming coarse or fine networks. Costs and rates are generally less than proportionately greater for longer hauls on one route, lower in the direction of lighter traffic flow, graduated discontinuously upward with increasing distance, lower for large shipments and large shippers, and lower for compact and easily handled goods and goods of low value in proportion to weight.

CHAPTER 3

Transfer Costs and the Location of the Individual Producer[1]

THE PREVIOUS CHAPTER indicated the principal variations in the cost of transferring a given type of goods or services a given distance. We are now ready to examine the way in which transfer costs help to shape the locational pattern. The present chapter deals with the adjustment, or "orientation," of a single production establishment to the transfer advantages of various possible locations; Chap. 4 will show what characteristic industry patterns arise from transfer considerations. The reader is warned that these two chapters are not easy. They will pave the way, however, for what is to follow.

[1] Below are listed some important references on the theory of the location of the individual producer in response to transfer costs. The first three are now mainly of historical interest. Wilhelm Launhardt, Der zweckmässigste Standort einer gewerblichen Anlage, *Zeitschrift des Vereins deutscher Ingenieure*, March, 1882, pp. 104–115, gave the first systematic geometric solution of the problem. H. J. MacKinder, "Britain and the British Seas," D. Appleton-Century Company, Inc., New York, 1902, gave a pioneer discussion of the transfer advantages of junction points, under the concept of "nodality." Alfred Weber, "Ueber den Standort der Industrien," Part I, Reine Theorie des Standorts, Tübingen, 1909, translated by C. J. Friedrich as "Alfred Weber's Theory of the Location of Industries," University of Chicago Press, Chicago, 1928. Weber further developed the theory of relative attractive forces of materials and markets but made serious analytical errors and failed to appreciate the full significance of route layout, junctions, and long-haul economies. Tord Palander, "Beiträge zur Standortstheorie," Almqvist och Wiksells boktryckeri-a.-b., Uppsala, 1935, corrected Weber's errors and presented the fullest analysis of the locational influence of routes and different transport mediums. Some of Palander's main conclusions are restated in a more accessible work: E. M. Hoover, "Location Theory and the Shoe and Leather Industries," Chap. II, Harvard University Press, Cambridge, Mass., 1937. August Lösch, "The Economics of Location," Yale University Press, New Haven, 1954, is the best work on the whole subject of location economics.

3·1 Incidence of the Locational Effects of Transfer Cost

Transfer costs can usually be reduced by bringing the seller and buyer closer together on the transport and communications network. Under most circumstances, each would gain something by closer proximity—the attraction is mutual.

There are situations, however, in which one party finds it possible and expedient to take most of the incidence of transfer cost upon himself, "absorbing freight," so that he is the principal gainer by proximity and the principal loser by distance. In such cases, the incentive for *rapprochement* may hardly be felt by the other party at all.

City stores that take orders by telephone and deliver free anywhere in the metropolitan area are absorbing the entire incidence of transfer cost on the goods they sell. Nearness means nothing to their telephone customers, but it is important for such stores to choose a location from which distribution costs will be small, *i.e.*, a spot at or near the transport focus of their market area. On a regional scale many kinds of manufactured goods, such as rayon yarns, are sold on a "delivered" basis, so that the customer pays the same price regardless of distance from the seller. Much more rarely, we find buyers systematically absorbing freight.[2]

Something will be said in the next chapter about the significance of geographical price discrimination for the location patterns of industries. At present we are concerned with the individual producer dealing with only a single supplier and a single market point, so the question of such discrimination *on his part* does not arise. It is necessary only to note that if he deals with a supplier or a customer who absorbs freight, his locational incentive to move toward materials or market, respectively, will be inhibited.

Actually this qualification is of minor significance. Freight absorption by buyers is confined mainly to a few goods which for

[2] For a conspectus of prevailing geographic price policies in the United States see Temporary National Economic Committee, "Price Behavior and Business Policy," Part II, Monograph No. 1, Government Printing Office, Washington, 1940.

the seller are by-products without much locational importance.[3] Freight absorption by sellers is quite common but is confined largely to finished goods and a few others in which transportation costs are a very small part of the price. Elements of transfer cost other than freight, moreover, are rarely absorbed; so distance remains a handicap for buyer and seller alike in respect to convenience of contact, flexibility of service, amount of inventory necessary to tide over delay in deliveries, and the like.

3·2   The Point of Minimum Transfer Cost

The profit-seeking individual enterprise responds to transfer costs by seeking to reduce them. Procurement costs can be lessened by moving to a point with better access to materials, or distribution costs can be lessened by moving to a point with better access to markets. These two considerations are quite likely to lead in different directions, so that the producer must strike a balance of relative advantages in order to decide where best to locate along the route connecting his materials source with his market.[4]

Let us examine the simplest case. Here the producer uses a single material from a given source and produces one kind of product, sold at a single given market point. In Fig. 3·1, the base line measures distance along the most economical route between the materials source and the market, and the gradients a and b show the variation of procurement cost and distribution cost, respectively, for all possible processing locations along that route. The diagram has been made as realistic as possible by giving these gradients their characteristic features: convexity upward and steplike progression.[5] Procurement costs show the usual steplike

---

[3] The best known examples are cottonseed and scrap metals, though within limited areas the intermediate buyers of milk and cream often absorb freight in purchasing from dairy farmers.

[4] For convenience in exposition, the individual producer is frequently treated in this book as if he were armed with all relevant facts and could make a scientific determination of the optimum location for his plant. Needless to say, this is not quite realistic. It was made clear in Section 1·6 that trial and error and the test of competitive survival play a large part in giving the location pattern such rationality as it possesses.

[5] Cf. Fig. 2·2.

slackening ascent with increasing distance from the materials source, while distribution costs rise similarly as production is moved farther from the market.

The best location is that involving the smallest total transfer cost. The topmost gradient on the diagram $(a + b)$ indicates total transfer cost for the various possible processing locations. For the case shown, it is clear that the best place is at the source of the

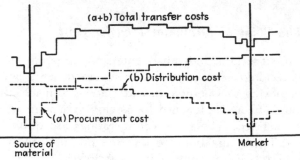

Fig. 3·1 Gradients of procurement cost, distribution costs, and total transfer costs per unit of product for processing locations along a route between a source of material and a market.

material. Closer examination will show that this is because the gradient of procurement cost as here drawn is steeper than the gradient of distribution costs. Had the latter been the steeper, the curve of combined transfer costs would have been lowest at the right, indicating that the pull of the market was the stronger and that the ideal location would be at the market.

Figure 3·1 demonstrates that in cases of this sort the best location will ordinarily be found either at the materials source or at the market and only exceptionally at any intermediate point.[6] As long as the gradients of procurement and distribution cost show their characteristic convexity, the combined transfer-cost curve must dip at both ends, with one end generally lower than the other.

An analogy in terms of equilibrium of physical forces may be helpful. The locational forces of procurement cost and distribu-

---

[6] Palander, *op. cit.*, was one of the first to call attention to this result of the characteristic economy of long hauls.

tion cost are each stronger at short range than at long range. Such forces are not like the pull of a weight on a string, which is constant regardless of the length of the string, nor are they like the pull of a stretched spring, which increases as the spring is stretched farther. Instead, they resemble gravitation or magnetism. Just as an iron ball placed between two magnets will roll to one or the other rather than remaining poised in the middle, so *the ideal location for a production process on the basis of transfer costs from a single materials source and to a single market will generally be at either the source or the market rather than anywhere between.*

At this point it is appropriate to ask what determines the relative locational influence of procurement and distribution costs on any given industry. It is a familiar fact that some operations locate characteristically as near as possible to the source of the materials they use while others locate as close as possible to their markets. What accounts for these differences in orientation?

3·3   *Orientation to Materials*

Let us go back a moment to Fig. 3·1 and see why it was that the best location for the producer in that hypothetical case was at the materials source rather than at the market. It is evident in the first place that gradients of transfer cost such as those used in Fig. 3·1 must apply to the *appropriate relative quantities of the material and product.* Thus if 3 tons of the material are required for each ton of product, the appropriate gradients to compare are those showing the costs of moving 3 tons of material and 1 ton of product. It is evident that a process entailing a larger volume of materials than of products is likely to be more influenced by considerations of nearness to materials sources. Thus, processes in which there is a considerable loss of weight through combustion or waste of part of the material are likely to be located close to the source of the material. Such operations as the smelting of ores and the crushing of sugar cane—in fact, the initial processing of most crude materials—belong in this category, since most raw materials as first obtained have a large proportion of waste, which it is economic to remove before transportation rather than after.

If freight rates per ton are anywhere near the same on material and product, such processes involving a high proportion of weight loss are most economically located at or near the source of the material.

Processes with large fuel requirements always involve a high proportion of weight loss and are likely to be found near sources of fuels or other materials, since the weight of the fuel used does not enter into that of the resulting product. Most of the industries using large amounts of fuel are found at early stages of processing —metallurgy and the making of cement, glass, calcium carbide, and synthetic nitrates are all examples.

Orientation to materials is also found when the relative weights of materials and product are roughly equal but procurement costs per ton-mile are for some reason greater than distribution costs. This is the case, for example, in the preserving of foods of all kinds. Another example is the ginning and baling of cotton. Since both the cotton and seeds are shipped on to other processing plants, there is no great weight loss; but after ginning, the cotton is compressed into more compact bales which take a lower freight rate. Cotton gins are thus more economically located near their materials, which means they are scattered at fairly short intervals through the cotton belt. Still other examples are furnished by establishments whose primary function is the collecting, sorting, and forwarding of the products of small-scale local producers. The many small commercial transactions with suppliers makes nearness to them a necessity, while the product itself can be more economically shipped in carload lots after consolidation and sorting. Grain elevators, freight forwarders, and junk dealers illustrate this case.

3·4 *Examples of Material-oriented Industries*

The accompanying maps (Figs. 3·2 through 3·5) show the actual location patterns of some representative material-oriented manufacturing industries in the United States. Figure 3·2 shows the extent to which beet-sugar factories are located near the beet fields, in order to economize on transportation of a bulky raw

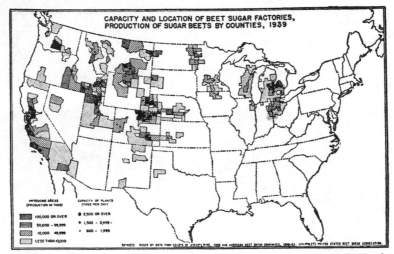

FIG. 3·2 Location of sugar-beet production and beet-sugar factories in the United States, 1939. (*Reproduced from National Resources Planning Board, "Industrial Location and National Resources," Fig. 58, p. 137, Washington, 1943. Based on data from U. S. Census of Agriculture, 1939, and United States Beet Sugar Association, "American Beet Sugar Companies, 1940–1941."*)

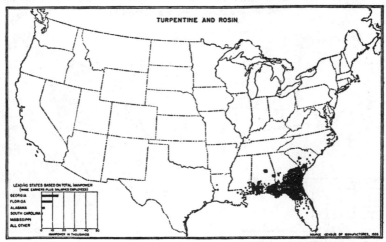

FIG. 3·3 Location of the turpentine and rosin industry, 1935. Dots represent individual establishments; counties with five or more establishments are shown in solid black. (*Reproduced from National Resources Committee, "The Structure of the American Economy," Part I, Map A-69, p. 361, Washington, 1939. Based on data in U. S. Census of Manufactures, 1935.*)

33

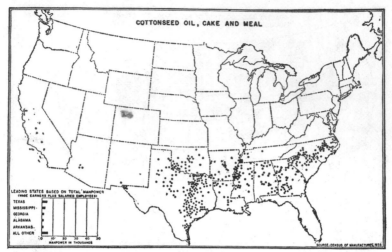

FIG. 3·4 Location of the cottonseed-crushing industry, 1935. Dots represent individual establishments; counties with five or more establishments are shown in solid black. (*Reproduced from National Resources Committee, "The Structure of the American Economy," Part* I, *Map* 9, *p.* 39, *Washington,* 1939. *Based on data in U. S. Census of Manufactures, 1935.*)

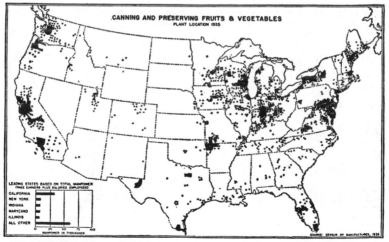

FIG. 3·5 Location of the fruit and vegetable canning and preserving industry, 1935. Dots represent individual establishments; counties with five or more establishments are shown in solid black. (*Reproduced from National Resources Committee, "The Structure of the American Economy," Part* I, *Map A*-15, *p.* 343, *Washington,* 1939. *Based on data in U. S. Census of Manufactures, 1935.*)

material.[7] Only about one-sixth of the weight of the beets is represented by the sugar extracted. Figure 3·3 shows how the "naval stores" (turpentine and rosin) industry, which comprises nearly a thousand small plants, blankets the southeastern region where the trees are tapped—here again the process entails a considerable reduction in bulk. A similar situation appears in the map of the cottonseed-crushing industry (Fig. 3·4). The striking material orientation of the canning and preserving industry (Fig. 3·5) is, of course, due primarily to the perishability of the material.

3·5 Orientation to Markets

We have seen that orientation to materials may be based either on a "weight loss" in the process or on higher transfer costs per ton-mile on materials than on products. Analogously, orientation to markets may be based either on a "weight gain" in the process or on higher transfer costs per ton-mile on products than on materials.

In processes involving incorporation of large quantities of some local "ubiquitous" material like water, the weight of products to be distributed often exceeds the total weight of materials transported. A ubiquitous material is defined as one obtainable nearly everywhere, at costs so nearly the same that it does not enter into the producer's transfer-cost reckoning at all. It does add to the weight of such products as beverages and inks, however, and gives the producer an incentive to locate as near the market as possible in order to reduce distribution costs. Beverages containing a large proportion of added water (soft drinks and beer) are generally made in the proximity of the market,[8] while wines and spirits are made nearer the source of the materials.

7 "Beets are now being grown as far as 30 miles from a beet plant or receiving station, whereas 5 miles was about the limit when the beets were hauled by horses." Works Progress Administration, National Research Project, "Changes in Technology and Labor Requirements in Crop Production: Sugar Beets," p. 8, Philadelphia, 1937 (processed).

8 The manufacture of soft-drink syrups (requiring mainly sugar) is commonly a separate operation, quite differently located.

In intermediate and late stages of production the weight of transported materials (including fuels) is not much greater than that of the products and may be less. Distribution costs are quite likely to be higher per ton of product than procurement costs. This means a tendency toward market orientation of the industry.

The reasons for this situation are basic. As products pass through successive steps of production after the primary bulk-reducing, purifying, and preserving operations already discussed and approach by stages the form in which they will be delivered to the final consumer, they become progressively more fragile, more cumbersome to pack and handle, more valuable in relation to their weight, and differentiated into more separate types and sizes. The customers buy in smaller and more varied lots and are more insistent on prompt delivery of goods ordered at short notice. Demand reflects more and more the passing whims of the final consumer, and goods not closely tailored to market trends and rapidly produced and delivered are likely to miss the market. In the case of many prepared foods (bread, pastry, ice cream, candy) the product is also much more perishable in a physical sense than the materials of which it is made.

In view of all the above factors, it is not surprising that the stages of production closest to the final consumer in the sequence of processing and handling are also closest in the locational sense.

To sum up, it appears that the goods going into any given final product assume their most easily transferable forms (in the sense of ease of physical carriage and simplicity of commercial exchange) at the intermediate stages of production.[9] The earliest stages usually involve bulk reduction, preservation, grading and standardization, or heavy fuel consumption, so that the resulting products are more easily shipped and sold than the initial ma-

[9] It is at these intermediate stages that most of the "foot-loose" industries are found; neither procurement nor distribution cost is an overruling locational factor. It has been estimated that in 1935 about 28 per cent of the working population of the United States were in activities "close to resources," about 48 per cent in activities "close to consumers," and about 24 per cent in "relatively foot-loose" activities. National Resources Committee, "The Structure of the American Economy," Part I, p. 36, Government Printing Office, Washington, 1939. In an appendix to the same report, each manufacturing industry is classified as to locational determinant ("consumer," "raw material," or "other") and as to scope of market ("national," "regional," or "local"). *Ibid.*, Appendix 8, Table I, pp. 264–269.

terials. On the other hand, the final stages in processing and handling goods usually involve differentiation, subdivision of consignments into smaller lots, more bulk and more value in relation to weight, and greater perishability in both physical and style terms. The products are more costly to ship and sell to the buyers than are the products of which they were made.

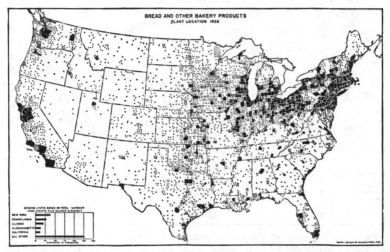

Fig. 3·6 Location of the baking industry, 1935. Dots represent individual establishments; counties with five or more establishments are shown in solid black. (*Reproduced from National Resources Committee, "The Structure of the American Economy," Part* I, *Map* 16, *p.* 43, *Washington,* 1939. *Based on data in U. S. Census of Manufactures, 1935.*)

This is, of course, only a generalization. The relative locational importance of procurement and distribution for any specific industry depends on the way in which distance involves increased costs of selling and delivering a unit of the product and of securing enough of the necessary materials to make a unit of the product.

3·6 Examples of Market-oriented Industries

Figures 3·6 and 3·7 show representative location patterns of manufacturing industries oriented to the consumer. The baking industry (Fig. 3·6) is distributed in close correspondence to the pattern of population, except that it is significantly underrepresented in the poorer agricultural areas where a large proportion of households do their own baking. The manufactured-ice industry (Fig. 3·7) also sells a perishable product and uses ubiquitous

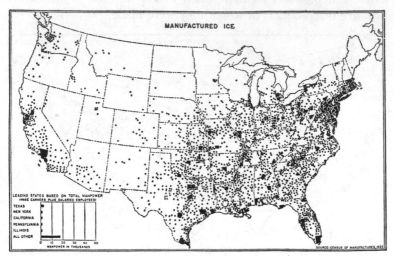

Fig. 3·7   Location of the manufactured-ice industry, 1935. Dots represent individual establishments; counties with five or more establishments are shown in solid black. (*Reproduced from National Resources Committee, "The Structure of the American Economy," Part I, Map 10, p. 39, Washington, 1939. Based on data in U. S. Census of Manufactures, 1935.*)

water as its principal material. The distribution of ice plants follows that of population in general but thins out notably in rural northern areas where natural ice is easily obtained and stored.

3·7   *Location at Intermediate Points*

Thus far it would appear that transfer-cost considerations normally lead producers to locate at materials sources or at markets rather than anywhere between. However, there are important exceptions.

It has already been mentioned in Section 2.7 that "fabrication-in-transit" privileges are often granted on railroads, whereby a material may be processed en route and then shipped on to its destination at a total freight cost equal to the through rate. In cases where the pull of materials and that of the market are nearly equal, this artificial removal of the dis-economy of short hauls makes an intermediate location feasible. It does not, however, give the intermediate location any particular advantage over a

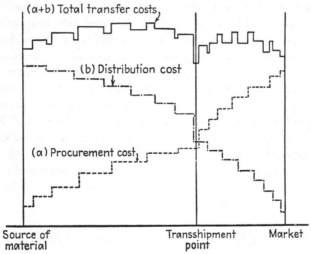

FIG. 3·8 Gradients of procurement cost, distribution cost, and total transfer costs per unit of product for processing locations along a route running from a source of material to a market via a transshipment point.

location at either terminus, and there may be substantial inconvenience and delay in having to arrange two hauls rather than one even when the freight bill itself is the same; so most intermediate locations of plants must be explained on other grounds.

Sometimes there is a peculiar conformation of the gradients of procurement and distribution cost that makes the total transfer cost least at some intermediate point, usually where two different mediums of transport, *e.g.,* water and rail, meet. Thus in Fig. 3·8, the route between the material source and the transshipment point is a water route, while that from the transshipment point to the market is a rail route. The expense of transshipping the material or the product (as the case may be) is shown by the abrupt vertical jog in each gradient.

It is clear that the transshipment point is a better processing location than any nearby points on either side, since neither the material nor the product has to be reloaded. It can even happen (as in Fig. 3 · 8) that this point will be better than a location at either the source or the market.

It is more likely if transport costs on material and product are nearly equal and both material and product are cheap and bulky so that the expense of transshipment is relatively great. Flour milling is a case in point. The principle has an obvious bearing on the strategic advantages of ports and railheads as manufacturing centers. For commercial activities (in which the same commodity is passed on with little or no physical processing) it is particularly significant, since in this case the weight of the "material" is about the same as that of the "product," and there is increased likelihood that a geographically intermediate location will be feasible for the handling process. It is not surprising, then, that ports and railheads are practically always commercial centers even when they have little manufacturing activity.

3·8   *Effect of Route Configuration on Orientation*

When a process uses more than one important material or turns out more than one important product, the simple tug-of-war analogy previously developed is inadequate. In this more complicated resolution of locational forces the outcome depends largely on the configuration of transfer routes and the geographical sequence of sources, junctions, and markets along these routes.

Figure 3·9 and the explanatory note (Appendix, page 301) demonstrate that plants of a given industry, with identical procurement and distribution requirements, may find ideal locations sometimes at a materials source, sometimes at a market, and sometimes at an intermediate junction. The following principles apply: [10]

[10] See also J. A. Quinn, The Hypothesis of Median Location, *American Sociological Review*, vol. VIII, No. 2, April, 1943, pp. 148–156, for an interesting contribution to this problem.

a. If transfer relations with several materials and/or market points are required for a production process, and if any one of the attractive forces (as measured by marginal procurement or distribution cost per added mile per unit of product) is greater than the sum of all the other forces, the location of minimum

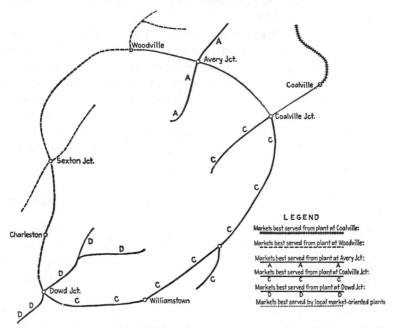

Fig. 3·9 Various orientations of production on a hypothetical transfer system. (A discussion of this map will be found in the Appendix, page 301.)

total transfer costs will be at the materials source or market responsible for that predominant force.

b. If no single force exceeds the sum of the others, the point of minimum transfer cost can be at any of the materials sources or markets or at some intermediate junction point.

As shown earlier in this chapter, the relatively high cost of short-distance transfer provides a special incentive to reduce the number of different transfers incident to a production process even if it means some increase in the total ton-miles of transport per ton of product. The effect is to encourage location at materials sources or market points rather than between them. On the other hand, intermediate points may escape this handicap if they are transshipment points or if fabrication in transit on through rates is allowed, while the direct saving in ton-miles by locating at junction points may be very considerable if routes between materials and markets are circuitous and if many materials or many markets are involved.[11]

Thus an ideal "distributing center" is a junction point from which the total distribution cost to a large number of markets is a minimum. A plant serving those markets is attracted to the distribution point rather than to any of the individual markets. Similarly, a material-oriented establishment such as a cottonseed oil mill, which can handle the materials from a considerable area of material supply, seeks a good "collection center," *i.e.*, a junction with minimum procurement costs for a sufficient supply of the material.[12]

3·9 *Variety of Orientations in the Iron and Steel Industry*

The various types of orientation indicated are well illustrated by the iron and steel industry, which uses two principal materials (coke and iron ore) and two minor materials (limestone and scrap). Table 3·1 shows typical material requirements in American steel-producing districts. The coke is generally made at or near the iron works so as to utilize the by-product gas from the coking process; so the fuel is brought from the mines in the form of coal. The iron is generally converted into steel in the immediate neighborhood of the blast furnaces also (mainly in order to conserve fuel, by using the iron in a still molten form); so the product shipped is mostly steel.

---

11 In terms of the simplified conditions of Fig. 3·9, the force pulling away from a junction along any one route is the sum of the forces of sources and markets located away from the junction along that route, while the force opposing departure from the junction along any one route is the sum of the forces of sources and markets located away from the junction point on all other routes plus the forces of sources and markets (if any) at the junction itself. It is evident that *the more arms a junction has the greater its advantage as a production location is likely to be.*

12 Factors determining the size of market areas and supply areas will be discussed in Chaps. 4 and 8.

Table 3·1   *Materials Consumed per Long Ton of Finished Steel Produced in Selected U. S. Steel Centers, 1939*

(*All figures in long tons*)

Location	Total, all listed materials	Iron ore	Coal	Lime-stone	Scrap *
Eastern New York state.............	4.36	1.71	1.79	0.61	0.25
Youngstown †......................	4.70	1.90	1.84	0.67	0.29
Chicago, Gary ‡...................	4.97	2.19	1.93	0.56	0.29
Birmingham......................	5.87	2.66	2.51	0.46	0.24
Utah............................	4.62	1.98	1.57	0.70	0.37

* Excludes "home" scrap (produced at the works and turned back into the furnaces).
† Figures for Pittsburgh and Cleveland would be similar.
‡ Figures for Detroit would be similar.
SOURCE: Board of Investigation and Research, "The Economics of Iron and Steel Transportation," 79th Congress, 1st Session, Senate Document No. 80, Table 27, p. 114, Government Printing Office, Washington, 1945.

The relative weights of ore and coal required vary according to the richness of the ore, the heat value of the coal, the technology used, and the availability of scrap to supplement the ore charge. The relative freight rates on ore and coal depend partly on the predominant direction of traffic flow. A region producing little else but ore or coal is likely to have an excess of outbound tonnage, which provides the basis for a low back-haul rate on inbound shipments of the other material and encourages metallurgical development in such regions. On the other hand, coal-producing areas usually attract a variety of industries on the basis of cheap fuel supply, and a highly industrialized area usually exports a smaller tonnage of goods than it imports (because manufactured products are less bulky per unit of value than most foods and raw materials). In that case, no back-haul concessions can be expected. However, industrialized areas provide a local market for iron and steel and a local supply of furnace scrap—both factors that encourage further expansion of metallurgical activities.

Pittsburgh, Pueblo, Birmingham, and the Ruhr are blast-furnace locations at or very near sources of coking coal, whereas

Lorraine and Duluth illustrate orientation to iron-ore supply. Cleveland and Buffalo are centers located at transshipment junctions intermediate between ore and coal, whereas the Ford steel plant in Dearborn, Mich., is located at its market. The new Volta Redonda steel works near Rio de Janeiro benefits, like Duluth, from back-haul rates on coal; a large part of its coal is supplied from the United States. Ore is brought from Brazilian mines by rail, and the product shipped out by rail. Only limestone is found near the plant site.

3·10 *Substitutability of Materials or Products*

One unrealistic feature of the analysis thus far is that it has assumed fixed proportions of the materials required and the products forthcoming in any industry. Actually it is possible to vary most industrial processes so as to use relatively less of a given material where it is expensive and more where it is cheap. Thus the proportions of materials required are not, in fact, constant but vary according to the relative delivered prices of the respective materials at different production locations.

Table 3·1 showed that blast furnaces in different parts of the United States use quite different proportions of the principal materials. In part, this reflects differences in the quality of the materials (iron content of the ore and heating value of the coal). In part, it is a response to differences in the relative costs of materials. The percentage of scrap used, for instance, can be curtailed where (and when) scrap prices are high relative to ore prices.

In many industries, also, it is possible and profitable to vary the proportions in which various products are turned out so as to get more of those products which can be sold more profitably. Oil refineries, for instance, can vary their yields of various grades of refined products in response to changes in relative demand and price.

Interregionally, the locational effect of flexibility in the proportions of materials and products is to give some processing industries a greater choice of locations than they would have if the specifications and proportions were rigid. In terms of orientation, the variability of product yields increases the advantage of locations at markets over intermediate locations, while the substitutability of materials increases the advantage of materials sources over intermediate locations. This last principle is demonstrated by example in Table 3·2.

Table 3·2   Hypothetical Case Illustrating Effect of Substitutability of Materials on Plant Orientation

Miles from source of material A	Procurement costs when 1 ton of each material is used			Procurement costs when either material can be substituted for the other, up to ½ ton			Saving in procurement cost due to substitutability (4) − (7)
(1)	(2)	(3)	(4)	(5)	(6)	(7)	(8)
	A (*1 ton*)	*B* (*1 ton*)	*Total*	*A*	*B*	*Total*	
0	0	40	40	0 (1½ tons)	20 (½ ton)	20	20
10	10	36	46	15 (1½ tons)	18 (½ ton)	33	13
20	18	30	48	27 (1½ tons)	15 (½ ton)	42	6
30	24	22	46	12 (½ ton)	33 (1½ tons)	45	1
40	28	12	40	14 (½ ton)	18 (1½ tons)	32	8
50	30	0	30	15 (½ ton)	0 (1½ tons)	15	15

In Table 3·2 the plant in question uses, in the first instance, 1 ton of each of the two materials A and B to make a ton of the product. For selected points at 10-mile intervals along the 50-mile route between the source of A and the source of B, the procurement costs on this basis are shown in columns 2, 3, and 4. It will be observed that total procurement costs are highest at intermediate points and lowest at the source of B (50 miles from the source of A).

It is now discovered that the two materials are partly substitutable; at least ½ ton of each must be used, but within those limits the total 2 tons can represent any combination of A and B. Procurement costs on the best combination for each assembly point are shown in columns 5, 6, and 7, with the tonnages also indicated.

Column 8 shows that the saving in procurement costs due to substitutability is much greater at the sources than at intermediate points.

The principle just stated refers to substitutability per se, assuming no change in the total weight of transported materials per ton of products. In some actual instances the effects are more complex, because a purer material may be substituted for one less pure or vice versa. Dr. Walter Isard has directed attention to the increased substitutability of scrap for iron ore in the manufacture of steel, which has lessened the total weight of materials to be transported for each ton of steel made, thus weakening material orientation and permitting the steel industry to operate in countries like Italy and Japan, where no adequate ore supplies exist. A corresponding qualification applies to the effect of variability of product yields as described in the previous paragraph.

SUMMARY

Transfer costs affect the locational preference of a producer unless his supplier and customer "absorb" these costs completely, which rarely happens. The relative economy of long-distance transfer favors location at material sources and markets, but intermediate points have special transfer advantages when they are transshipment points or junctions and the processing establishment draws from several material sources or sells to several markets. In this last case, the sequence of material sources, junctions, and markets on the transfer network plays a large part in determining the orientation of production in different regions.

As a rough generalization, one can say that early stages of production are material-oriented and late stages are market-oriented while intermediate stages are relatively "foot-loose" as to transfer considerations. Flexibility in the combinations of materials used or of products turned out increases the area of locational choice and generally favors orientation to material sources or markets rather than intermediate points.

CHAPTER 4

Transfer Costs and Industry Patterns

THE PREVIOUS CHAPTER was concerned with "orientation," *i.e.*, with the types of location that are attractive to an individual producer under various conditions. It appears that advantageous production points from the standpoint of transfer costs as a whole are found sometimes at material sources, sometimes at markets, and sometimes at specially situated intermediate points. In any given case the choice will depend on the relative proportions of materials and products, the structure of transfer costs, and the sequence of material sources, junctions, and markets on the transfer network.

The present chapter explores the effect of transfer costs on whole industries. We now inquire not what kind of locations may suit an individual producer, but what kinds of geographic groupings and spacings this producer and his rivals will develop by virtue of their competition for materials and markets.

These and other questions will occupy our attention:

a. In what types of business is each production center likely to have an area tributary to it alone, either as a market or as a source of supply of materials?

b. What determines the shape and size of such areas and thus the spacing of producing and consuming centers for any given commodity?

c. What conditions favor the overlapping of market or supply areas?

d. In what types of business may rival sellers or buyers feel a mutual locational attraction rather than repulsion?

e. What is the locational significance of price policies involving geographic discrimination?

4·1   *Market Areas and Supply Areas*

The locational relation among producers competing for markets is generally one of mutual repulsion represented by the efforts of each seller to find a market where there is not too much competition.[1] To the extent that this mutual repulsion outweighs conflicting locational considerations, producers tend to be spread out in a pattern similar to that of market demand.[2]

It is convenient at this point to refer to Fig. 3·9, which presented the multifarious possibilities of orientation with respect to Woodville, Coalville, and other points. If markets are assumed to exist everywhere on the transfer network shown, no single production location will be ideal for serving them all. One or more producers can operate at Woodville, serving the markets indicated as tributary to that center; one or more at Avery Junction, Coalville, and each other place that has the advantage of minimum total transfer costs with respect to some stretch of markets, or "market area."

If a little more realism is introduced into the assumptions of Fig. 3·9, it can be made clear that market areas must really exist even in those stretches where production "at markets" was indicated as most economical of transfer cost. After all, industries rarely sit in the very laps of their customers. Breweries may be "market-oriented," but that does not mean that a brewing firm establishes a branch in every customer's back yard. The main reason for this is the high cost of small-scale operations (including procurement and distribution as well as processing). This point will be taken up in some detail in the next chapter; for the present it is enough to note that an even mildly realistic view of Fig. 3·9 would envisage a discrete distribution of production centers along the two stretches in which "market orientation" prevails. Here as elsewhere in the imagined region, there will be market areas served by a production center where one or more producers

---

[1] An important exception is discussed in Section 4·6.

[2] A good analogy is a process utilized in the making of sandpaper, in which an electric charge is imparted to the abrasive particles and an opposite charge to the adhesive-coated paper. The particles are individually *attracted* to the paper but *repelled* by each other. The result is that they distribute themselves over the paper in an exceedingly uniform pattern.

operate. Output at each of these "market-oriented" production centers will be small, however, relative to output at the material sources and junctions.

Interpreted in this way, Fig. 3·9 shows the locational relation of an industry to its customers as a system of *market areas*. But that is only one aspect of the actual locational relationships among successive stages of production. In this case the customers were assumed to be highly scattered, so that any single producer had to sell to customers at more than one place in order to do enough business to survive. The converse situation is equally realistic: Sellers are small and highly scattered, so that the individual buyer has to buy from more than one place in order to operate on a large enough scale to survive. In the latter case the interindustry locational relationship appears as a system of *supply areas* rather than market areas. In real life, for example, neighborhood grocery stores have market areas, and grain elevators have supply areas.

Actual locational relations among the industry patterns of successive stages often involve a mixture of market-area and supply-area systems. This is more likely to be the case at intermediate stages of production. For example, one textile town supplies cloth to garment factories in several different places, while each of these garment factories may buy cloth from several different textile towns. For present purposes, however, this complication will be ignored. In describing a system of market areas we shall begin by assuming that there is no collateral system of supply areas—in other words, that buyers at each point do all their buying from one selling point and market areas do not overlap. Circumstances leading to mixed relationships and overlapping trade areas will come up for discussion later.

Each industry plays a part in at least as many different systems of market or supply areas as it has materials and products. Individual cotton gins, for example, appear as collecting points in a system of local supply areas for unginned cotton. They appear again as units making up the ginned-cotton supply areas of individual cotton-spinning centers. They appear yet again as units making up the cottonseed supply areas of individual seed-crushing centers. Finally, to the extent that they supply seed directly to planters, they have their individual market areas as well.

Most of what has to be said about market areas applies in converse fashion to supply areas also; so for convenience the market-area situation will be discussed in greater detail first. We shall return briefly to supply areas in Section 4·7.

4·2   The Shape of Market Areas

If the product is standardized, affording no grounds for customer preference except cheapness, each market point will buy from whatever production center can supply it most cheaply. The cost of laying down the product at any market is equal to the cost at the factory plus distribution cost. Consequently, if the costs of the product at rival production centers are equal, those centers will divide the market on the basis of relative distribution costs alone. Markets nearer one production center are likely to have lower distribution costs from that point, hence will be served from it rather than from any other; they will belong to its market area. Points so situated that the distribution cost is the same from two production centers will be "boundary" points, equally well served from either.

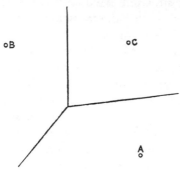

FIG. 4·1   Market areas of three producing centers with equal f.o.b. costs, i.e., costs of procurement plus processing.

Thus in Fig. 4·1 three production points are shown (A, B, and C) and the lines indicate destinations to which the distribution cost is the same from two of these points, i.e., market-area boundaries. At one point all three market areas touch.

If procurement plus processing costs less at one production point than at another, the outcome will not be as shown in Fig. 4·1, for the favored production center will be able to meet a less favored rival more than half way.[3] Figure 4·2 shows a somewhat

[3] The effect on market competition is the same here, regardless of whether the cost advantages of some production points are due to differences in procurement cost or to differences in processing cost. In either case production centers with

more realistic case, in which costs are unequal at the three selling points. It will be observed that the market-area boundary between any two centers is nearer the center with the higher costs and is curved back around it. The greater the cost differential the more circumscribed will be the market areas of the higher cost points.

An interesting and important special case of unequal costs at different selling centers in a region occurs when the latter are major distributing points for a product that originates somewhere outside the region. The market areas of wholesale distributors of manufactured goods in a nonindustrial region (or of food products in a region that does not produce its own food) are asymmetrical because the wholesalers nearer the points of "import" into the region get the product cheaper and have an advantage over wholesalers who must procure from a greater distance.

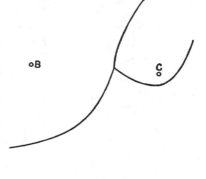

FIG. 4·2   Market areas of three producing centers with unequal f.o.b. costs. Costs of procurement plus processing are assumed to be lowest at *A* and highest at *C*.

The accompanying map of wholesale drygoods market areas in the United States (Fig. 4·3) illustrates this characteristic. Most of the main distributing centers in the West and South are not in the middle of their areas but nearer the northeastern manufacturing region whence the bulk of the goods comes.

Actual distribution costs are of course not proportional to air-line distance. Transfer is canalized along established routes and is much cheaper and quicker on some routes than on others. Along any one route, the rates are lower per ton-mile for longer hauls and for hauls between important and competitive terminals. The progression of transfer costs along a route is stepwise rather

higher total "f.o.b." costs (procurement plus processing) can serve more cheaply than their rival only those markets in which they have a distribution-cost advantage at least great enough to offset this handicap.

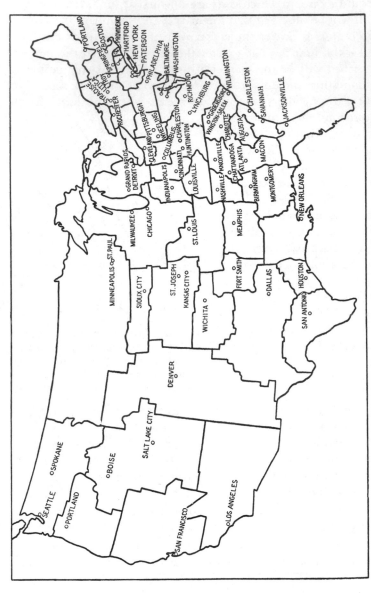

FIG. 4·3 Market areas for wholesale drygoods in the United States. Boundaries are drawn along county lines. The cities shown are the major distributing centers supplying the respective areas. (Based on a map in U. S. Bureau of Foreign and Domestic Commerce, "Atlas of Wholesale Dry Goods Trading Areas," Washington, 1941.)

than continuous. Finally there are innumerable special exceptions and localized advantages in any actual rate structure, involving still further departures from the direct distance relation. As the result of these features of the transfer-cost structure, actual market areas have irregular boundaries.[4]

The existence of certain especially cheap or convenient routes of transfer has the effect of expanding the market areas of producing centers that the routes serve. Thus, although the usual inland brickyard distributes its product over only a very restricted radius, a brickyard located on navigable water can cope with competition over much greater distances.

When one production center has especially cheap service available, it may acquire a market area entirely enclosing that of some less favored center. An important example is intercoastal trade via the Panama Canal. Producers located on either seacoast of the United States can ship to the other coast by water more cheaply than many of their inland rivals can by land. Similarly, British coal producers located on tidewater have competed in coastal market areas nearly all over the world, whereas the coal of the Ruhr and Silesia, farther from ocean transport, has been confined primarily to inland European markets.

The effect of the characteristic long-haul economies of transfer is to increase the curvature of market-area boundaries. With a uniform rate per mile, such boundaries would approximate straight lines or hyperbolas.[5] With transfer costs increasing less than in proportion to distance, we have instead a type of curve that eventually bends back to enclose the higher cost production center.[6]

---

[4] The market-area boundaries in Fig. 4·3 were drawn arbitrarily along county lines.

[5] For an extended discussion of "natural" market areas, see F. A. Fetter, "The Masquerade of Monopoly," Harcourt, Brace & Company, Inc., New York, 1931. A hyperbola can be defined as the locus of points which are a fixed distance farther from a point A than from a point B. If distance and transfer cost were proportional, this fixed differential in distance would then correspond to the distribution-cost differential needed to offset point A's assumed advantage in costs of procurement and processing.

[6] As we go from one production center through its rival and farther and farther beyond, the difference in distribution costs from the two centers becomes less and less. If we go far enough, the distribution-cost differential is no longer enough

4·3   Overlap of Market Areas

Anyone attempting to trace out actual market-area boundaries will be struck by the fact that such boundaries are usually blurred. Instead of a sharp line, one finds a zone of transition or indifference, in which part of the trade goes to sellers at one location and part to sellers at another location. *The overlapping of market areas implies an "absorption" of distribution costs by one of three parties: the transfer agency, the seller, or the buyer.* There are thus three distinct bases for overlap.

Transfer agencies absorb the added distribution cost when they engage in the universal practice of bracketing their rates by "mileage blocks." As noted in Section 2·7, this gives transfer-cost gradients a steplike rather than a continuous rise with increased distance. Where rates are bracketed, there may be a considerable zone in which the distribution costs from two or more different production points are equal.

Further overlapping of market areas is involved in sellers' absorption of freight costs. Still a third basis of overlap is the imperfect interchangeability of the goods of rival production centers. These last two causes are somewhat complex and will be examined in greater detail in the sections that follow.

4·4   Geographical Price Discrimination and Market-area Overlap

It was noted in Section 3·1 that the extra costs of longer distance distribution are not always reflected in the price of the commodity at its destination. Just as a transfer agency may find it desirable to charge rates that fail to progress regularly with distance, so the seller of a commodity in separated markets may profit by geographical price discrimination, *i.e.,* by taking control of the delivered prices of his product and arranging these in a pattern not in accord with that of transfer rates. The guiding principle in such cases is naturally that of shading the delivered

---

to offset the difference in procurement-and-processing cost; from that point on, the low-cost production center has the field to itself.

price downward at markets where intense competition makes the demand for the seller's individual product particularly elastic and shading the delivered price upward at markets where competition is relatively less intense and the demand is particularly inelastic.

Geographical price discrimination may show a spotty and fluctuating pattern in some lines where market conditions are very unstable and competition is "cutthroat," but commonly there is some evidence of a systematic discrimination against either the more remote or the nearer buyers.[7] Discrimination against the nearer buyers (known as "freight absorption") is by far the more usual, and the reason is not far to seek. Evidently it will frequently happen that a seller has more intense competition in some remote market than he does at home, for he will have to compete in the remote market not only with the other producers in his own location—who can ship there just as well as he can—but also with other producers in locations closer to the market in question. Thus freight absorption is common and occasionally is carried as far as the quoting of a lower delivered price in the remote market than in the home market.

On the other hand, it is not easy to conceive of a situation in which a seller has *less* competition in a remote market than he does in the home market; systematic "freight inflation" or discrimination against more remote buyers is rather rare. It is practiced occasionally by industries in which the sellers are geographically highly concentrated.[8]

[7] It can be demonstrated deductively that if the demand for the individual seller's goods is of uniform and equal elasticity at various markets, it will pay him to discriminate against more remote buyers; whereas if the demand for his goods is a linear function of price, with equal slope at various markets, it will pay him to discriminate against nearer buyers, *i.e.*, to absorb some of the freight. *Cf.* E. M. Hoover, Spatial Price Discrimination, *Review of Economic Studies*, vol. IV, No. 3, June, 1937, pp. 182–191.

[8] One example is the pricing of automobiles in regions served by branch assembly plants. Since in any particular area not all firms are likely to have assembly plants, those which do are at an advantage that does not apply in the area served by the main plants. It is possible and profitable, then, for the assembly-plant firm to charge a delivered price based not on cost of shipment of parts to the assembly plant but on the shipment of the completed car. In other words, more freight is charged for than is actually incurred.

A factor that sometimes hinders discrimination against remote buyers is the possibility of evasion by collusion between buyers. If the remoter buyers can do their purchasing through the nearer ones, they cannot be charged much more than the actual freight and any discrimination scheme would collapse.

Of the various forms of freight absorption, the most frequent is that involving one or more uniform delivered prices, extending over the whole range of the market or broad zones of the market. Several conditions favor such a pattern in particular instances. If the article is a finished consumer good with a relatively low price, the price is likely to be a matter of convenience or custom, say some multiple of a frequently used coin or some particular figure like $1.98 that is regarded as especially irresistible to the bargain-seeking buyer. In this case there is an incentive to keep the price uniform over the whole market. Distribution costs, in the case of compact and nonperishable branded goods, may be quite high and yet only slightly related to distance. Finally, the existence of highly popular channels of nation-wide advertising is an increasingly important incentive to development and maintenance of a nation-wide market. Nation-wide selling requires uniform or at least zoned delivered prices unless the bulk of the sellers are in one area.

Another fairly common price pattern is the basing-point system, in which delivered prices of all sellers grade up according to freight costs from some designated basing point or points, usually important producing or distributing centers. A producer not located at a basing point can sell in the direction of the basing point only by more than 100 per cent freight absorption, *i.e.*, by charging a lower delivered price and getting doubly lower net receipts on sales to more distant destinations.

Usually the basing-point system is a reflection of originally lower production costs at the basing point, although even after new producing centers have attained comparable efficiency, there is a tendency for their installation as new basing points to be restrained out of consideration for the interests of the older production district.

The chief effect of these various systems of delivered prices is upon the pattern of locational advantage for the users of the product. For example, a flat delivered price on a certain material means that nearness to the source of supply of that material need not be considered at all by subsequent processors. Under a basing-point system nearness to a basing point rather than nearness to an actual supplier becomes the determinant of cost of materials for the subsequent processor. It should be kept in mind, however, that in basing-point industries where most of the production is at or near basing points, the delivered price pattern might be about the same in the absence of any formal arrangement and that the ignoring of transport costs in the case of uniform price zones is generally a matter of little consequence, since it involves commodities in which delivery costs are small.

An important reason for the establishment and persistence of uniform, zoned, or basing-point price systems is that they provide a simple and easily policed price structure. The interest of the sellers as a group is in curbing price competition, while the individual seller might feel tempted (especially when trade is slack) to grab a larger share of the business by quietly making price concessions. The simpler the price formula the more conspicuous and difficult do such deviations become.

The effect of geographic price discriminations upon the locations of the sellers who practice it is an intricate question, to which no complete theoretical or factual answer has yet been given. Its importance, however, is easily overestimated. Regardless of the pricing tactics used, it is still advantageous for a seller of a commodity to be located at or near the center of a large market with as few near competitors as possible. The seller under flat delivered prices gets a smaller net return the greater the average length of shipment. The difference between market competition under f.o.b. pricing (with strictly delineated market areas) and under discriminatory delivered pricing is something like the difference between trench warfare and guerilla warfare. In the former case all the fighting takes place along a definite battle line; in the second case the opposing forces are intermingled over a broad area. It should be noted that the principal systems of geographically discriminatory pricing—flat delivered prices and basing-point systems—grow out of conditions that would lead to market-area overlap even in the absence of any formal arrangement. The seller under a flat delivered price system chooses to extend his market area even in the face of lower net yields on more distant sales, because freight costs are a small item anyhow and because his main concern is that of "selling" the customer on the distinctive merits of his brand. The basing-point system grows out of situations in which the plants remote from main centers of the industry have not enough capacity to meet the whole demand in their vicinity, which continues to be supplied partly by plants in the main centers. Under these circumstances prices naturally grade upward from the "surplus" to the "deficit" areas. The market sharing involved in this case is no more anomalous than the fact that both New York and Minnesota grain growers help to supply the New York grain market. It illustrates the mixture of market-area and supply-area situations mentioned at the outset of this chapter.

"Crosshauling" represents a special case of market-area overlap in which the same kind of goods travels in both directions over the same route. This, too, is common under discriminatory pricing. Where the goods are really interchangeable, it makes distinctly less sense than the simple sharing of markets. Even crosshauling, however, can be explained and justified in some industries on the basis of geographical instability of demand. Producers of building materials, for example, may find a dearth of business in their vicinity at some times, while at other times, when several large construction projects happen to be under way there at the same time, they may be unable to supply the demand and their competitors elsewhere may have capacity to spare. Under these conditions it would be absurd to expect each seller to confine himself to the fluctuating demand of a fixed market territory, and crosshauling appears not only natural but desirable.

4·5 *Variations in Consumer Preference and Market-area Overlap*

Another basic cause of market-area overlap is the fact that two production centers sometimes cater to the same want by supplying different though substitutable products. Thus, coal of various kinds competes with oil, wood, or natural gas as a fuel; brick and stone compete with wood as a building material; fresh meat and vegetables compete with the preserved forms; and last but not least, different styles or brands of the "same" product compete with each other.

If all the customers agreed on the relative merits of the alternatives, there would be no special reason here for overlap of market areas—an inferior product would simply find its market area restricted. But in actual fact, the customers are not agreed on how large a price premium they should pay on fresh tomatoes as against canned tomatoes or Milwaukee beer as against home-town beer. This produces an overlap of market areas; in the case of some high-value branded goods, where distribution costs are small and price differentials small or nil, the market areas of different production points may overlap to the point of coinciding.[9]

[9] Interesting locational results of another sort arise from the fact that substitute commodities are quite likely to take different transfer rates on equivalent quantities. For instance, two kinds of coal pay the same rates per ton, but one kind has greater heating value than the other and consequently pays less freight per B.t.u., which is what the consumer is really buying. Two rival building materials may be about equally "concentrated" in their utility, i.e., a ton of one may be about equivalent to a ton of the other, but they may for some reason have to pay different freight rates per ton. In either case, the freight charge per unit of actual utility is different on the two commodities.

A frequent result is that one market area surrounds the other. The outer area must always be that of the more cheaply transferred product, regardless of which product has the lower production cost. If the more cheaply transferred product happens to be the one with higher production costs, and if the two rival production points are sufficiently close together, it may even happen that the high-cost cheaply transported commodity cannot compete on its own home ground but must seek its market in a ring of more distant territory where its transfer advantage comes into play.

An example of this is in coal fields where both low-grade and high-grade fuel are produced in close proximity. In such cases, the low-grade product is consumed locally and the high-grade, i.e., that which is the more cheaply transferable per heat unit, is shipped to more distant markets. It is commonly said of such cases that the high-grade or more concentrated product can "bear" greater transportation charges than the other and for that reason is sent out. It is likewise a familiar phenomenon in fruit- and vegetable-producing districts that the best are shipped out and the lower quality crop is consumed locally or processed into more transportable form, e.g., fruit juices, or starch and alcohol from potatoes.

4·6 Coalescence of Market Areas: The Special Case of "Shopping Goods"

Ordinarily we think of a seller as avoiding a location where there are many competitors. In some market situations, however, the reverse is more nearly true.

A woman intending to buy a hat engages first in an arduous and complex operation known as "shopping," in the course of which she may inspect and compare a vast number of different styles. The various kinds of hats displayed before her are certainly in market competition, since if she buys one, she is less likely to buy some other. Yet each different style contributes to the variety of the offering that led her to seek out that market in which to make the selection. Marketing specialists apply the term "shopping goods" to products of this character, in which the customer likes to look at several different varieties before making his selection.

The locational effect is a concentration of marketing outlets. In the final retail stage the buyers are unwilling to come very far to make their comparisons and purchases because these are on a small scale; so the concentration is local. Shopping goods are sold in the centers of towns and particularly in larger shopping centers to a greater extent than other consumers' commodities. Rival shops cluster in the same small district or even side by side on the same street.[10] Thus there are in most cities particular neighborhoods devoted to the selling of specific kinds of shopping goods.

At the earlier stages of production and distribution, there is room for concentration on a grander scale, since more money is

[10] R. U. Ratcliff, in The Problem of Retail Site Selection, Table 9, *Michigan Business Studies*, vol. IX, No. 1, Ann Arbor, Mich., 1939, pp. 32–33, presents the results of an investigation of the relative tendency of individual lines of trade and service to cluster in the same city blocks. The several lines, in order of their degree of cluster, are as follows: men's furnishings, women's clothing, shoes, furniture (new), furs, variety stores, food specialties, grocery stores, general markets, haberdasheries, paint and wallpaper, hardware, restaurants, jewelry, millinery, parking lots, banks, theaters, curtains, upholstery, department stores, hosiery, tailoring, shoe repairing, beer, radios, candy, music, barbershops, cleaners, drugstores, cigars, bakeries, and florists.

involved in any one transaction. Thus the buyers of millinery at wholesale find it worth their while to make long trips, if necessary, to a center where a particularly varied offering is on display; consequently the wholesale "market" tends to concentrate in one or at most a few leading cities. This bottleneck through which most of the goods pass then becomes a point of attraction for both buyers and producers. Each additional producer sending his goods to such a shopping market increases the attractiveness of the market to the buyers and thus indirectly increases its attraction for other sellers.

The manufacturer may, of course, merely maintain a showroom in the market center and operate his factory elsewhere, but such a separation involves extra expense and inconvenience that can be justified only by relatively large economies in production costs or material supply at the outside location. Characteristically, shopping-goods manufacturers are highly dependent on a flexible and trained labor supply and on quick access to suppliers and contractors as well as to buyers; so such industries show extreme concentration.

4·7 *Supply Areas*

It was indicated at the outset of this chapter that the locational relations between two successive stages of production can be pictured either as a system of market areas or as a system of supply areas, depending on whether the earlier or the later stage is the more concentrated. The formation of supply areas is thus analogous to the formation of market areas; practically all that has been said in this chapter in regard to market areas can be applied, with obvious modification of terms, to supply areas. A very brief recapitulation should suffice.

The economies of long-haul transfer make supply-area boundaries more sharply curved than hyperbolas. Particularly cheap routes make it possible for one production center to obtain materials from sources behind and beyond a rival production center or to extend its range of procurement to exceptional lengths in particular directions. Either of these features may produce situations in which the supply area of one production center is entirely surrounded by the supply area of another [11] or in which a particular production center's supply area consists of two separated pieces of territory. The same effect may likewise occur if the transportation rates on equivalent quantities of two substitute materials are different.

Supply areas may overlap just as market areas often do. The steplike progression of transfer rates is one factor making this possible. The other causes of overlap, however (differences in consumer preferences as between varieties and the pricing policies of producers), operate generally with less force in the case of materials than with products. Materials, for one thing, are more standardized and are bought and sold in larger quantities and on a more scientific and objective basis in most cases. There is less room for quasi-irrational preferences based on individual tastes or advertising. The importance of uniform prices over a wide area is much less. Then, too, freight costs are likely to be more important in the costs of materials and accordingly less likely to be disregarded by either buyer or seller in connection with the price.

Probably the most familiar kind of supply area is the "milkshed" of a city. Figure 4·4 shows the pattern of these areas for a few major cities in the northeastern part of the United States. It will be observed that these milksheds overlap considerably and that the Philadelphia and Washington milksheds each include exclaves surrounded by territory tributary to another major market center.

4·8   Satellite Supply Areas and Market Areas

In Fig. 4·4 one must imagine the small milksheds of all the smaller cities as being carved out of the larger areas indicated on the map. *The economies of longer hauls* play a significant part in giving small buying centers their own supply areas even when those centers are located on a route through which the product

---

[11] As, for instance, the Albany milkshed is surrounded by the New York City milkshed.

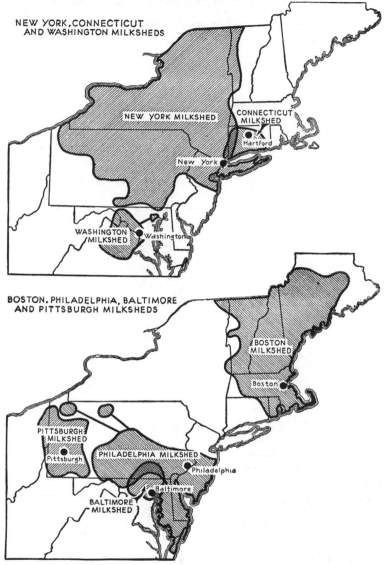

FIG. 4·4 Principal urban milksheds in the northeastern United States. (*Reproduced, by permission, from Leland Spencer, The Surplus Problem in the Northeastern Milksheds, Fig. 12, p. 30, New York State College of Agriculture in cooperation with Farm Credit Administration, Bulletin 24, Washington, 1938.*)

passes to reach a larger buying center. Comparison of the two diagrams in Fig. 4·5 will make this clear.[12]

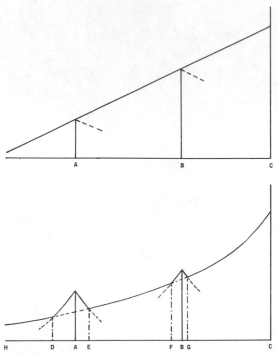

Fig. 4·5   Net returns to the producers of a good consumed at a principal buying center C and also at two small buying centers A and B. In the upper diagram transfer costs are assumed to be proportional to distance along the route through A, B, and C. In the lower diagram transfer costs are assumed to increase less than proportionally with distance. Supply areas of individual buying centers are indeterminate in the case shown in the upper diagram; each buying center draws from suppliers on its left. In the lower diagram A is supplied by producers in the range DE, B is supplied by producers in the range FG, and C's supply area is HD plus EF plus GC.

The upper diagram in Fig. 4 · 5 shows the gradient of net returns to the producers on sales as it would be if transfer costs were proportional to route distance. It is evident that the supply areas of

[12] For the sake of simplicity, geographical price discrimination and the usual steplike progression of transfer costs are both ignored in this illustrative case.

the small buying centers A and B would be indeterminate in extent, since all suppliers to the left of A will get the same returns from sales to A, B, or C and it will be a matter of indifference to them where they sell. If the price of the good at A were any higher than that shown, the large buying market C would lose the output of all territory to the left of A; on the other hand, if the price at A were to be lower than that shown, A would receive no supplies at all.

The lower diagram is more realistic, representing the price gradients as they will be when transfer costs increase less than in proportion to distance. In this lower diagram it is evident that A and B can each have a supply area of appropriate size and definite limits without interfering with the through shipment of the product to C from points to the left of A (and from between A and B) under cheap long-haul rates.

The same effect applies likewise, of course, to the formation of market areas when small producing centers supply local markets within the area dominated by a larger producing center.

SUMMARY

The geographic relation between successive stages of production can be described in terms of market areas or supply areas, depending on whether the earlier or the later stage is the more concentrated. The shape of market or supply areas is influenced by the advantages of different locations for procurement and processing and by the structure of transfer costs. Actual market and supply areas sometimes enclose one another, and usually they overlap.

Overlapping of market or supply areas may result from an absorption of the extra transfer costs on the part of the transfer agency, the seller, or the buyer. In the case of transfer agencies, this means the bracketing of rates in mileage blocks. Sellers absorb freight to extend their market areas and in many cases have formalized a structure of uniform, zoned, or basing-point prices. Such pricing systems grow out of situations conducive to market-area overlap, although they are not themselves responsible for imposing it. Finally, the preferences of different buyers for substitutable goods vary, producing a further overlap of market areas. Where the customer wants to compare alternatives before buying, market areas tend to coalesce, as the sellers find it desirable to cluster for display of their wares. In a few industries this concentration of "shopping" markets extends back to the manufacturing stage.

The analysis of market areas applies, *mutatis mutandis*, to supply areas. Less emphasis, however, should be placed on overlap factors in the latter case, on account of the greater importance of actual freight costs relative to other commercial considerations.

CHAPTER 5

Processing Costs and the Location of the Individual Producer

THE THREE PRECEDING CHAPTERS have described the web of transfer connections that determines how economic units trading with one another are locationally related. We now turn to the locational effects of processing costs.

These approximate what the census calls "value added by manufacture" for a manufacturing establishment—the difference between cost of materials (including fuel and purchased energy) and value of the finished product at the place of production. Processing costs include direct labor costs, costs of administration, interest, rents and royalties, maintenance and depreciation, and taxes.

In some lines of business it is evident that transfer costs vary so little with location, in comparison with processing costs, that the latter must be the significant locating factor. This is true of industries that use compact materials (with high value in relation to weight or bulk) to make compact products and in which the production process is complex but transfer operations are not, *i.e.,* the customers and suppliers can be dealt with at long distance. The manufacture of typewriters, alarm clocks, and similar light and staple devices is illustrative. In such cases an explanation of location must run primarily in terms of processing advantages.

5·1 The Factors of Production

Why does it cost more in one place than in another to grow a bushel of wheat, weave a yard of cloth, or assemble an automobile? Any of a large number of cost items may be responsible in a specific case. To throw light on the general principles involved, we can break down the producer's expenses into payment for four broad classes of productive services. The producer needs (*a*) equipment, (b) a site, (c) labor, and (d) government services such as law enforcement and fire protection. His contribution to government (taxes) is, of course, less directly related to specific services received than the other three kinds of expenses.

There may seem to be little ground for the distinction between expenses for equipment and expenses for land, i.e., a site. Each can take the form of either interest or a rental. Farmer Jones may hire the services of a combine harvester; alternatively he may buy one outright, in which case he should expect his investment to yield interest. He has a similar choice in regard to farm land and buildings. Certainly the choice of contractual arrangements by which the producer acquires command of resources need not detain us here.

But in the ultimate determination of locational patterns there is good reason to distinguish between a producer's payment for a *site* and his other costs. It is, after all, his choice of sites that constitutes our problem. The value of a site, which can neither be replaced nor moved, merely reflects the bids of various would-be users for that particular location. To hire the services of reproducible capital equipment, on the other hand, one must pay a price that takes into account the reproduction cost of the equipment and the alternative demands for it at other locations.[1]

The difference is shown by the effect of geographic differentials in interest rates and tax rates. Both rates enter into the costs of holding reproducible capital goods—other things being equal, a location with high interest rates or high taxes on capital equipment will involve extra cost. But the cost of holding a site as such is not directly affected by either interest rates or taxes on sites. A site cannot be shifted elsewhere to avoid the tax; so its price represents a capitalization, *at expected interest rates,* of the expected net returns to the user *after payment of taxes.* Higher interest and site-tax rates are at least roughly offset by low sale prices for sites of a given rental value.

[1] For a short period this need not apply. Capital investment in buildings or other quasi-immobile forms has to take whatever return it can get during its lifetime at the location to which it is committed. Only when it comes time to consider replacement or new investment does the question of reproduction costs or better rates of return at other locations become relevant.

The producer locating with an eye solely to processing economies will presumably look for the site where the combination of productive services necessary to make the product can be had at minimum cost per unit of output. This means that the prices of production factors will help to determine the relative advantage of different possible processing locations. The rent or price of land, the rate of wages, tax rates, and interest rates are all relevant. In the short run, the price or rental of capital equipment already in place will likewise be considered.

5·2 Mobility and Geographic Differences in the Prices of Factors of Production

Differentials in the prices of productive services arise primarily from the difficulty or expense of moving factors from one place to another. The important but elusive concepts of labor mobility and capital mobility thus underlie geographic differences in processing costs.[2]

To the extent that any factor of production is mobile, it moves to places where it is better rewarded. This tends in turn to reduce geographic differentials in its price. Thus the mobility of investment funds (notably enhanced in the United States by the introduction of the Federal Reserve system) reduces differentials in interest rates, and the mobility of labor reduces differences in wages. The price of a freely mobile factor would be the same everywhere and would not affect the location of production or other factors at all.[3]

Labor and capital move "stickily"; the migration response takes time. Labor with deep-set economic and social roots in its community may not move for many years in response to a differential in wages or employment opportunities. Some forms of capital equipment such as tools and light machinery are moved, but most

---

[2] In this chapter little specific attention is given to taxes, since the effect of most forms of tax can be expressed as an equivalent differential in pay-roll or interest expenses. Taxation as an instrument of locational policy will be taken up in a later chapter.

[3] A qualification, to be discussed in Chap. 7, must be noted in regard to labor Full labor mobility would equalize real wages, but one type of labor-cost differentials would remain.

kinds of equipment are regarded as "sunk" in a particular location; the capital involved can be shifted only gradually and indirectly by a diversion of replacement and new investment. Sites and many of their features (such as climate) are not mobile even in this indirect way.

The magnitude of price differentials corresponds inversely to mobility. Land shows the largest differences, partly because it is immobile and partly because there is such wide variation in the natural endowments of sites. Wage differentials are considerable, but small by comparison. For example, wages in Detroit in 1943 were estimated to be about 90 per cent higher than those in Atlanta,[4] but rents or land prices can vary over a much greater range within a few city blocks. The price of capital equipment in place generally varies between the limits set by replacement costs and junk value. Capital funds for new investment, however, are highly mobile and show relatively small geographic differentials in price. Interest rates exhibit a tendency to vary with distance from major financial centers [5] but are rarely a significant factor of location within any one country.

The explanation of geographic patterns of land costs, labor costs, and interest rates lies beyond the province of this chapter, as it involves the competition of different producers and industries in local markets for factors. The next two chapters will deal with the patterns of land and labor costs respectively, while the role of capital costs will come in for incidental attention at later points.

---

[4] Intercity Variations in Wage Levels, *U. S. Bureau of Labor Statistics Bulletin* 793, Table 5, p. 12, 1944. This comparison is based on a weighted average of hourly rates in 35 selected occupations and takes no account of differences in man-hour productivity.

[5] This point is discussed by August Lösch,"The Economics of Location," pp. 461ff., Yale University Press, 1954. From data in the *Federal Reserve Bulletin*, he finds that prevailing rates on prime commercial loans in major centers in 1919 to 1925 varied roughly with distance from New York at the rate of about 0.5 per cent per 1,000 miles. The highest rates, however, were in the Mountain region, with somewhat lower rates prevailing in Pacific Coast cities. Rates on bank loans and on time deposits in Texas cities in 1936 varied consistently according to distance from the nearest Reserve Bank city. Lösch also cites data from the 1928 report of the Federal Reserve Board to indicate that member-bank discount rates were systematically higher in smaller cities in that year. Finally, Lösch finds generally higher yields on state, municipal, and utility bonds with increased distance from New York.

For the present, we take geographic differentials in the supply of land, labor, and capital for granted and inquire merely how they affect an individual producer's locational preferences.

5·3   The Producer's Adjustment to Differences in the Relative Prices of Production Factors

The comparative costs of a process at different locations cannot be arrived at by simply pricing a fixed recipe of productive factors, such as 2 acres of land, 500 unskilled laborers, and $100,000 of invested capital. Land, labor, and equipment are never required in absolutely inflexible proportions. Wheat can be grown under "extensive" cultivation, meaning that labor and equipment are thinly spread over a large acreage, or under "intensive" cultivation, meaning that much labor and equipment are employed per acre. Similarly, the investment in equipment per man may be large or small depending on the degree of mechanization adopted. Of all the possible combinations of factors that *could* be used on a given site to produce, say, a bushel of wheat, the *most economical* combination is the one to appraise and compare with the cost of other appropriate combinations at other locations.

The appropriate combination of factors for any given process depends on the relative prices at which the several factors are available. At locations where some one factor, *e.g.*, labor, is particularly expensive, it will be more profitable to use it intensively —to economize on labor and substitute land or capital. There is no such thing as a "most efficient" combination for a given process in a purely technical sense without regard to the relative prices of the factors used.[6]

Since geographic differences in price and quality are particularly prominent in the case of land, it is convenient to illustrate the producer's adjustment of factor combinations by referring specifically to *intensity of land use* in relation to rents and the qualities of sites. The reader will see, however, that the same

[6] Ideal economic proportioning of factors requires that the marginal product of each factor be equated to the marginal cost of that factor. That is, each kind of input should be increased up to the point where any further addition would add just as much to total costs as to total returns.

principles apply to the intensity of use of each factor. Adjustment of the relative proportions of labor and capital in particular is closely associated with the question of scale of production, which will be taken up later in this chapter.

The way in which intensity of land use on a given site is adapted to land cost [7] is indicated in Fig. 5·1. As is there shown graphically, the user of the site for any given production process can maximize the net returns on the resources at his command by proper adjustment of the intensity of land use. With higher rents, more intensive land use is appropriate. There is, however, a definite "ceiling" rent payable. At this level of rent, it is just possible for the producer to remain in business on the site, assuming he adopts the most appropriate intensity of land use. With any higher rent, loss would be inevitable.

Location involves a choice of sites that may have different advantages both for processing and for transfer. These advantages have to be weighed against the respective rents charged. In Fig. 5·2, four different sites are considered, which may be regarded as located at different distances from a market, so that the net realized price of the product is different at each.[8] At each of the sites shown, the possible returns (assuming the optimum adjustment of land-use intensity) will depend on the rent charged, decreasing as the rent increases. For each site, there is one ceiling rent figure, associated with zero profits. Sites available for rents below their ceiling rents (as are two of those shown in Fig. 5·2) afford profit possibilities and are presumably acceptable to producers in this industry.

Figure 5·3 represents the case in a still different light, showing how the ceiling rent in a given use varies with the advantage of the site. This advantage is here supposed to be measured in terms of access to market. The rents and market advantages of five sites

---

[7] For convenience, the cost of acquiring the services of land will henceforth be called simply "rent." We should remember, however, that in practice the producer may choose to buy the land and pay interest instead. A discussion of the relation between rents and site values will be found in Section 6·8.

[8] The picture would be similar if the sites all had equally good access to market but different procurement costs or different degrees of advantage, e.g., soil fertility, in the production process itself.

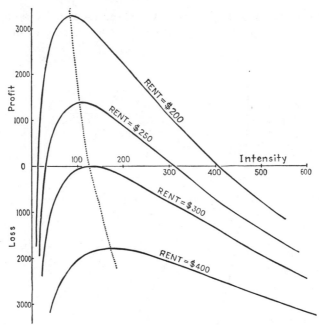

Fig. 5·1   Relation of rent, intensity, and producer's net return. This diagram indicates the annual net return on a hypothetical annual outlay of
$10,000 for rent, interest, and wages combined. Each curve shows how returns
vary with intensity of land use when a given rent per acre is charged. Intensity
is defined as the annual outlay per acre for the hire of production factors
other than land.

For each level of rent, the returns are low for the lowest intensities, rise
to a maximum at the intensity representing the optimum combination of
production factors, and fall away again as intensity is further increased. Thus,
in the case represented in the diagram, an intensity of about $107 is the best
choice when rent is $250 per acre.

The higher the rent the lower the returns at any given intensity. With
higher rents the point of optimum intensity moves to the right, i.e., it pays
to use more labor and capital per acre when the land costs more. The dotted
line passes through all such optimum points and traces out the relation
between rent and returns under the assumption that for each level of rent
the appropriate optimum intensity is adopted.

Finally, the diagram indicates the maximum, or "ceiling," rent that the
user of land of this quality could afford to pay. The curve of returns when
rent is $300 just touches at its point of optimum intensity the zero-profits
line. If intensity is properly adjusted to rent, then, the user could just afford
a $300 rent per acre. This is his top demand price for the use of the land.

are shown, but presumably only those represented by points on or below the curve of ceiling rents will be acceptable to this type of user.

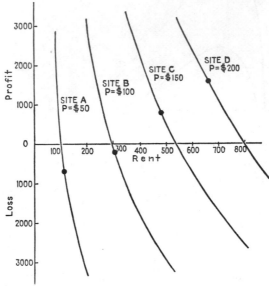

FIG. 5·2   Relation of rent and returns (at optimum intensity of land use) on four sites. This diagram is based on the same hypothetical production function as Fig. 5·1 and shows the relation between rent and returns (at optimum intensity in all cases) for four sites. The net realized unit price of the product (P in the figure) is taken as $50, $100, $150, and $200 respectively at the four sites, to reflect differences in ease of access to market. For each site, the effect of increased rent in curtailing returns is shown by the way the curves drop off to the right. The "ceiling" rent for each site is shown on the rent axis where the curve crosses the zero-profits line. In the four cases shown, these ceiling rents are approximately $100, $300, $540, and $800 respectively.

If the rents actually asked by the owners of the land were as shown by the abscissas of the large dots on the curves, the user could make a profit by renting site D or a smaller profit by renting site C but would lose money on either of the other two.

It will be noted in Fig. 5·3A that the curve showing the relation of ceiling rents to net realized price of the product is concave upward. That is, if the transfer costs on the product were simply proportional to distance, the maximum rent this user could afford

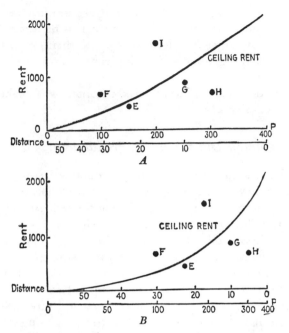

FIG. 5·3   Relation of rent and distance from market. These diagrams are based on the same hypothetical production function as Figs. 5·1 and 5·2 and show by "rent gradients" the way in which the ceiling rent varies with distance from market. Optimum adjustment of land use intensity is assumed in all cases.

The effect of distance from market is represented in each diagram by the two scales at the bottom, both in terms of the net realized price of the product at the producer's location (P) and in terms of route mileage. Equal changes in the net price P correspond to small added distances close to the market and to increasingly larger added distances as we go away from the market. This is in accord with the principle that transfer costs increase less than in proportion to length of haul, as explained in Chap. 2.

The curve (rent gradient) in each diagram shows the highest rent this user can afford to pay for sites at each distance from market. If certain sites are available, at distances and rents as shown by the five dots on each diagram, sites E, G, and H would be acceptable to this user, but not site F or I.

In Fig. 5·3A the horizontal scale is proportional to transfer cost and the rent gradient appears only slightly concave. Figure 5·3B shows the same hypothetical data plotted with the horizontal scale proportional to distance from market; the concavity of the rent gradient is markedly increased.

to pay for land of a given quality would decline first rapidly and then more and more gradually with increasing distance from market. Actually, since transfer costs rise less than proportionately with distance, the gradient of ceiling rents as a function of distance is still more concave, as shown by Fig. 5·3B. The analysis of land-utilization patterns in the next chapter will make use of such "rent gradients."

5·4 Geographic Differences in Productivity

In most of the discussion thus far, productive factors have been treated as if they were of uniform quality at all locations, so that only price differentials needed to be considered. Actually this is far from true. Both rent and wages may be high in a given farming area, for instance, and yet the fertility of the soil and the skill of the labor there may result in very low processing cost. Qualitative differences are particularly important for types of use that exploit rare natural features of sites, such as mineral content or unique scenic advantages, and for those which demand rare skills.

As a rule it is impossible to ascribe the processing advantages of a site wholly to the quality of any particular factor of production such as land or labor, and the resultant economies may show up in almost any item of the cost statement. For present purposes it is enough to note the three principal origins of productivity differentials.

Some such differentials are traceable to differences in natural resources or the land itself. Soil, climate, and topography are important direct determinants of yield in agriculture and forestry and affect the efficiency of almost any process. A hot climate, for instance, is likely to curtail output per man-hour in manufacturing or trade and thus to raise unit labor costs—though the employer may prefer to shift the extra cost to other items such as interest and electric power by installing air conditioning. Cold climates necessitate heavier and more costly construction. Construction and maintenance costs may also be higher when soil and topographic features are unfavorable.

Other productivity differentials are based on economic and social organization rather than original natural resources. The efficiency of labor, for example, depends partly on education and adaptability. The laws and customs of a society help to determine how fully a producer can utilize the resources at his command. Though a few generalizations and tentative "laws of development" can be laid down, a complete explanation of any local productivity advantage of this sort would require an analysis of the history of the area.

Finally, efficiency is associated with large-scale production as such, though the relationship depends to some extent on the institutional milieu just mentioned.

Subsequent sections of this chapter will discuss productivity differentials involving the degree of utilization of the producer's resources and productivity differentials involving the scale on which production is organized.

5·5 Flexibility and the Utilization of Production Factors [9]

Not all the land, labor, and capital a producer owns or hires are fully employed all the time. The requirements of a process for these factors may thus vary from one location to another if some locations permit fuller utilization than others.

Production factors, being imperfectly mobile and imperfectly divisible, cannot quickly adjust to fluctuations in the producer's need for them. In most businesses it is impracticable to pay the entire working force on a piece-rate basis or to hire and fire or adjust working hours to meet day-to-day variations in the work load. As a result, some of the pay roll is wasted some of the time, and total direct and indirect labor cost [10] per unit of output rises during recessions of production. It is much harder still to vary the input of capital and land in an enterprise in response to such fluctuations; so more of these factors are idle more of the time, and the fluctuations in capital and land cost per unit of output are generally greater than those of labor cost.

[9] A more detailed treatment of the subject matter of this section will be found in M. C. Daly, The Effect of Overhead Costs upon the Structure of the American Economy, Southern Economic Journal, vol. VIII, No. 1, July, 1941, pp. 22–39.

[10] Direct labor cost here refers to those wages which are easily assignable as costs to particular lots of output; indirect labor cost here includes the wages and salaries of all other employees.

What is commonly known as overhead cost includes those elements of outlay that are relatively fixed over time and consequently on a per-unit basis vary inversely to output during recessions.[11] The relative importance of overhead is perhaps greatest in independent household agriculture, but it is increasing in modern manufacturing.

Overhead costs are locationally significant for an industry if some locations allow either more continuous and stable production or more flexible adjustment of inputs. Thus, the overhead costs of operating an outdoor swimming pool are likely to be greater in Minnesota than in Florida, because the season is shorter. The overhead costs of a firm employing organized labor are likely to be higher than those of an otherwise identical firm employing unorganized labor, to the extent that organization restricts or penalizes hiring, firing, or overtime.[12] The overhead costs of a firm operating under agreements or legislation restricting regular night and Sunday work will also reflect the less constant use of fixed investment that such controls impose.

5·6 *Economies of Concentrated Production*[13]

Preceding sections have indicated how the producer's search for a low-cost processing location is affected by the possibility of

[11] Some elements of procurement and distribution cost also involve use of production factors by the consignee or shipper and thus some overhead cost. Most taxes belong in the overhead category, except excise taxes on the product or a material or energy source, income taxes, and pay-roll taxes on such wages as can easily be varied according to work done.

[12] Some of the overhead burden imposed on the firm by such restrictions upon "treating labor like a commodity" represents social costs that the employee or the community would otherwise have to bear.

[13] This section is adapted from a passage by the present author in the National Resources Planning Board report, "Industrial Location and National Resources," p. 242, Government Printing Office, Washington, 1943, and owes the basic formulation to P. Sargant Florence, "The Logic of Industrial Organisation," Kegan Paul, Trench, Trubner & Company, Ltd., London, 1933. More detailed discussions will be found in E. A. G. Robinson, "The Structure of Competitive Industry," Harcourt, Brace & Company, Inc., New York, 1932, and in Joseph Steindl, "Small and Big Business," Oxford Institute of Statistics, Monograph No. 1, Oxford University Press, New York, 1945.

It should be made clear that the economies of larger output here referred to are long-run economies, involving the superiority of a large establishment to a small varying the combination of factors and the possibility of fuller utilization of factors in some locations. A third important feature of the behavior of production costs is their relation to the size of the plant and the firm.

Three basic principles operate to reduce costs in a plant with larger output: "multiples," "massing of reserves," and "bulk transactions."

MULTIPLES. The principle of multiples rests on the imperfect divisibility of units of equipment and labor. A machine, for instance, can be designed for a certain rate of output while at the same time it is impossible to design a machine to perform the same operation at a lesser rate without a substantial increase in the cost per piece. Another way of stating the same thing is to say that there is a minimum efficient capacity for any kind of productive apparatus.

In the case of labor the same point is equally in evidence. Ten men may be hired for an operation or two or one, but part-time use of one man usually entails loss in efficiency, especially if the rest of his time is spent on work not fully utilizing his training and ability.

These rather elastic limits to the divisibility of the human and mechanical units employed in production are the main basis of the economies of large-scale production organization. It is evident that the larger the scale of output the more nearly will it be possible to have each operation performed by a fully utilized and efficient-sized unit adapted to that operation alone and unencumbered by the necessity of shifting from one operation to another. The principle of "multiples" states that maximum efficiency in the use of the combined units would require a total plant capacity equal to some common multiple of the capacities of the individual units and that the *smallest* fully efficient size would be the *least* common multiple.[14]

---

one rather than the operation of a given establishment at a higher percentage of capacity.

[14] Thus if four machines are used in successive steps in a process, with daily unit capacities of 100, 200, 300, and 500 respectively, the plant's daily output must be 3,000 or some multiple of 3,000 in order to use all machines to their full capacity. A daily output of 3,000 would call for 30 machines on the first step, 15 on the second, 10 on the third, and 6 on the fourth.

The advantages of detailed specialization in production thus tend to make larger scale forms of organization in a particular industry more efficient than smaller scale, provided that the relative prices of materials and services are no greater and that the product can be disposed of just as favorably.

MASSING OF RESERVES. Massing of reserves is another basis of economies in larger sized units. Some reserves of materials, supplies, and equipment must normally be held in any plant to provide for accidents, routine maintenance, interruptions of supply, and sudden variations in demand. The size of this necessary margin is not proportional, however, to normal output; it is much less than proportional. A larger operating unit can safely get along with a smaller percentage of its resources tied up in this way, since to a considerable extent the fluctuations of requirements in different parts of the establishment will cancel out. Essentially the same actuarial principle applies here as in any form of insurance.

BULK TRANSACTIONS. A still further incentive to large-scale production is the reduction of the unit price of materials, supplies, and services purchased from other enterprises. Gas, electricity, and water, for instance, are sold to industrial consumers at graduated rates roughly reflecting the economies of large-scale supply of these essentials. As noted in an earlier chapter, transportation rates on both materials and products go down considerably when larger, *e.g.,* carload, trainload, or shipload, consignments can be made at one time, and scheduling and other features of transportation service are more likely to be adapted to the interests of large than of small shippers and receivers.

The greater bargaining power of the large enterprise and its ability to provide its own transport, facilities, and other services if necessary work in the same direction. The complexities of administering antidiscriminatory price legislation attest the difficulties of separating the "genuine" economies of bulk transactions from the ulterior concessions gained by bargaining power.

5·7   *Limits to the Economic Size of Production Units*

The existence of all these advantages in the operation of larger plants does not mean, however, that cost decreases indefinitely with added size. In many industries all the important economies depending on size can be fully realized in a moderate-sized plant, and a still larger one would have little further to recommend it.

The development of specialized mechanization beyond a certain point is often of doubtful advantage because it involves a corresponding loss of adaptability to changing conditions and consequent risk of high overhead costs. The economy of mechanized methods depends on repetitiveness. For this reason, the very large plant may actually produce at about the same level of mechanization as the moderate-sized plant and thus lack any purely technical advantage over the latter. Equipment, procedures, and personnel that are specialized elaborately for a particular rate and type of production may be impossible to use efficiently at times of slack production or when the character of the product has to be changed to keep abreast of competition. Every new annual model of automobiles, for instance, requires expensive plant retooling. If model changes took place, say, only every five years, undoubtedly still further elaborations of the existing specialization would become profitable. On the other hand, if specifications were changed still more frequently, some of the highly specialized machinery that is now set up for a year's run in an automobile factory would doubtless be replaced by more versatile equipment, less efficient on some specific jobs but easier to adapt from one job to another. The style clothing trades are an instance of drastic limitation of mass-production economies by variations in the product.[15]

5·8 Characteristics of Location When Plant Size Is Effectively Limited by Enterpriser Capacity

The foregoing considerations of flexibility and adaptability do not necessarily penalize the large plant; they merely impose cer-

[15] Cf. the discussion of "building flexibility into plants" in George Stigler, Production and Distribution Theory in the Short Run, *Journal of Political Economy*, vol. 47, June, 1939, pp. 305–327. Actually three somewhat different kinds of limitation on large-scale organization are involved here: (a) the need to provide for quantitative flexibility in time (variations in the rate of output), (b) the need to provide for qualitative flexibility in time (variations in the style or character of the product), and (c) the fact that at any one time the market insists on variety so that only a limited portion of total output can be uniform.

tain limits to specialization in productive processes and make the economies of increased size eventually taper off.

There is one item, however, that will ultimately lead to increased processing costs with increased size. We may think of this as a reflection of the imperfect "multipliability" of leadership in a firm, just as the high costs of very small establishments reflect the imperfect divisibility of units of labor and equipment. Every concern must head up to a single leader with ultimate responsibility for coordination. Although the leader may delegate many tasks, there remains an irreducible final responsibility that *cannot be shared*. The larger the business the greater becomes this task for one individual and the more elaborate the machinery of delegation and coordination.

It is important to note that this consideration limits the size of the unit of control (the firm) and may or may not be the effective limit on the size of the production unit (the plant). In some businesses there are so many unpredictable variables in the production process (including procurement and distribution as well as processing) that the limits of ordinary human administrative capacity seem to be reached in a small enterprise operating only a single plant. Only a few enterprisers who possess exceptional abilities or have developed some relatively protected or stable line can operate on a larger scale.[16]

Table 5·1 lists some of the manufacturing industries that show the least development of branch plants and belong in the class just discussed. In none of the industries listed is as much as 10 per cent of the employment accounted for by firms that operate more than one establishment.

Most of these industries turn out highly differentiated products for unstable markets. Individual exclusive features, reputation of the maker, and seasonal styles are important factors in determining the market for any one firm's output. Variety of products, irregularity of demand, and low capital requirements facilitate the

---

[16] Strictly speaking, the consideration under discussion belongs under the heading of transfer costs to the extent that top management problems are purchasing or merchandising problems. It has nothing directly to do with distance, however, and it seems more convenient here not to insist on a distinction between the management of production proper and the management of purchasing and sales.

Table 5·1. *Manufacturing Industries with Least Development of Branch Plants, 1937*

Industry *	Wage Earners in Concerns with Two or More Plants, as Percentage of Total Wage Earners in the Industry
Blouses, women's, misses', and children's—contract factories	0.0
Engraving (other than steel, copperplate, or wood), chasing, etching, and diesinking	0.0
Knitted outerwear—contract factories	0.0
Wool scouring	0.0
Fur goods—regular factories	0.9
Clothing, men's, youths', and boys', not elsewhere classified—contract factories	1.5
Dresses, except house dresses	2.2
Millinery—regular factories	2.5
Coats, suits, and separate skirts, women's, misses', and juniors'—contract factories	3.3
Jewelry	6.1
Shirts (except work shirts), collars, and nightwear—contract factories	9.3
All manufacturing industries	51.1

* Industries with fewer than 1,000 wage earners have been omitted. For a considerable number of other industries, data have been withheld by the Census Bureau to avoid disclosure of individual establishment data.

SOURCE: Willard L. Thorp and others, "The Structure of Industry," Appendices A and B, pp. 211–226, Temporary National Economic Committee, Monograph 27, Washington, 1941.

entry of new competitors into many of these fields. These conditions are typical of such lines as jewelry, fur goods, women's shoes, and apparel in general.

Farming is an unexpected bedfellow of this group. Enterpriser capacity seems to set the effective limit on growth of the individual farm,[17] and multiple-farm enterprises are relatively rare. The basic reason, however, is not so much the character of the product or its demand as the nature of the productive process

[17] It is commonly found that in a given type of farming in a given area, the larger farms are the more efficient and more profitable, but this does not necessarily mean that any representative farmer in the area could make a better living if his farm were larger.

itself. A farmer's intimate connection with the soil requires a complex dovetailing and planning of diverse operations (a farmer is notoriously a jack-of-all-trades), a relatively extensive land use, and an adaptation of the operator's whole way of life. Weather is a special factor of uncertainty, which hardly enters into the calculations of most other businesses.

The accompanying maps (Figs. 5·4 and 5·5) show the location patterns of two manufacturing industries of the "clustered" type mentioned: jewelry and "women's, misses', and children's apparel, not elsewhere classified." At the time to which the maps refer (1935), the jewelry industry comprised 994 establishments with an average of 17 wage earners in each, and the women's, misses', and children's apparel industry comprised 8,464 establishments with an average of 31 wage earners in each. It is apparent from the maps that most of the plants in each of these industries are concentrated in and near the large metropolitan centers.[18] Detailed maps show a still more striking concentration in particular neighborhoods and streets of those cities.[19] It is clear that the scatter of *ultimate* consumers all over the United States has little bearing on the location of either of these lines of manufacturing. They produce for concentrated intermediate "shopping" markets of the type discussed in Section 4·6. Concentration is further encouraged by the advantages of sharing a labor market —a factor to be discussed in Chap. 7.

5·9 Characteristics of Location When Considerations of Distance Limit Concentration

At the other extreme are industries in which it is customary for firms to have many branches. The optimum size of a firm is here larger than that of a plant, and enterpriser capacity does not impose the effective limit on plant size. In these industries the

[18] Jewelry establishments were reported at the 1935 census in only 73 of the 3,000-odd counties of the United States, and women's, misses', and children's apparel factories in only 258 counties. National Resources Planning Board, "Industrial Location and National Resources," Table 15, pp. 252–254, Government Printing Office, Washington, 1943.

[19] *Cf.* M. A. Magee, "Trends in Location of the Women's Clothing Industry," University of Chicago Press, Chicago, 1930.

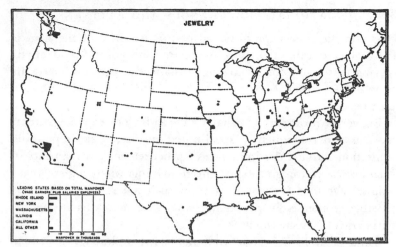

FIG. 5·4 Location of the jewelry manufacturing industry, 1935. Dots represent individual establishments; counties with five or more establishments are shown in solid black. (*Reproduced from National Resources Committee, "The Structure of the American Economy," Part* I, *Map A-59, p. 358, Washington, 1939. Based on data in U. S. Census of Manufactures, 1935.*)

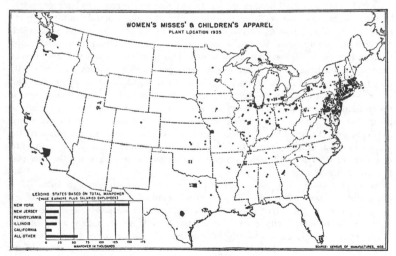

FIG. 5·5 Location of the women's, misses', and children's apparel industry, 1935. Dots represent individual establishments; counties with five or more establishments are shown in solid black. (*Reproduced from National Resources Committee, "The Structure of the American Economy," Part* I, *Map 20, p. 46, Washington, 1939. Based on data in U. S. Census of Manufactures, 1935.*)

characteristic reason for dispersal of the activities of the firm is that a larger scale of operations at any one point would entail serving markets at greater average distances or drawing materials from greater distances or perhaps both, and thus would increase transfer costs.

Breweries, for example, usually have to be located close to their markets and consequently are limited in size. A corresponding limitation through the influence of procurement costs appears in such cases as cotton ginning or cheese making, where a giant plant would have to draw materials from such a large area that any possible economies in processing would be more than offset by extra costs of procurement.[20]

Table 5·2, listing some manufacturing industries in which branch-plant organization is especially prevalent, furnishes an interesting contrast to Table 5·1. In each of the industries listed

[20] Another good illustrative case of the limitation of plant size by procurement-cost considerations is the grain-elevator business. A grain elevator is essentially a group of large storage bins for grain awaiting transshipment by rail or water. "Local" elevators, as distinct from the giant ones at major ports or milling centers, receive grain direct from the farmer's truck. Running the elevator is a relatively simple task, usually done by one man, and the costs of construction and maintenance increase much less than in proportion to increased capacity. Consequently, various studies have found that elevator costs per bushel decrease markedly with larger volume of business. From the distribution standpoint there are certainly no compensating disadvantages of size, since the shipments of one elevator are an insignificant part of the total entering the main markets and have no effect on price. But increased volume can be attained only by inducing more remote producers to join the supply area of that particular elevator, and the costs of trucking grain additional distances sets a limit on this. Consequently, we find the representative local elevator a small and high-cost establishment, serving a supply area of a few dozen square miles.

In North Dakota alone there were 1,101 country grain elevators in 1939. (U. S. Census of Business, "Wholesale Trade, 1939," Table 1, p. 263, 1940.) This is one elevator for every 64 square miles of land area in the state, or one for every 54 square miles of farm land, or one for about every 15 or 20 square miles of harvested grain acreage. Even allowing for the fact that some towns have more than one elevator, it is clear that the supply areas of most individual elevators do not extend for many miles.

As is to be expected, the majority of country grain elevators are branches of multiple-unit organizations. No data on this point are available for the cooperative elevators, comprising 20 to 25 per cent of the total; but of the noncooperative elevators in North Dakota in 1939, three out of four were "line," *i.e.,* branch, establishments.

in Table 5·2, at least 90 per cent of employment is accounted for by firms operating two or more plants.

Table 5·2   Manufacturing Industries with Greatest Development of Branch Plants, 1937

Industry *	Wage Earners in Concerns with Two or More Plants, as Percentage of Total Wage Earners in the Industry
Copper smelting and refining	98.1
Blast-furnace products	96.5
Cars, electric and steam railroad	92.3
Coke-oven products	91.4
Petroleum products	91.2
Cigarettes	91.1
Beet sugar	90.0
All manufacturing industries	51.1

* Data for a considerable number of industries have been withheld by the Census Bureau to avoid disclosure of individual establishment data.

Source: Willard L. Thorp and others, "The Structure of Industry," Appendix A, pp. 211–225, Temporary National Economic Committee, Monograph 27, Washington, 1941.

The location patterns are quite different from those of the "clustered" type discussed in the previous section. Plants are spaced out to serve distinct market areas or to tap distinct supply areas as the case may be, and clusters of similar plants at any one location are the exception rather than the rule. The demarcation of exclusive sales or purchasing territories for individual plants is naturally more rigid between the various branches of one firm than between plants of competing firms.

Figure 5·6 shows the branch warehouses of General Foods, Inc., on a map especially drawn to make the areas of states and major cities proportional to their populations. The approximately uniform scatter of points on this map shows the extent to which this system of branch establishments has been spread over the market pattern.

Other representative location patterns in industries of this general type are shown in Figs. 3·2 through 3·7.

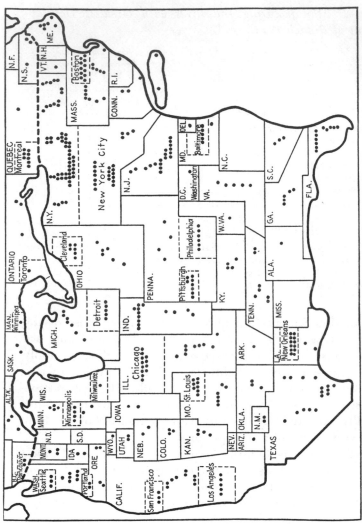

FIG. 5·6 Location of warehouse stocks of General Foods Corporation in the United States and Canada. The areas of the states, provinces, and principal cities have been made proportional to the respective populations. (*Redrawn by permission from a map prepared and distributed by the General Foods Corporation, 1946.*)

An interesting contrast between the "clustered" type of industries discussed in the previous section and the type here shown is that the former tend to have smaller plants in the major production centers, whereas the latter tend to have larger plants in such centers.[21]

SUMMARY

The basis of geographic differences in processing costs is the fact that units of land, labor, and capital are imperfectly mobile and imperfectly divisible. To minimize his processing costs, the individual enterpriser seeks a location conducive to high utilization of the productive capacity of factors and scale of output appropriate to that location.

The best combination of factors involve more intensive utilization of any factor where its price is high, the most conspicuous variations occurring in the rent of land.

The scale of production is determined primarily by the economies of larger scale processing as against either increasing transfer costs over wider areas or the diseconomies of larger administrative control units. Where concentration at one location is limited by transfer costs, firms may outgrow single locations and establish branches. Where the diseconomies of the larger firm are the limiting factor, branch plants are the exception and many similar plants may cluster in the same town or city.

[21] *Cf.* National Resources Planning Board, "Industrial Location and National Resources," Tables 18 and 21, pp. 257 and 260, Government Printing Office, Washington, 1943, for data illustrating this point in regard to the shoe and ice-cream industries.

CHAPTER 6

Land-use Competition

IN THE PREVIOUS CHAPTER the individual producer was confronted with a pattern of land costs (rents), along with patterns of cost for the other items: capital, labor, taxes, materials, and distribution expenses. In any given situation the producer's profits at any particular location will, of course, be determined by all these factors, and his preference for location will be determined by whether or not he thinks he could find a more profitable combination of circumstances somewhere else. Rent is one of the many factors he must consider.

Each producer may be regarded as having in mind a maximum, or "ceiling," rent that he could just afford to pay for the privilege of occupying any site. For better sites his ceiling is, of course, higher.[1] If the pattern of actual rents asked happened to coincide with his pattern of ceiling rents, all locations would be equally desirable for him. In practice, however, he finds that in many locations the rent asked is more than he could afford, while if he is fortunate, there may be a few locations where he is asked less than his ceiling and therefore can make an extra profit.

This chapter will explore the way in which competition among such land users leads to systematic geographic patterns of land utilization and rent.

6·1 Processing Advantages and Transfer Advantages of Sites

A producer requires a site on which to operate and can afford to pay different rents for different sites, depending on their advantages for his business. These advantages are of two sorts.

In some uses the value of a site depends primarily on the access

---

[1] Some of the ceilings are likely to be subterranean, *i.e.*, the business could not survive on some sites even rent-free unless subsidized.

the site affords to other parties with whom the occupant may want to trade. A good site in this sense is one entailing low *transfer costs*. For downtown urban land uses in general, transfer costs are the important locational factor, and land is rented, bought, and sold on the basis of its positional advantages alone.

At the other extreme are types of land use for which transfer costs are unimportant compared with differences in *processing costs* at good and bad sites. The more valuable the product in relation to its distribution costs per mile the greater is the significance of resource quality as against access to markets. Metal ore mining is an example—the chemical and physical make-up of the site rather than its location is the main basis of value. Other factors of intrinsic quality are the availability of water on the site in adequate amount and quality, the suitability of the soil and climate for agriculture, the natural flora and fauna (for trapping, fishing, hunting, forestry, or grazing), the amenities of the site (climate, view, and terrain), and finally those features of the site which determine construction and maintenance costs (primarily terrain, soil structure, and climate). All these aspects of intrinsic quality join with the advantages of position, in different combinations for different industries, to determine the economic attractiveness of the site.

This distinction between processing and transfer advantages of sites is worth emphasizing. Even if all land were of uniform quality, patterns of differential advantage and preferred land use would still arise on the basis of relative position alone. This is the case first analyzed theoretically more than a century ago by von Thünen [2] and exemplified most nearly in plains regions where the pattern of occupance is based almost entirely on transfer relations.

For the purposes of the present analysis it is appropriate to devote attention mainly to position. On the basis of its transfer advantages, a site can attract a wide variety of bidders. It is this competition of alternative uses which sets the over-all pattern of

[2] "Der isolierte Staat in Beziehung auf Landwirthschaft und Nationalökonomie," 3 vols., Hamburg and Rostock, 1826–1863. For a more recent and accessible exposition, see R. T. Ely and G. S. Wehrwein, "Land Economics," The Macmillan Company, New York, 1940.

rents and land utilization. Specific quality advantages of a site, on the other hand, are often relevant only to one industry and rarely to more than a few.

6·2 Rents as the Outcome of Competitive Bidding for the Use of Sites

In so far as there really is competition and an active and informed pursuit of maximum individual advantage (which is by no means always the case), better sites will be bid up in rent and purchase price. Complete competitive equilibrium, in fact, would imply that rents on better sites were just enough higher to offset the advantages of those sites to the highest bidder, so that no producer would have any further incentive to move. The existing pattern, of course, never attains this state of equilibrium.

The landowner in general will attempt to exact the maximum rent any user will pay for the site; or if he uses it himself, he will choose a form of use that yields as great a return on the land as possible. Thus the outcome of competition for the limited and immobile supply of land tends to allocate each site to the user and type of use capable of paying the *highest rent per acre.*

Note should be made of the distinction between this principle and the one regulating the policies of the individual land user, which is the maximization of the rate of net return on his total outlay inclusive of rent.[3] The reason for this difference is that for the individual the total resources at his command are fixed but the supply of land may be just as elastic as the supply of any other factor, whereas for the whole economy of an area, the supply of land is fixed.

6·3 Rent Gradients for Specific Types of Land Use

To understand how the process of competitive allocation of sites leads to systematic patterns of land use we must inquire what determines the maximum, or ceiling, rents that particular types of use will pay for different sites. We are interested here not in the location of individual producers but in the location pattern of

[3] *Cf.* Section 5·3.

an industry or type of land use, such as wheat growing or hard-ware selling. Within any such relatively homogeneous group of producers, the factors of locational preference are similar despite the latitude afforded by the possibility of varying the intensity of land use according to rent charged.

Figure 5·3 showed that with increasing distance from a market there is a rather consistent decline of the ceiling rents payable by any one type of land use. Since increased distribution costs reduce the net receipts of the producer, such producers can afford less rent if they are farther from the market and finally none at all at a point beyond which it would no longer pay to use the land for that purpose even if rent free.

There is such a "rent gradient," or progression of ceiling rents, for each kind of use, and no two such gradients are identical. What determines their shape?

The level of transfer costs naturally influences the slope of rent gradients. When transfer is costly, the ceiling rent for any given kind of use drops off rapidly with increasing distance; but along a route of cheap transfer, the corresponding rent gradient is rela-tively flat.

The structure of transfer costs influences the shape of rent gradients. It has already been noted that the characteristic long-haul economy of transfer is reflected in an accentuated concavity of the gradients; [4] *i.e.,* ceiling rents fall off rapidly with distance from market as long as the distance is short but less and less rapidly as longer hauls are involved. Over any stretch of distance for which the rate is uniform, the gradient will be horizontal, ex-cept as influenced by considerations other than freight cost. Thus the steplike characteristic of transport-rate progressions may be reflected by steps in the gradient of land use return as well.

As between different products, the slope of the gradient will differ according to the *amount and transferability of the product produced per unit of land.* This is not at all the same thing as the intensity. Intensity of use is measured by the input of capital and labor per unit of land; what is in question here is the cost of delivering the products of a unit of land. Some very intensive

---

[4] *Cf.* Fig. 5·3 and the accompanying discussion.

uses, like diamond mines, yield compact and easily transferable products; some uses of low intensity, like city parking lots, are forced by transfer considerations to be very close to their markets. Within any single kind of use, however, larger output per unit of land (of a given intrinsic quality) is directly dependent on increased intensity.

Regardless of relative intensity of land use, processes that yield a large volume of output per unit of land, particularly if the product is expensive to distribute, have relatively steep rent gradients. This is because each addition to distance adds a relatively large amount to the expense of distributing the products of an acre and thus makes a relatively large reduction in the rent earnable on an acre.

The ultimate extreme in this direction is the production of direct personal services, such as shoe shining. Where the potential customers pass, *i.e.*, on main shopping streets, the use of space for a shoe-shining establishment may justify paying a high rent; a short distance away on a side street it may be impossible to earn enough to pay any rent at all. In other words, the rent gradient in this kind of use is so steep as to be almost vertical. It is limited by the extent to which the customers themselves are willing to detour in order to get the service, and in the case of small-scale "convenience" transactions this is a very short distance indeed. At the other extreme are land uses producing small amounts of easily transferable products per unit of land. Sheep grazing, for example, is profitably practiced thousands of miles from the markets for wool and mutton.

Evidently the gradients and patterns of ceiling rents will show different characteristic forms for different land uses even in the absence of any intrinsic-quality differentiation in the land itself. Some kinds of use can afford to pay more than others for the occupance of sites convenient to markets.

The same can be said with reference to the effect of procurement costs on the location of different industries around material-supply points. That case, however, is far less significant. It is rare for a number of industries, requiring considerable space, to be competing for sites as close as possible to a single materials source.

On the other hand, nearly all types of industry find a *market* in towns and cities, and for many of them the ease of access to that market is the dominant locational factor.

6·4 *Characteristic Patterns of Land Uses around Markets*

The way in which the different slopes of rent gradients around a market produce an orderly sequence of land uses is illustrated schematically in Fig. 6·1. Four representative types of use are included, with the rent gradient for each rising to a peak in the market city, since that would be the optimum location for each use from the standpoint of distribution costs alone. The rent gradients fall at different rates, so that each use in turn appears as the highest bidder.[5] The resulting idealized pattern of land uses—a series of four concentric zones—is indicated mapwise in the lower part of the figure.

In the actual world it is rare to find so neat a pattern. One reason for this is the irregularity with which transfer costs correspond to distance. Another reason is that each product or kind of land use has its own geographic pattern of supply areas and market centers.

In Fig. 6·1 the influence of only a single market center is

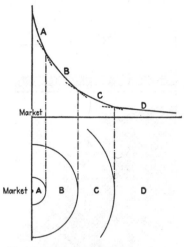

Fig. 6·1 Rent gradients and zones of land use tributary to a single market center. The upper part of the diagram shows the relation between distance from a market and rent in four different types of land use *A*, *B*, *C*, and *D*. Each of the four rent gradients is drawn as a solid line over the interval in which the corresponding land use is the highest rent use. The lower part of the diagram is a map of the resulting pattern of land-use zones.

[5] The composite gradient of actual rents, as determined by the sequence of "highest bidder" uses, must be even more concave than the gradients for individual uses. Figure 6·1 adequately demonstrates this.

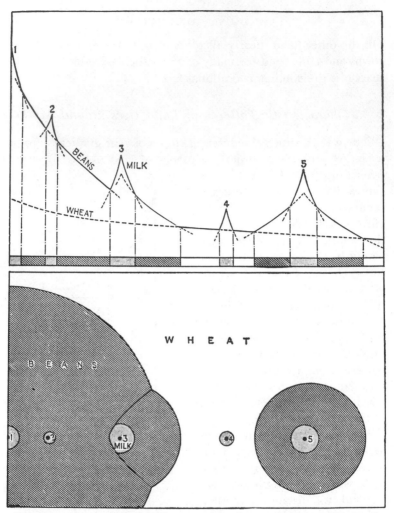

FIG. 6·2 Rent gradients and zones of land use tributary to five market centers, 1, 2, 3, 4, and 5. Three types of land use are involved: milk, beans, and wheat production. It is assumed that a market for milk exists at each of the five market centers, that markets for beans exist at market centers 1, 3, and 5 only, and that a market for wheat exists only at market center 1.

The upper part of the diagram shows the rent gradients for the three types of use, each rent gradient being drawn as a solid line over the interval in which the corresponding land use is the highest rent use.

The resulting progression of land uses along the route running through the five market centers is shown by the shadings on the strip near the middle

shown. But some products (such as fluid milk) have a primarily local sale, whereas others (such as wheat) are produced largely for national or even world markets, and their whole geographic price structures are based on the prices quoted at a few major market centers. A more complete picture, which takes account of this diversity of patterns, is shown in Fig. 6·2. The flatter rent gradients of the more easily transferable products are intermittently penetrated by the more closely spaced peaks of the steeper local gradients.

The over-all pattern of land uses shows broad regions of supply for the most easily transferable products, interrupted occasionally by smaller enclosed supply areas for less easily transferable products, which are, in turn, interrupted frequently by the very small enclosed supply areas of the least transferable products. The rather complex pattern of land-use areas derived in Fig. 6·2 for only three products under highly simplified assumptions should make it clear why in the much more complicated actual world, with many rival products and sets of markets, we see a patchwork that sometimes appears utterly unsystematic.

6·5 *Influence of Differences in Land Quality on Rent Gradients and Land Use*

Little attention has been given thus far to differences in the intrinsic quality of the land, which affect ceiling rents by determining processing costs in specific uses. Areas of especially low processing cost could be shown as humps on the rent gradients; areas of especially high cost (such as swamps, mountains, sterile soil, etc.), by depressions or gaps in the gradients.

The circumstances that make for low processing costs in one type of land use may be less advantageous or even a handicap for

of the figure: Stippled stretches of territory are devoted to milk production; shaded stretches to bean production; and white stretches to wheat production.

The lower part of the diagram is a map of the resulting pattern of land use zones. Dots represent the five market centers. Stippled areas are devoted to milk production; shaded areas to bean production; and white areas to wheat production. The bean-supply areas of market centers 1 and 3 meet along the boundary that curves around market center 3.

another type of use. On industrial sites, for example, soil fertility is irrelevant. Again, most good vineyard land is poor onion land and vice versa. The gradients for different uses have quite different configurations, though all share the tendency to rise with nearness to market centers.

Rent gradients for the production of valuable materials—or more generally, for activities restricted to a few scarce and highly specialized sites—consist only of short segments or isolated stalagmites. In such cases, the presence and the richness of the specific resource in question is a much more important factor than access of market.

6·6 Impediments to Optimum Utilization of Land

The foregoing simplified exposition of the principles of land-use competition ignores practical problems of great importance. Every change in production techniques, markets, transportation rates, etc., alters the conditions of profitable land use and raises, lowers, or reshapes the various gradients. The adjustments consequent to these changes often take a long time and create maladjustments of the locational pattern, which will be given some attention in a later chapter.

It must also be recognized that the land use adopted by the user is not always the best one, despite competitive pressures and incentives. The user may cling to an inferior use because he knows no other; he may be indifferent to the prospect of greater returns; rent charges may fail to be readjusted in response to potential returns; or the user may decide on a use that is most profitable for him in the immediate future but not so good from a long-run standpoint or from a broader social point of view. He may abuse and even destroy the land resources through ignorance or through unwillingness or inability to take a long-range view. He may use his land in such a way as to handicap others, e.g., by stream pollution or by cropping practices that lead to erosion and floods, silting of reservoirs, etc. All these problems of locational dynamics and possible conflicts of private with public interest lie, however, beyond the scope of the present chapter.

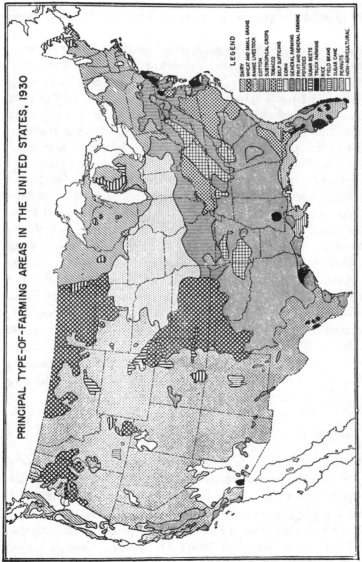

FIG. 6·3 Principal type-of-farming areas in the United States, 1930. (*Reproduced from National Resources Planning Board,* "*Industrial Location and National Resources,*" *Fig. 46, p. 74, Washington, 1943.*)

6·7   *Types of Farming in the United States*

The general pattern of agricultural land use in the United States, as depicted in Fig. 6·3, shows the effects of all three of the influences discussed: distribution costs, quality of the site (principally soil and climate), and impediments to best utilization. Most apparent, of course, in an area as large and climatically diverse as the United States, are the effects of quality differences. Products requiring a warm climate, like cotton, rice, sugar cane, peanuts, and the category "subtropical crops," are naturally restricted to the South, while most of the intermountain area is too dry for anything but range livestock. The influence of access of major markets is shown primarily in the densely settled Northeast, which specializes in bulky or perishable crops such as dairy products, vegetables, small fruits, poultry, and eggs. Similar specialized zones are found around large urban centers outside the northeastern industrial region, but most of these zones are too small to show on the generalized map before us. Finally, the pattern of land utilization shown on the map includes some departures from what could be regarded as the ideal from the standpoint of the long run or the national economy. The wheat belt, as we learned to our sorrow in the dry 1930's, should never have extended so far west into the Great Plains. Much of the cotton territory would be better utilized by more diversified farming. Some of the problems of misuse and maladjustment of land resources will be discussed in Chap. 11.

6·8   *Relation of Site Values to Rents*

The sale value of a site is, of course, related to the amount of rent the land can be made to earn. When, for instance, the opportunities for investment of capital are such that the going rate of return is 5 per cent per annum, someone with $10,000 to invest would be just willing to pay $10,000 for a piece of land expected to yield an annual rental of $500.[6] The general formula for this

---

[6] After taxes and any necessary or customary maintenance expenses payable by the landowner. There is so much variation in customary arrangements between

process of "capitalization," or conversion of rate of annual income into value of an asset, is to divide the annual income by the rate of interest.

But many different rates of interest exist, depending on the alternative potentialities for investment, the degree of risk involved, and other factors. Furthermore the annual income rate that has to be considered in determining what a piece of real estate is worth is not so much the present or past rate of earnings as the *expected future* rate. If conditions are expected to improve, the value of land will be high in relation to present earnings; if prospects are gloomy or highly uncertain, the value of land will be low in relation to present earnings.

With these complications in mind, one can see why there is actually great variation in the relationship between land income and land value. It is noticeable in particular that land values are high relative to actual income on farm lands near growing cities. The basis for this is speculative: it is hoped that the land can soon be subdivided and begin to earn relatively high returns in urban uses. Consequently its sale value may be out of all proportion to its current earnings in agriculture.[7]

The following quotation is descriptive of this situation: [8]

As the city limits of the different cities have spread out farther and farther, efficiency of farm production has been reduced in the areas immediately surrounding the cities. When one farmer in a community sells his land for subdivision into city lots or suburban tracts, many other farmers in the community hope that they may soon be able to sell their farms for a sufficiently large sum to enable them to retire. The psychology of the situation seems to be that the hope of sale is so strong that there is little interest in improving the efficiency of operating

landlord and tenant that the relation between prevailing rentals and sale values also varies widely as between different areas or classes of tenancy. For an elaborate analysis of such differences, see C. R. Chambers, Relation of Land Income to Land Value, *U. S. Department of Agriculture Bulletin* 1224, 1924.

[7] *Ibid.*, and Influence of a City on Farming, *U. S. Department of Agriculture Bulletin* 678, 1918, p. 11.

[8] What Is Happening to Agriculture in Northwestern Indiana?, *Purdue University Agricultural Experiment Station Bulletin* 321, 1928, pp. 42–43.

the farm. The chief concern seems to be to carry on until the sale can be made.

Examples are numerous where farm operators are delaying liming, deferring building a chicken house, refraining from improving the dairy barn or from doing some similar pieces of work because there is at least a remote possibility that the farm may be sold. When it is sold for subdivision purposes it will bring no higher price if it is well limed, has a new poultry house or if the dairy barn is in better condition. As the cities become larger, the zone of "watchful waiting" widens.

It seems then that capitalization ratios have an upward trend with increased distance from points of peak land-use intensity locally through the suburban development zone of growing cities and on a regional or national scale as interest rates rise with greater distance from financial centers.

SUMMARY

Competition for land tends to distribute various types of land use in such a way that each site is occupied by the use that can earn the highest rent there. Different industries competing for space with distribution advantages thus tend to settle in a complex pattern around major and minor markets with the relative position of each industry depending on the "transferability" of what it produces per acre of land. In some uses, however, transfer costs are less important than the advantages in processing cost offered by certain sites to particular uses. Actual land uses are often neither the most profitable for the user nor the best for the economy as a whole.

CHAPTER 7

Location and the Labor Market

THE TWO PREVIOUS CHAPTERS have given some indication of the way in which processing costs at different locations reflect the supply of all the factors of production. Labor, like land or capital, is not required in rigidly fixed quantity for any given process—a firm can economize on labor, chiefly by mechanization, where wages are high. Like land, labor varies greatly in productivity from place to place, and the quality of a local labor force is subject to improvement or deterioration with use or disuse. Unlike land, however, labor is both mobile and reproductive, so that differences in labor cost rest partly on migration responses and on geographical differences in rates of reproduction. Labor costs are a locational factor of importance in many industries and the decisive factor in a few.[1]

This chapter aims to indicate the principal ways in which locations come to have labor supplies conducive to efficient production.

7·1 Fundamental Bases of Labor-cost Advantage

Locations with high wage rates do not necessarily attract job seekers or repel employers. The employer is interested essentially in low processing costs, which depend on labor productivity and also on how the local labor supply lends itself to low overhead, *i.e.*, good utilization of fixed investment, and to improvements in production techniques. The best labor supply from the employer's standpoint is often found in places with relatively high wage rates.

Employees, on the other hand, should be and usually are in-

[1] In manufacturing industries in the United States in 1939, wage and salary payments accounted for 47.1 per cent of total value added by manufacture. This ratio rises to 70 to 80 per cent in shipbuilding and some apparel industries. National Resources Planning Board, "Industrial Location and National Resources," Chap. 11, Government Printing Office, Washington, 1943.

terested in the long-run living standard that their annual earnings will buy. This involves, in addition to wage rates, the questions of living costs, stability of employment, agreeable working and living conditions, and opportunities for advancement.

It appears, then, that at least three kinds of locations might have a labor supply conducive to low-cost production:

a. Places especially attractive from a consumer standpoint, *i.e.,* having low living costs or such amenities as a pleasant climate (either physical or cultural). If such places are sufficiently attractive, people will be willing to work there for smaller money wages than elsewhere.

b. Places afflicted by "population pressure" in the sense that expansion of employment opportunities has lagged behind the growth of the labor force, so that people must work for lower real incomes than elsewhere.

c. Places where the nature of local employment and the size and structure of the local labor market develop an unusually productive or adaptable labor force, worth more to the employer per man-hour.

The mobility (and in a very broad sense the divisibility) of labor are involved in the evolution of these three types of low-cost labor locations. The greater the degree of mobility, the more nearly can migration equalize levels of real income, and the more important are money-wage differentials of the first type mentioned—those resting on consumer considerations. Ohlin applied the term "equalizing" to such wage differentials, to distinguish them from differentials in real wages.[2] On the other hand, wages are low at the second type of locations—those with population pressure—precisely on account of imperfect mobility. Finally, the advantages of the third type of location mentioned rest partly on the imperfect divisibility of labor, which affects the efficiency of a local labor force in some ways analogous to the economies of specialization and large-scale organization in a firm.

The three types of low-cost labor location will now be considered separately in greater detail.

[2] Bertil Ohlin, "Interregional and International Trade," pp. 212–220, Harvard University Press, Cambridge, Mass., 1933.

7·2   *Living Costs and Labor Costs* [3]

Concentration of economic activity in particular areas raises the rent of land and likewise the prices of such products as are extensively produced and costly to ship. An important consequence is that the cost of living is usually higher in areas and regions of concentrated economic activity and dense nonagricultural population.

Living in congested areas entails expensive housing or expensive and time-consuming commutation. Typically, the urban worker compromises by choosing a residence involving some of both. That is, he pays a higher rent but also spends more money and time on transportation than he would in a smaller town.

Another major item is food, which is similarly affected over even broader regions, because most kinds of food are produced fairly directly from the soil and thus become more costly when a concentration of local demand necessitates more intensive production and longer hauls. This applies particularly, of course, to such perishable foods as milk, eggs, fresh meat, fresh vegetables, and fruit. Not only in big cities but in any region that does not grow enough food to feed itself, the cost of food is relatively high.

Thus the cost of living as a whole is likely to be higher in areas where nonagricultural activity is disproportionately developed, because of the pressure upon local resources both by industry directly and by the needs of the employees of industry.

Where the cost of living is high, wages also are likely to be high. Of course, a complete proportionality between living costs and wages—in other words, uniform *real* wages—would imply perfect mobility of labor, which does not exist. But there is generally enough mobility to give rise to some similarity in pattern as between wages and living costs. It is well known that wages are higher in cities and industrialized areas.

There is even a certain compounding of effects tending to reinforce this relationship. The consumer's budget consists partly

[3] On the historical role of "equalizing differences" in industrial location, see W. H. Dean, "The Theory of the Geographic Location of Economic Activities" (selections from Harvard doctoral dissertation), Edwards Bros., Inc., Ann Arbor, Mich., 1938 (processed).

of services, which are themselves related to the living costs of those who perform the services. Thus in a city where food, lodging, and commuting costs are high, the effect will be felt not only in the food, lodging, and commuting items of the budget but likewise in the service items.

Despite the very real nature of the forces giving rise to equalizing differences in wage rates, such differences are small in advanced economies where transport is cheap and wage earners spend a large part of their incomes on manufactured goods.[4] The influence of higher prices for living space and foodstuffs and the longer commutation distances in crowded areas are partly offset by lower costs of some types of manufactured goods and services in such areas. Under present conditions in the United States, for instance, it appears that geographic differentials in living costs cannot account for any major part of the existing differentials in wages.[5]

[4] In a country with high living standards, only a small part of consumer expenditures consists of remuneration to farmers; so access to surplus food-producing areas has far less to do with over-all living costs than it does in poorer countries. Even the foods we eat are often so highly processed that they cost the same all over the country.

[5] There are no satisfactory measures of comparative living costs in different regions and in towns and cities of various sizes, largely on account of differences in consumption requirements and habits that make such comparisons ambiguous. Differences in consumption habits, however, are presumably becoming less and less marked in the United States. A survey of relative costs of "emergency" and "maintenance" budgets for wage earners' families in 59 United States cities in 1935 (Works Progress Administration, Division of Social Research, "Intercity Differences in Costs of Living, March 1935, 59 Cities," Research Monograph XII, Washington, 1937) found slightly lower costs in South Central cities and (independently) in smaller cities as such. Housing and transportation expense were rather consistently higher in larger cities, while heating expense varied regionally with climate. Remarkably little pattern of variation was found in food and clothing costs. Some small items such as clothing upkeep and gas seemed consistently lower in larger places.

Subsequent investigations have disclosed no further noteworthy systematic variations and show mainly the temporary inflation of all budget items in crowded war production centers. See, for example, the U. S. Bureau of Labor Statistics mimeographed release of Apr. 1, 1946, "Relative Differences in the Cost of Equivalent Goods, Rents and Services in 31 Large Cities, March, 1945."

In a comparison of living costs of wage earners in a few selected small cities (10,000 to 20,000 population) in the North and South, the only consistent regional differential was in fuel costs, reflecting climatic conditions. (Differences in Living

7·3 *Labor-cost Differences Based on Population Pressure*

The basis for labor-cost differentials just discussed depends on some degree of human mobility. In contrast, population pressure depends on a lack of mobility.

The reasons for shifting patterns of employment opportunity, or labor demand, lie outside the scope of this chapter.[6] What concerns us here is why the pattern of labor supply fails to adapt itself to these changes, thus creating pools of surplus cheap labor.

The usual hindrances to migration are all too familiar. It is likewise well known that improved labor-market organization, under public auspices, can greatly reduce such obstacles as ignorance of job opportunities and fear of the risks and trouble of job-seeking in a new place.

The whole problem is aggravated, however, by two "perversities" in the response of labor supply to geographic differences in labor demand.

The first perversity is that the migration response of the unemployed often diminishes rather than increasing as their resources dwindle.[7] This reflects primarily the fact that the act of

Costs in Northern and Southern Cities, *Monthly Labor Review*, July, 1939, Serial No. R963.) H. M. Douty, investigating the same question (Are Living Costs Lower in the South?, *Southern Economic Journal*, vol. V, No. 3, January, 1939, pp. 363–370), concluded: "(*a*) There is no *wide* cost differential for equivalent standards of living between the South and the rest of the country, although a small favorable differential may exist; (*b*) Variations in living costs within the South are considerable."

[6] See Chaps. 9–11.

[7] The 1935 Michigan Census of Population and Unemployment seems to bear this out. An analysis of its findings makes the comment: "The 'unemployment' entry . . . represents persons who had no private employment during the time they were in the labor market, which in many cases was for the entire period, April 1930 to January 1935. The proportion of persons in this group who made one or more moves was distinctly less than that of all workers, and lower than that of all but one of the industrial groupings ('Casual employment and unknown industries'). Moreover, the proportion of continuously unemployed workers making interstate moves was smaller than that of any of the groups. It should be noted, however, that a long-time unemployed group usually includes a high proportion of older workers, which in itself tends to lower the mobility of the group. Aside from the age factor, however, the most probable reason for the relatively low mobility of this group is the inertia produced by long-continued unemployment. Another reason is that many persons in this group received relief, which normally tends to hold population in place." J. N. Webb and Albert Westefeld, Industrial

migration itself requires cash outlay, effort, and perhaps the risk of falling from the frying pan into the fire. The greater a family's need the less able may it be to surmount the threshold of migration.

The second perversity is much more important and operates from generation to generation. It has to do not with migration but with the renewal of the labor supply through births.

The reasons for great differences in human fertility in different areas are imperfectly understood, though racial, social, economic, climatic, and even political influences are all known to play some part. As among the different parts of a single country, the most important controlling factor seems to be economic. Malthus' gloomy view was that higher levels of well-being bring more rapid increase of population, but it now seems fairly well established that except for a bottom stratum near the margin of starvation, higher real income is associated with lower fertility.[8]

City dwellers, whose living standards are relatively high, show almost universally a lower rate of natural increase than rural people. Table 7·1 shows that despite a recent rise in fertility, urban net reproduction rates in the United States have been

Aspects of Labor Mobility, *Monthly Labor Review,* April, 1939, Serial No. R917. The authors' statement as to the effect of relief payments on mobility is controversial.

[8] A spectacular table evidencing this tendency was presented by Frederick Osborn before the Population Association of America in 1935. It appears in *Social Forces,* vol. XIV, No. 1, October, 1935, Table III, p. 30, and also in Carter Goodrich and others, "Migration and Economic Opportunity," Table 60, p. 498, University of Pennsylvania Press, Philadelphia, 1936. For the United States as a whole and within each of four regions, the various counties were arrayed in order of a composite index of "economic level," and each array was divided into six groups, with the first group containing the most prosperous sixth of the counties in that region and the last group the least prosperous sixth. For each sextile group of counties a fertility index was calculated, based on a ratio of the number of children under five years old to the number of women of ages twenty to forty-four. Almost without exception, the fertility ratio was lowest for the most prosperous sextile of the counties in each region and in the country as a whole and steadily higher for each succeeding sextile of counties descending the economic scale. The Goodrich report sums up the conclusions as follows *(ibid.,* pp. 498–499): "To an almost astonishing degree . . . the areas which now have the least economic opportunity per capita tend to be the very ones in which natural increase is the greatest. Unless these differentials are eliminated it is obvious that they will furnish a continuing pressure toward migration."

Table 7·1   *Net Reproduction Rates for Urban, Rural Nonfarm,*
and Rural Farm Populations, United States and Southern
States, 1935–1940 and United States 1941–1946 *

| Residence | 1935–1940 | | 1941–1946 |
	South †	U. S.	U. S.
Total	1,182	978	1,202
Urban	712	726	976
Rural nonfarm	1,211	1,150	1,359
Rural farm	1,812	1,661	1,928

* The net reproduction rate is the number of girls who will be born to a group of 1,000 new-born girls during their lifetimes, under a given set of mortality and fertility rates by age groups. A net reproduction rate of 1,000, indefinitely continued, would ultimately produce a stationary population; a net reproduction rate of 1,200, indefinitely continued, would ultimately produce a population increasing at the rate of 20 per cent per generation.

† South Atlantic, East South Central, and West South Central regions combined.

SOURCE: "Differential Fertility, 1940 and 1910—Standardized Fertility Rates and Reproduction Rates," Sixteenth Census of Population Special Report, and Bureau of the Census, "Differential Fertility: June, 1946," Current Population Reports, Series P-20, No. 8, Dec. 31, 1947.

generally below 1,000. Our cities and towns can be kept from eventual depopulation only by continued migration from rural areas if the 1941-to-1946 fertility and mortality rates of specific urban age groups should prevail in future generations.[9]

[9] A population can show an excess of births over deaths for many years after its net reproduction rate has fallen below 1,000 if it has inherited a favorable age distribution from its previous fertility and mortality experience, but a net reproduction rate of, say, 950 that persisted for a long time would finally develop a population of a stable age distribution, diminishing in size at the rate of 5 per cent per generation.

The Census Bureau makes the following comment on recent increases in fertility: "The past few years have been markedly an apparent resurgence in the re-productivity of the American people. With the age-specific birth and death rates prevailing in the period 1940 to 1945, and with no immigration, the population of the United States would eventually increase at a rate of 14.0 per cent per generation, whereas with those prevailing in the period 1935 to 1940, the population would eventually have decreased at a rate of 2.2 per cent per generation. This change to a potentially increasing population from a potentially declining population is largely the result of the unprecedented upsurge in birth rates as a conse-

Table 7·1 also shows the differential in population replacement rates between the United States as a whole and the Southern states. It should be noted that the South's high over-all fertility is almost wholly accounted for by the fact that that region is more rural than the rest of the country. The Southern urban population actually had a lower net reproduction rate (based on 1935 to 1940 data) than the urban population of the United States as a whole.

The relatively high rates of natural increase associated with the low income levels of "pioneer" regions may be regarded as simplifying the migration problem, since they tend to reduce the need for actual migration in the proper settlement of such regions. However, in more mature areas where incomes are low because of limited economic opportunities, the characteristically high rates of natural increase aggravate the need for migration. In a settled country it can almost be said that the increase of population comes in just the wrong places. Even if no change took place at all in the geographic distribution of employment opportunities, a large amount of migration would have to occur in order to offset differentials in natural increase and maintain the same relative distribution of population. In practice, migration sometimes more than offsets the differences in natural increase; but since mobility is imperfect, it never brings the distribution of population quite into correspondence with the distribution of employment opportunities. Wide differences in real income and money wages persist.

The effect upon comparative labor costs is generally smaller, since conditions associated with population pressure (poor and backward populations, narrow outlooks and occupational opportunities, unprogressive technology) are likewise unfavorable to

---

quence of the favorable psychological and economic conditions of the war years. Another factor is a reduction in mortality, despite overcrowded housing in war production centers and shortages of medical personnel and facilities. It is almost certain that there will be some decline in fertility rates in the next few years, but opinions differ as to whether or not our population will resume its historic secular trend toward smaller families, which has been in progress for over a century. The prospect of a declining population has probably not been eliminated; but, at least, the time of occurrence has been postponed, and the maximum population will be somewhat larger than formerly expected."

Bureau of the Census, "Recent Trends in Population Replacement," Special Report Series P-47, No. 2, Mar. 27, 1947.

productivity. Low-wage labor deriving from such conditions offers advantages in production only for processes requiring little skill.

7·4 Migration from Farm Areas in the United States

The large and persistent population overflow from American farms is shown in Table 7·2. This table covers the period since 1915, when our farm population reached its maximum of 32,440,-000 and began to decline. In every year, births have exceeded deaths by 345,000 or more, but in all but two years (1932 and 1945, which mark the nadir of depression and the end of the war) there has been a net excess of migration away from farms. The ups and downs of urban employment opportunities can be clearly traced in these migration figures.

The consequent change in farm population has been downward except in 1930 to 1932 and 1945, with the result that only about 20 per cent of our population now lives on farms as compared with nearly 33 per cent in 1915.[10] Meanwhile a large differential in living standards persists between nonfarm and farm areas as a whole. Farmers are worse off than townspeople by almost any measure of real income one may choose. The conclusion is that migration from farms has more than offset high rural reproduction rates but has not been rapid enough to equalize real income levels. Population pressure remains.

7·5 Size and Other Characteristics of Local Labor Markets as Determinants of Locational Advantage

Even if the two bases of labor-cost differences thus far discussed did not exist, i.e., if both money wages and real incomes in the broadest sense were geographically uniform, some locations would have a more attractive labor supply than others from the standpoint of the employer interested in low-cost production.

Local concentration of an industry fosters the development of a labor force particularly productive in that industry. A rubber-manufacturing center like Akron or a clothing manufacturing

[10] Cf. Table 9·1.

Table 7·2   United States Farm Population and Changes through Natural Increase and Migration, 1915–1945

(*All figures in thousands*)

Year	Natural increase	Net migration			Change due to reclassification of residence	Total net change	Farm population at end of year or 5-year period
1915–1919 (average)	*	*			*	−165	31,614
1920–1924 (average)	+509	−666			†	−157	30,830
1925–1929 (average)	+461	−593			†	−132	30,169
1930	+377	−325			+264	+316	30,485
1931	+387	−79			+235	+543	31,928
1932	+398	+325			+282	+1,005	32,033
1933	+375	−482			+19	−88	31,945
1934	+383	−415			−112	−144	31,801
1935	+375	−642			−157	−424	31,377
1936	+363	−690			−44	−471	30,906
1937	+375	−529			−132	−286	30,620
1938	+405	−420			−125	−140	30,480
1939	+410	−491			−130	−211	30,269
		Civilian	*Military* ‡				
1940	+400	−606	−75		†	−281	29,988
1941	+417	−1,146	−211		†	−940	29,048
1942	+390	−1,920	−859		†	−2,389	26,659
1943	+355	−988	−505		†	−1,138	25,521
1944	+345	−476	−200		†	−331	25,190
1945	+348	0	+452		†	+800	25,990

* Data not available.

† Estimated for 1930 to 1939 only. In other years, this item is included in the "net migration" figure.

‡ Represents net transference of personnel between farms and the military forces.

SOURCE: U. S. Bureau of Agricultural Economics, "Farm Population Estimates, United States and Major Geographic Divisions, 1910–1946," Tables 1–4, pp. 3–6, Washington, 1946 (processed).

center like New York City comes to have an advantage over rival locations in the form of skilled and experienced labor. The effect is to reinforce and perpetuate the concentration of plants using similar skills.[11] Where the degree of labor skill required is high and at the same time the product is a nonstandardized "shopping good," there is consequently a double incentive to concentration in a few centers for at least that part of the industry in which demands on workmanship are most exacting and the product most individualized.

To some extent, such advantages reside in the superior skill of the individual workman and can be carried by him to a new location if he sees inducements to move.[12] But the character of the local labor force as a group is perhaps even more important.

One characteristic of a local labor force that influences production costs, independently of the skills of individuals, is the size of the group within commuting distance. The principle of "massing of reserves," which was introduced in an earlier chapter in relation to the internal economy of firms, can be applied likewise to the economy of a local labor market. A shoe manufacturer in one of the big centers like Brockton or Chicago can normally get additional or substitute help with adequate experience at a few hours' notice, whereas an isolated shoe manufacturer in a small town cannot. For an industry with specialized requirements, the advantage runs in terms of the size of the local supply of labor already trained or suitable for specific processes. In other cases such as the confectionery industry, where previous training is not essential for most of the jobs, the over-all size of the local labor supply is the important factor. The seasonal character of employ-

---

[11] "When a locality is highly specialized industrially, all its institutions are apt to be transformed to aid that industry and the population dependent upon it. The school and library systems of Grand Rapids, Michigan, have been specialized to meet the needs of the furniture industry. The schools teach woodworking and furniture designing and the library claims to have a collection of books on furniture equal, or superior, to any other existing in the country." A. M. Simons, "Production Management," reviewed by H. P. Dutton, p. 37, American Technical Society, Chicago, 1940.

[12] Many historical examples of shifts of industries made possible by migration of skilled workers are cited in Laurent Dechesne, "La Localisation des diverses productions," pp. 115–122, Les Editions Comptables, Commerciales et Financières, Brussels, 1945.

ment in both of the examples just cited, of course, contributes to the firm's need for access to a sizable labor "reservoir."

It appears, then, that concentration of production offers opportunities for more flexible adjustment of labor input and consequent economies which show up in lower overhead costs. Whether or not these potentialities are realized, however, depends on two other characteristics of the local labor market: organization and attitudes.

In some apparel and textile centers concentration appears to have brought its own nemesis. A large group of skilled and essential workers producing stylized products for what is generally a seasonal and unstable market has great potential bargaining power vis-à-vis the employers (who under the same conditions are usually small, financially weak, and fiercely competitive). The concentration of a large part of the industry in one place, the above-average intellectual level of the employees, the weakness of the employers, the seasonal nature of the work, and the dependence upon experienced man power all combine toward raising wage levels in such situations faster than they are raised elsewhere or among other groups of workers. Even more generally important than high wages is the development of restrictive practices embodied in agreements, tradition, or legislation or the more frequent interruption of work by disputes. As noted in an earlier chapter, the effect of restrictions and interruptions is to increase overhead—in effect, to make a greater input of capital, land, and "overhead" labor necessary for a given rate of output.[13] Thus the potential advantage of flexibility in large labor markets may be converted into disadvantageous inflexibility, with high overhead as well as high direct labor costs of production.

The reaction of employers under such circumstances is to resort either to laborsaving techniques or to a change of location. These two steps are, in fact, often related, since the entrenched workers in the old-established centers of the industry have a vested interest in their acquired skills and a short-run interest at least in opposing the introduction of laborsaving techniques; therefore

[13] This point is amply emphasized by M. C. Daly in The Effect of Overhead Costs upon the Structure of the American Economy, Southern Economic Journal, vol. VIII, No. 1, July, 1941, pp. 22–39.

the only way to introduce these harmoniously may be in a new location. At the same time, the relatively inexperienced labor force of a new location may be able to cope with its tasks only if a more mechanized technique is adopted.

The result is that those operations of the industry which can most easily dispense with expert labor are transferred to new locations, resulting in a partial decentralization of the industry, while the plants remaining in operation in the old centers have to specialize more and more on high-quality work, requiring special skills, in order to survive the competition. This specialization is thus likely to be quite persistent, although in time some of the new centers will mature and go through the same cycle.[14]

It should be recognized that the process just described is merely something that has very frequently occurred in the past and carries no aura of inexorability. Improved labor-market organization and procedures for conciliation and mediation and more enlightened attitudes on the part of both employers and employees may bring to a better fruition the mutual advantages of large labor markets.

SUMMARY

Low labor costs, an important locational factor for many industries, are found at several distinct types of location. They may arise from the willingness of people to accept lower wages in order to be where living is pleasant and cheap, from people's tendency to reproduce faster in places providing poorer employment opportunities, from the inability of people to migrate promptly out of depressed or stagnant areas, and from the production advantages of a diverse, experienced, and adaptable local labor supply. The strengthened bargaining power of skilled and specialized labor in mature industrial centers has often encouraged a search for new locations and new processes adapted to those locations.

[14] See, for example, the case of the shoe industry, in E. M. Hoover, "Location Theory and the Shoe and Leather Industries," Chaps. XIII, XIV, XVI, Harvard University Press, Cambridge, Mass., 1937. Some of the observations in the text above apply to the rubber and automobile industries—though in neither of these could the employers be described as small or financially weak. For other cases, see Dechesne, *op. cit.*, pp. 122–124.

CHAPTER 8

The Economic Structure
of Communities

IT IS NOW TIME to bring together the major conclusions of previous chapters as to the locational effects of transfer and processing costs in order to arrive at an understanding of the characteristic industrial patterns of communities and larger areas.

The analysis of transfer costs showed that early stages in production are most often located near the point of extraction of their principal materials, whereas later stages are located near their markets. All types of production, however, find favorable locations at nodes (transshipment and junction points) on the transfer network.

The analysis of rents as a locational factor showed that land costs are significant chiefly in determining which of several industries oriented to the same markets shall, in fact, occupy the sites nearest those markets and in what sequence the other uses arrange themselves with increasing distance from markets. For specific uses, differences in the intrinsic qualities of land are likewise important.

The analysis of labor costs disclosed important advantages in processing cost at large urban centers, which, however, are offset in some cases by the lower wages prevailing in areas of surplus population (chiefly rural) and by institutional inflexibilities in long-established urban labor markets.

Those earlier chapters, however, have not disclosed the extent of interrelationship among locational patterns. It may well have appeared that since the determining locational factors are not identical for any two industries, there must be as many different sets of production locations as there are industries.

The purpose of the present chapter is to show how in many cases the locations of different industries coincide, greatly reducing the total number of different locations and giving rise to more or less diversified economic communities with fairly well-defined areas of external influence and characteristic patterns of internal geographic structure.

8·1   *"Linkage" of Industries by Transfer Economies* [1]

Perhaps the most obvious cases of locational juxtaposition of different industries are those involving a close transfer, *i.e.*, trade, connection between them. If the "selling" industry is strongly market-oriented or the "buying" industry strongly material-oriented (or both), then the two industries will usually be found together. In extreme cases the two may even be considered locationally as a single industry. Thus, the economies of "locational integration" between blast furnaces and steel furnaces are peculiarly great. Both processes involve high temperatures, and a great deal of fuel can be saved if the intermediate product, iron, is transferred in a molten state rather than in pigs. In this case the utilization of by-product gases from the manufacture of coke and the use of process scrap in furnace charges further extend the economy of integration, bringing in coke ovens and rolling mills. Four technologically distinct stages—coking, iron smelting, steel making, and rolling—are normally found in such close association that for purposes of locational analysis we can almost lump them all together as the "coke, iron, and steel" industry, considered as a consumer of coal, limestone, and iron ore and a producer of primary rolled products (plus smaller quantities of pig iron, slag, ingots, and castings).

There are several other instances of close locational integration between successive stages, *e.g.*, the shoe-findings and shoe-manufacturing industries, which are linked both by the importance of proximity for commercial contact and by the use of factory scrap in making findings. This kind of juxtaposition is clearly limited,

[1] For statistical measures of the extent of geographical linkage in both British and American industry, see PEP (Political and Economic Planning), "Report on the Location of Industry in Great Britain," pp. 82, 293, London, 1939, and National Resources Planning Board, "Industrial Location and National Resources," Chap. 5, Government Printing Office, Washington, 1943.

however, by the principle disclosed in an earlier chapter on transfer costs: that in general the earlier stages of a production
sequence are unlikely to be market-oriented and the later stages
are unlikely to be material-oriented while intermediate stages are
generally less dependent on either procurement or distribution
factors in their location. Only under somewhat special circumstances then (often involving the feeding back of by-products from
the later stage to the earlier stage) will two successive stages of
processing locate together.

Another basis of linkage is a little less direct but not without
significance. It is really a sort of corollary to the direct integration
attraction discussed above. Two industries using jointly produced
materials or turning out complementary (jointly demanded) products have an incentive to be together. At some stages in their
history, the woolen and worsted industries (which use different
staple lengths of wool, separated in the combing process) have
been close neighbors, though the cost of materials is hardly the
dominant factor at present in either case. The producers of a
wide variety of automobile parts and accessories cluster together
around the main centers of automobile manufacturing, while tanneries, glue factories, and other processors of the by-products of
the packing industry are found together in packing centers.

8·2   Linkage by Complementary Use of Labor

A distinct type of interindustry linkage involves the complementary use of production factors, primarily labor. As noted in
an earlier chapter, the labor supply in a community comprises a
number of groups suitable for different kinds of tasks on the basis
of skill, sex, strength, age, and even racial or national background.
A town in which the main industry employs only certain groups
has an available surplus of some other groups which can be hired
cheaply by other industries to which they are suited. A classic
example is the migration of silk mills from the New York metropolitan area (chiefly Paterson, N. J.) to Pennsylvania anthracite-
mining centers like Scranton, where the wives and daughters of
miners constituted a surplus labor supply. "By-product women"
also played a large role in the beginnings of the shoe and textile

industries in New England at a time when the men were occupied mainly in farming, fishing, lumbering, shipbuilding, and shipping.[2]

The kinds of linkage thus far discussed, however, are only special cases. A much more general basis for conformity between the locational patterns of different industries is inherent in the internal economics of the transfer system and in the fact that the locations of all industries are influenced, even though indirectly, by the same pattern of ultimate-consumer income.

8·3 Concentrating Effect of the Structure of Transfer Costs

The structure of transfer costs reduces the number of advantageous procurement and distribution points. For reasons already discussed, the transfer of goods and services does not proceed "as the crow flies," but is channeled along organized transfer routes, with costs depending primarily on the character of the terrain and the density of the traffic. Industry patterns, as shaped by transfer costs, reflect this economic pressure toward concentration of traffic on main routes and on routes where basic physical conditions are favorable.

The concentrating effect of the structure of transfer costs goes even further. The existence of terminal costs, reflected in relatively lower rates for long hauls, gives terminals and junctions a locational advantage over intermediate points, while the advantages of junctions as such becomes very great for enterprises trading with several material or market points.

On the organized transfer network, then, are certain strategically located transfer "nodes," with special locational advantages as procurement and distribution points and therefore as processing centers for all kinds of activities in which transfer costs are locationally important.[3] There is only a limited number of such

[2] Cf. E. M. Hoover, "Location Theory and the Shoe and Leather Industries," Chap. XIII, Harvard University Press, Cambridge, Mass., 1937.

[3] The general locational advantage of nodal points, and the resulting concentration of production, trade, and population at such points, was ably analyzed by H. J. MacKinder more than a generation ago in "Britain and the British Seas," D. Appleton-Century Company, Inc., New York, 1902. More elaborate treatments

nodal points, and each is a production center for manufacturing as well as for trading and intermediate handling operations. Since the transfer advantages of these points rest partly on large-volume traffic and frequent and flexible service, there is evidently a cumulative pressure toward concentration of transfer advantage.

8·4   *The Principles of Large-scale Economy Applied to Urban Concentrations of Production*

The incentives toward agglomeration of diverse types of business into a relatively small number of clusters at transfer nodes may be summed up under the head of "economies of urban concentration."

Just as a single production unit gains in efficiency, up to a point, with added size, so a city as a whole has certain large-scale economies to offer its business enterprises. The advantages of better transfer services and a broader, more flexible labor market have already been mentioned. In addition there are many kinds of auxiliary services catering to business in general—banks, utilities, fire and police protection, and others—which can do a more effective job in larger communities. Interest, property insurance, and utility rates are generally lower in larger cities.[4]

The economies of urban concentration rest on the same basic principles as those of the individual producing unit: multiples, massing of reserves, and bulk transactions.[5] The principle of multiples means here that in a large industrial concentration the specialization of functions as between firms can be carried further. Certain operations and services that a firm in a smaller place would have to do for itself can, in the city, be farmed out to separate enterprises specializing in those functions and operating on

---

will be found in Tord Palander, "Beiträge zur Standortstheorie," Chap. XII, Almqvist och Wiksells boktryckeri-a.-b., Uppsala, 1935, and in August Lösch, "The Economics of Location," Yale University Press, 1954. The discussion of "interposts" in R. G. Hawtrey, "The Economic Problem," Longmans, Green & Co., Inc., New York, 1926, is also noteworthy.

[4] Electricity rates in New York City are a conspicuous exception to an otherwise consistent tendency for electric energy to be cheaper in larger cities.

[5] See Section 5·6.

a large enough scale to do them more cheaply.[6] The principles of massing of reserves means that in a large city the individual firm can operate on hand-to-mouth basis of materials and supplies, secure in the knowledge that more can be obtained at short notice if necessary. The principle of bulk transactions refers here esssentially to the economies of large-scale transfer and terminal handling, already mentioned in Chap. 2.

Exploitation of the advantages of urban concentration does not necessarily require a downtown location. For many types of business it is sufficient to be somewhere near the city—say within the "labor-supply area" or the local telephone rate zone—and the suburbs may be most suitable. Some attention will be given at a later point to the changing patterns of location within metropolitan areas.

8·5 Degrees of Concentration of Market-oriented Industries

Businesses that produce or handle goods for final consumption usually locate primarily with an eye to distribution. This means that a large sector of the productive economy—including consumer services, trade in finished consumer goods, and the later stages of consumer-goods manufacture—is all oriented the same way, toward the consumer market. For any line of business in this category, the first approximation to an index of potential sales in an area is simply the aggregate income of the people there.[7]

---

[6] This specialization is illustrated in the printing business. City printers often have their machine typesetting done by special composing shops. Similarly, garment manufacturers rely on contract shops and specialized producers who may concentrate on such single steps as buttonhole making.

[7] Collections of basic data for market surveys, as compiled by the Department of Commerce and many private market-research firms, always feature indicators of over-all income and consumer expenditure by areas, including the number of income-tax returns and total retail sales. Since demand for any particular product or service depends on other factors too, such as the size distribution of incomes, the proportion of rural to total population, age distribution, number of car owners, family size, education, and climate, the suppliers of basic marketing-research data also attempt to include series bearing on those variables. With such information it is possible to gauge fairly accurately the relative demand for any given product in various sales territories. The individual firm seeking a location or planning its sales effort must in addition, of course, face a problem that need not concern us here: the evaluation of competition.

In view of this generally similar orientation and the previously discussed incentives toward grouping of businesses at a small number of nodal transfer points, we should expect a particularly high degree of coincidence among the locational patterns and market-area systems of the later stages of distribution and manufacturing.

Considerable coincidence does in fact exist, but an important qualification must be made. Market-oriented industries differ considerably in the intimacy of their adjustment to market. The location pattern of each represents a compromise between the distribution advantages of small decentralized units close to the customers and the processing and procurement advantages of larger centralized units.

Where the operations involved are mostly simple and non-mechanized, as in a retail store, they can often be subdivided down to the point where each establishment employs only one or two people, without undue increase in "processing" costs. At the same time, if the individual sales are small (as they are particularly in the case of "convenience goods"), the customer will not go far out of his way even for lower prices or to reach a well-advertised outlet; so the establishment must be very near the market. A highly decentralized location pattern is indicated.

On the other hand, where the processing operation is mechanized and subject to considerable economies of larger scale (as in the case of breweries), a more centralized locational pattern is indicated, particularly if the product is sold in large standard lots, *e.g.,* to middlemen rather than direct to the consumer, or comes in large individual units, *e.g.,* furniture or automobiles, so that the customer is not too averse to coming some distance to shop.

A "decentralized" location pattern in this context means a highly intimate adjustment to markets, with an outlet in every village and in every neighborhood of each city. A more centralized pattern means a less intimate adjustment, with, say, an outlet in most towns of 10,000 population or more and in every important business district of each large city. A still more centralized pattern means that outlets are found only in large cities.

The various main types of retail trade show considerably different degrees of concentration. Much the most numerous and widely scattered of these main types in the United States is the grocery store. Filling stations come next in numbers, followed in order by eating places, drinking places, apparel stores, and automotive, furniture, building-materials, and hardware stores. Within each of these broad types, of course, there are more specialized types of stores found only in the larger places.

In manufacturing, four industries seem to have the most intimate locational adjustment to the general consumer market, as judged by the fact that they each operate in more than a third of the 3,000-odd counties of the United States. They are newspaper plants, bakeries, artificial-ice plants, and soft-drink bottling plants.[8] All four products are sold in small quantities for immediate consumption; the first three are highly perishable, and the last is very bulky in relation to transported materials.

8·6 The "Trading Area" of a Community

A community has at least as many "trading areas" as it has industries. But if we were to map out all these areas around some representative community and arrange them in order of size, they would probably not show a smooth continuous distribution of sizes. Instead, certain boundaries would recur especially often; most of the community's trade areas would coincide fairly well with one of a small number of characteristic types.[9]

There are, in fact, good reasons for expecting many of a community's retail trade areas to coincide. The out-of-town buyer rarely comes in with just one item on his shopping list. He finds it convenient to get hardware, shoes, chicken feed; visit his bank; and take in a movie, all on the same trip. Moreover, if he brings

[8] Based on data from the U. S. Census of Manufactures, 1935. See National Resources Planning Board, "Industry Location and National Resources," Chap. 14, Table 15, p. 252, for the complete tabulation of all 1935 census industries by number of establishments and number of counties.

[9] This assertion has yet to be demonstrated satisfactorily—it is hardly more than an accumulated impression from incomplete data, since no one has traced all of a community's trade areas. It is commonly accepted, however, among marketing analysts.

produce of his own along to sell, he will naturally try to combine his buying and selling on the same trip to the same town whenever possible. The close resemblance between the patterns of supply areas for farm produce and market areas for small-town retail trade bear this out.[10] Probably few farmers regularly trade, either as buyers or sellers, in more than one or two different towns. Generally they go to the nearest village for convenience goods and to a larger, more distant town for shopping goods and specialties. We should expect, then, that any given market town should not have hundreds or even dozens of different retail trade and service areas but only a few.

It should be mentioned in passing that churches, schools, and other noncommercial community institutions likewise have their areas, which share the same tendency toward coalescence into a small number of composite areas for any one community. Areas of local-government jurisdiction are, of course, more rigid and unlikely to match economic or social boundaries.

Outside the category of retail trade and services, there seems to be less of a basis for generalized trade areas that fit whole groups of products. There is no obvious advantage to a wholesale buyer or seller in doing all his trading in different products in the same city.

However, where there are distinct breaks in the transfer-cost pattern, many kinds of trade areas will terminate together. National boundaries and in special cases state boundaries act as transfer barriers, so that a city may have a whole group of industries serving the same state-wide or national market area.[11] Natural barriers like the rugged and thinly settled Rocky Mountain region likewise cause trade-area boundaries to "pile up." Thus many products command a Pacific Coast market or an east-of-the-Rockies market. Finally, there are breaks in freight-rate structures at certain competitively strategic points like the Mis-

[10] See, for example, the pair of maps of Appanoose County, Iowa, in E. M. Hoover, "Location Theory and the Shoe and Leather Industries," Fig. 34, p. 106, Harvard Economic Studies, vol. LV, Harvard University Press, Cambridge, Mass. 1937.

[11] See Chaps. 12 and 13.

sissippi and Missouri River crossings, which create sharp breaks in transfer-cost advantage. These further concentrate wholesale distribution and manufacturing and make otherwise disparate market areas coincide.

The net effect of all these factors of area conformity can best be described as Procrustean. The variety of possible industry patterns and market-area systems is circumscribed and something like a "hierarchy" of minor and major distributing points exists.[12] Two market-oriented industries with about the same number of establishments in the country as a whole are likely to have most of their production points and sales territories in common.

Analogous Procrustean influences among material-oriented industries are of much less significance. For one thing, there is no common extensive "source of materials in general" for material-oriented industries, corresponding to the pattern of consumer income for the market-oriented industries. Moreover, material orientation rarely extends to more than the first or second stage of processing, and the total amount of employment involved is relatively small.

The accompanying maps, Figs. 8·1 and 8·2, show some of the characteristic features of community trading areas. In Fig. 8·1 areas tributary to the village of Dryden, N. Y., in a number of different respects have been mapped on the same scale for comparison. For the types of business represented in so small a community, the areas are all small and show considerable similarity, though no two precisely coincide. The reader may judge for him-

---

[12] The size of the smallest class of trade areas, *i.e.*, the spacing of the smallest trading centers, is determined by the distance that the buyer or seller is willing to travel for a routine marketing trip rather than pay a sufficient premium to allow still more decentralized centers to exist. In horse-and-wagon days this distance was only a few miles, and market towns carrying on a rather diversified and comprehensive trade developed at close intervals. As late as 1925 nearly half the farmers in Michigan were within 4 miles of a market town (J. H. Kolb and E. deS. Brunner, "A Study of Rural Society—Its Organization and Changes," p. 175, Houghton Mifflin Company, Boston, 1940). Most of the functions of the smallest centers have disappeared, however, with the increased mobility of the rural population since the spread of automobile ownership. The crossroads store these days is a filling station with a convenience line of candy, tobacco, soft drinks, and perhaps a few canned goods. The distance between real market towns, where most of the objectives of a weekly shopping expedition can be realized, has certainly increased.

self to what extent it is proper to speak of a single general "trading area" for the village.

In Fig. 8·2, the greater variety of activities found in a sizable metropolis gives rise to a wider range of trade areas. This Salt

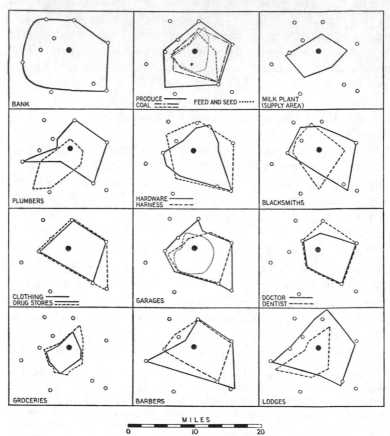

FIG. 8·1 Various tributary areas of Dryden, N. Y. (population 666 in 1930). Each of the 12 maps is drawn to the same scale. Where more than one area boundary is indicated for a single type of activity, the different boundaries apply to different establishments. The solid dot near the center of each map represents the village of Dryden; other settlements are shown as open circles. (*Redrawn by permission from maps in G. M. Kensler and B. L. Melvin, A Partial Sociological Study of Dryden, N. Y., Cornell University Agricultural Experiment Station Bulletin 504, Ithaca, N. Y., 1930.*)

Lake City case illustrates also the effect of state boundaries, a sparse network of transfer routes, and topographic barriers (on the east, north, and south) in forcing many area boundaries into exact conformity for parts of their circumference.

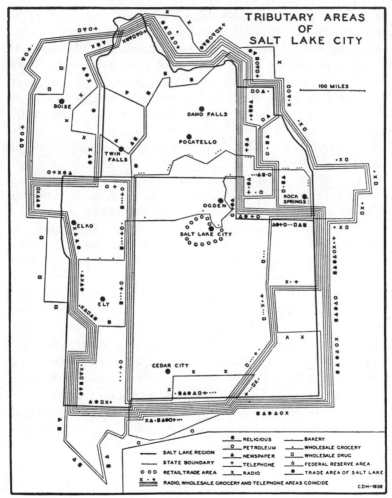

Fig. 8·2 Various tributary areas of Salt Lake City (population 149,934 in 1940). (*Reproduced by permission from Chauncy D. Harris, "Salt Lake City —A Regional Capital," University of Chicago Libraries,* 1940.)

8·7 Location Patterns within Urban and Metropolitan Communities

Characteristic patterns of urban structure arise from the different requirements of the various land uses with respect to the transfer and processing advantages of sites. Cities develop, as already explained, at nodal points on the transfer network and owe a large part of their growth to the advantages of close contact between different kinds of producers and consumers. They have their own characteristic internal geography, shaped very largely by factors of contact and therefore subject to change in keeping with the evolution of the means of transport and communication. Because of the competition for space among highly intensive rival forms of land use, the selective locational role of rents is prominent.

Certain economic activities within cities involve the handling of large quantities of goods either coming in from elsewhere or being shipped out. For these activities, which include the heavier types of manufacturing, warehousing, and wholesaling and the maintenance and servicing of transfer terminal operations, the only possible locations are those in the transshipment zone. This zone includes the dockside area (in port cities) and sites along railroad lines in the terminal and switching district. In the relatively small area thus served directly by heavy freight transport services, all the heavier manufacturing, storage, and distribution facilities are concentrated. In large cities this "industrial zone" is neither compact nor particularly central but stretches out along water fronts, radial rail lines, and belt railroads. In rolling country especially, it is likely to be restricted to stream valleys.

In the more central parts of the city, where general transfer advantages attract other intensive uses and rents are high, the industrial belts along transport lines are generally quite narrow and are occupied by the smaller and the older plants. Farther out the land is in less general demand, rents are lower, and the belts are wider. In these outlying locations are found the larger and newer factories, warehouses, and wholesalers.

Manufacturers, wholesalers, and warehousers of the less bulky goods need not be located on railroads or water fronts at all, since they can be served by truck. They have a much greater choice of locations than the heavier industries. Except as barred by zoning ordinances, they are free to locate anywhere in response to the attractions of labor supply, cheap land, and nearness to local suppliers or customers. As a rule, they are found interspersed with commercial and inferior residence uses.

Passenger terminals exert some effect on the location of hotels, theaters, and dealers catering to transient out-of-town buyers, *e.g.*, the garment-industry showrooms of New York. This attraction appears, however, not to be decisive. In many cities, such as Washington, the main passenger terminal has attracted only a minor cluster of hotels.

Businesses requiring frequent direct contacts with the local population are those most forcibly drawn to the main focus of intracity transit. This includes banks, offices, newspapers, and outlets for shopping goods at retail or wholesale. The important thing for these uses is to be accessible to the largest possible number of people during the daytime. They occupy the area referred to as "downtown" in the medium-sized city; in very large cities this area may split into a subdistrict specializing in finance (the Lower Broadway region in New York, LaSalle Street in Chicago, State Street in Boston) and another intensively developed district, with equally good transit facilities, devoted primarily to commerce, large hotels and theaters, and offices, *e.g.*, the midtown district of Manhattan.

In the less specialized branches of trade and service, centripetal attraction is weaker and the individual store or motion-picture house, say, can get along outside the main shopping center on the basis of easier access for the buyers of *one part* of the city. We find, then, outside the areas of peak intensity a broad zone in which trade, services, light industry, and residence are intermingled. In the inner parts of this zone, residence merely fills in the back streets, while the main street frontages are solidly commercial. Farther out, this belt assumes a more and more residential aspect, with shops mainly confined to occasional neighborhood subcenters. Where good transportation and relatively attractive surroundings occur together, *e.g.*, where an important transit artery approaches a park area, intensive residential occupance in the form of large apartment buildings is usually found, *e.g.*, some riverside areas, the environs of Central Park in Manhattan, and near Rock Creek Park in Washington.

It is evident from above that the main components of city structure are

a. Activities that must be located on rail or water terminal facilities and are therefore strung along the network of such facilities, with the larger establishments generally farther out.

b. Highly centripetal "downtown" establishments, which cluster near each other and in the area affording best access to the city as a whole.

c. Light industry, unspecialized commerce, and residence, which occupy those parts of the urban and suburban area not preempted by *a* and *b*.

d. Convenience-goods establishments (small nonspecialized stores, barber shops, motion-picture theaters, pool halls, eating and drinking places, newsstands, pressing and cleaning shops, and the like), which are distributed at important intersections and along principal streets in all parts of the city approximately in proportion to sidewalk traffic between home and work. They sell in too small quantities to entice the customer far off his beaten path.

The above discussion has run entirely in terms of transfer-cost factors. The distribution of various classes of residence use, however, involves an additional factor: the amenities of a neighborhood. In addition to wanting to live near their work, people like to live in quiet, spacious, clean, temperate surroundings. To this extent they are repelled from neighborhoods with dense traffic, noisy or dirty industry, or dense occupance of any sort. Likewise the local topography in certain directions from the center of the city usually provides much more pleasant residential sites than in other directions—areas of high ground, say, with breezes, preferably to windward of the industrial area, and perhaps with a view and near-by park space. Some of these same topographical features discourage the development of railroads, industrial zones, and cheap intensive housing. Consequently, the pattern of urban uses ordinarily is differentiated by *sectors* at least as much as by concentric zones, *i.e.*, varying according to direction as well as according to distance from the center. The irregularities introduced by the transit pattern and topography of the particular city and by accidents of historical development and promotion make the actual pattern of urban land uses highly complex.[13]

8·8   *Illustrations of Urban Land-use Patterns*

We may now look for some illustration of the tendencies just discussed in the actual patterns of land use of representative modern cities. Three broad types of use are to be distinguished: industrial, commercial, and residential.

Some characteristic patterns of *industrial* land use are shown in Figs. 8·3, 8·4, and 8·5, including six cities ranging from fairly small to very large. In every case the layout of rail and water routes is apparent from the disposition of the main continuous industrial tracts, though there is also a scattering of small industry (light manufacturing that receives and distributes by truck) throughout the more central parts of the city. This is most clearly shown in Fig. 8·4, which differentiates the zones of heavy and light industry in Chicago.[14] The other Chicago map, Fig. 8·5,

[13] A good recent collection of ideas and factual materials on this subject is Building the Future City, *Annals of the American Academy of Political and Social Science*, vol. 242, November, 1945, especially the article by C. D. Harris and E. L. Ullman, The Nature of Cities, pp. 7–17. A good insight into the factors relevant to urban site selection for retail stores is given by H. G. Canoyer, "Selecting a Store Location," Bureau of Foreign and Domestic Commerce, Economic Series No. 56, Washington, 1946. For similar materials relating to specific kinds of enterprises, see other reports in the Industrial (Small Business) Series of the Bureau of Foreign and Domestic Commerce.

[14] The Chicago Plan Commission has analyzed the industrial pattern as follows ("Master Plan of Residential Land Use of Chicago," pp. 20–21, Chicago, 1943): "Before the advent of railroads, industries in Chicago were almost entirely confined to areas along the Chicago River near what is now the central business district. The river at first was the only means of transportation for heavy raw materials and was the chief route for shipping finished products. The later disposition of manufacturing plants along both radial and belt railroads created an industrial pattern which extends throughout much of Chicago and into some satellite cities. Some establishments found sites for large-scale operations in areas adjacent to the Calumet River, others located on belt line railroads to obtain the advantage

shows the elaborate spider web of industrial zones in a giant rail center with flat local topography and also the lake-front development of heavy industry to the south as far as Gary.

The typical disposition of *commercial* areas is shown in Figs. 8·6 and 8·7, referring to the same six cities as the previous figures. Four elements of the commercial pattern are evident:

a. The main "downtown" shopping centers (crosshatched on Fig. 8·6).

b. Ribbons of commercial development along principal thoroughfares. These are especially noticeable in San Antonio and Chicago.

---

of fast freight handling, while still others preferred to remain near the heart of the city and a large labor supply.

"Four major varieties of industries may be differentiated. The first type includes the light manufacturing plants which are principally found in multistory buildings concentrated on the fringe of the central business district. Labor is a more important localizing factor than raw materials in these industries, and therefore they are concentrated at the focus of local transportation. Examples are the clothing and printing industries. The close intermingling of such establishments with the older homes near the heart of the city results in hybrid industrial residential neighborhoods.

"Another type of industry includes manufacturing plants in organized, integrated industries such as the Central Manufacturing District. These are located along radial and belt railroads and are served by highways for direct trucking. In such organized and large-scale districts, industry is segregated and its possible blighting effect on residential areas is therefore minimized.

"A third type is composed of large primary processing industries, such as steel mills and petroleum refineries which require tremendous acreage and handle large tonnages of bulky materials. Such industries create noise and emit odors obnoxious to adjacent residential areas. Establishments of this type were formerly concentrated on the Chicago River, but have shifted to the Calumet district, where lake transportation and large sites are available.

"The fourth type is composed of very large new war plants which have been built since 1940. These plants are located on the belt lines and on the major highway arteries outside the built-up suburban areas, both within and without the city, where large tracts of land were available. These extensive industrial sites made it possible to erect huge one-story buildings with the resulting economies of straight-line assembly operations. These plants will readily lend themselves to conversion for peacetime production after victory is achieved. They will serve as nuclei for the development of residential communities. Persons living inside Chicago will find employment in these plants, thereby bringing about a desirable two-way traffic movement, with the outflow of city workers to suburban industrial plants balanced by the inflow of suburban residents to their jobs in the central business district."

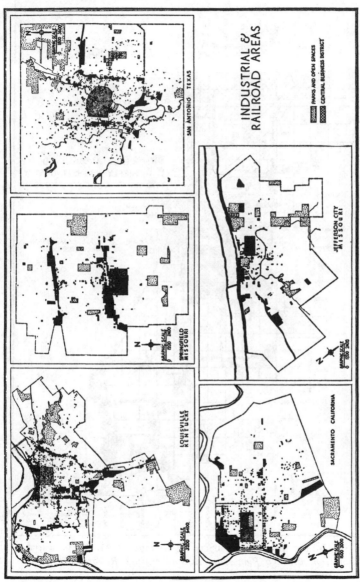

Fig. 8·3 Industrial and railroad areas in five representative "self-contained" cities. (*Reproduced by permission from Harland Bartholomew, "Urban Land Uses," Plate IX, Harvard City Planning Studies, vol. IV, Cambridge, Mass.,* 1932.)

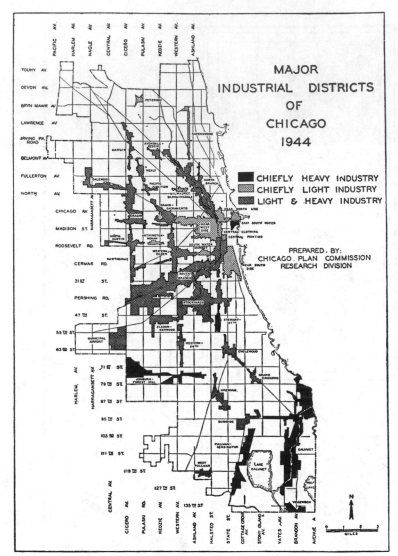

FIG. 8·4 Major industrial districts of Chicago, 1944. (*Reproduced by permission from Chicago Plan Commission, Annual Report, 1944.*)

Fig. 8·5 Principal industrial areas of Chicago and environs, 1945. (*Reproduced by permission from a map prepared by the Chicago Plan Commission.*)

    c. A few subordinate centers of concentration, *e.g.,* the one in the northern section of Springfield, Mo., which was once the center of a separate town.

    d. The "shotgun" scatter of neighborhood stores throughout the built-up area. In the Chicago map, Fig. 8·7, this is not quite so apparent, as not all stores have been shown.

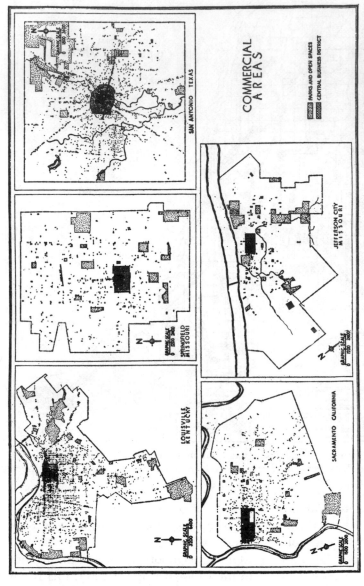

FIG. 8·6 Commercial areas in five representative "self-contained" cities. (Reproduced by permission from Harland Bartholomew, "Urban Land Uses," Plate VIII, Harvard City Planning Studies, vol. IV, Cambridge, Mass., 1932.)

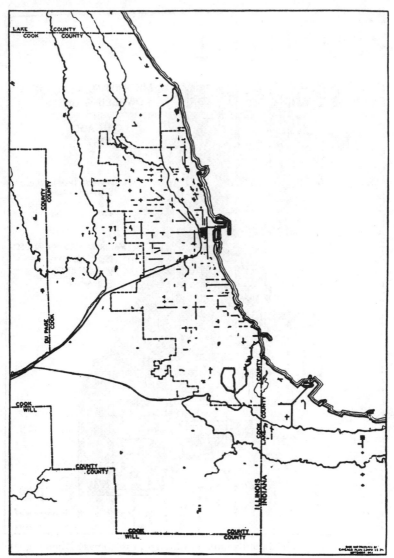

FIG. 8·7 Areas of concentrated commercial street frontage in Chicago. (*Reproduced by permission from Chicago Plan Commission, "Master Plan of Residential Land Use of Chicago," Fig. 2-G, p. 17, Chicago, 1943.*)

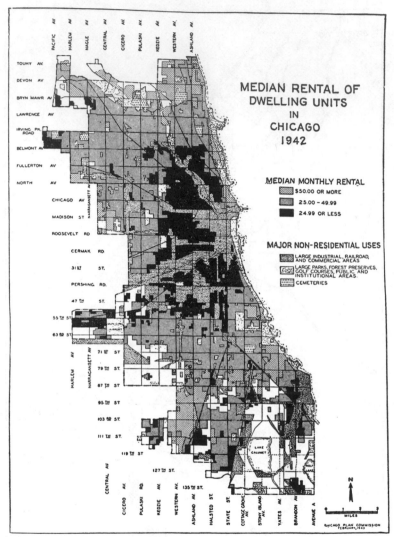

FIG. 8·8   Rental of dwelling units in Chicago in relation to adjoining land uses. (*Reproduced by permission from Chicago Plan Commission, "Master Plan of Residential Land Use of Chicago," Fig. 87, p. 65, Chicago, 1943.*)

Finally, the relation of *residential* land uses to other types is shown for Chicago in Fig. 8·8. Grades of residence areas, according to rental, have been distinguished. The generally low quality of residential property near the industrial sections is evident, as

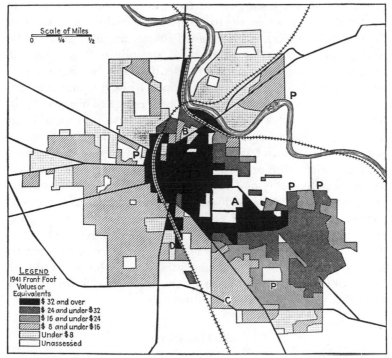

FIG. 8·9   Assessed valuations of property in Ann Arbor, Mich. Based on information supplied by the office of the city assessor and compiled with the assistance of the City Planning Commission. Most of the large tracts of "unassessed" land in the eastern section of the city are state university property. Major traffic arteries leading into the city are shown as heavy lines.

In classifying areas into land-value groups, valuations per front foot were used where available, with each block being rated according to the average value of its street frontage. Valuations on a square foot or acreage basis were converted into approximate front-foot equivalents. These methods would not be accurate for fine distinctions but are believed to be adequate for a generalized breakdown such as that here presented.

well as the relatively high quality of residence near parks and other open spaces.

A more detailed pattern of site values in all types of urban uses is shown in Fig. 8·9, which is based on assessments for taxation in Ann Arbor, Mich. (population 29,815 in 1940). Five ranges of land values are distinguished by shadings. The highest values (shown in solid black on the map) are in the industrial belts along the railroads, the central business district, and immediately adjacent property zoned for commercial or industrial use. Outside these areas, the predominantly residential land use shows the effects of a combination of factors. Property just east and southeast of the central business district, though occupied mainly by inferior housing, bears a high valuation because it is suitable for high-density residence or commercial use and has been zoned to permit one or both of these uses. There is a conspicuous southeastward orientation of the better residential districts in response to the location of the state university (centered at A but including also most of the "unassessed" areas shown in white in the eastern section of the city). Small residential areas isolated by through traffic streets or railroads, e.g., B, C, D, have depressed valuations. The worst housing in the city is found in the area between the central business district and the junction of the two railroads. Properties near parks and open spaces (some of which are marked P on Fig. 8·9) command a premium.

SUMMARY

The locational patterns of different industries are drawn into closer conformity in special cases by large transfer economies on the intermediate product or by complementary use of production factors. Still more generally, the economies of urban concentration and the transfer advantages of nodal points work toward still greater conformity. The market and supply areas of the various industries of a community are also subject to influences imposing some degree of uniformity.

Characteristic patterns of internal urban structure arise from the different requirements of the various land uses with respect to transfer and intrinsic qualities of land. Heavy industry is found along rail and water routes; commercial and service facilities needing contact with the metropolitan area as a whole are mainly at the focus of local transit routes; retailing of convenience goods and other activities serving only neighborhoods are strung along main commuting arteries; and residential uses are influenced by the advantages of access to workplace and the disadvantages of high site cost and nearness to industrial uses.

Part Two

Locational Change and Adjustment

CHAPTER 9

The Process of Locational Change

PREVIOUS CHAPTERS have described how individual producers and consumers develop locational preferences that lead toward certain more or less rational patterns of geographic distribution. But the world is full of change, necessitating a constant readjustment of patterns. Locational equilibrium is never attained, and many serious practical problems are due to difficulties and conflicts of interest in the process of adjustment.

Chapter 11 will explore some of those problems. The present chapter deals with four general points: (*a*) the principal types of locational change, (*b*) the way in which a specific firm or industry "migrates," (*c*) the way in which a shift in one industry affects the location of other industries, and (*d*) some important trends and developments in the location of population and manufacturing in the United States.

9·1 Long-run and Short-run Changes in Factors Affecting Location

The basic causes of locational change may be classified for convenience as seasonal, cyclical, secular, and structural, according to their character and duration.

SEASONAL CHANGES. Within the limitations of their mobility, consumers and producers shift their locations to meet changing seasonal conditions. Those who can afford it flock to summer resorts and winter resorts, while many tradesmen follow the seasonal tourist flow back and forth. Hundreds of thousands of families follow the progression of harvest seasons in the United States in order to get work for enough of the year to subsist. Many routes of trade, particularly in the colder and the rainier climates, are of a seasonal character. In California and a few other places beekeeping is seasonally migratory: hives are systematically moved about over great distances in order to give the bees access to the blossoms of different areas throughout the year.

The passing of the seasons and their effects on locational preferences are known in advance. For this reason adaptation to seasonal shifts has always been a routine procedure, and the locational problems caused thereby are generally of minor importance. The main question is the extent to which the use of the less mobile production factors can be regularized and thus made more efficient by reducing seasonal shifts or by combining different employments with complementary seasonal patterns.

CYCLICAL CHANGES. These last longer than seasonal ones. Moreover, they are much less predictable, though an enormous amount of effort has been devoted to trying to forecast them. Most important of all is the fact that in any given country, at least, the cyclical changes are likely to affect all activities in the same direction at about the same time,[1] whereas there is considerable diversity in seasonal patterns.

Cyclical changes are essentially fluctuations in the total rate of investment with accompanying effects on the total demand for production factors and for new goods, especially durable goods. Changes in the geographic distribution of productive equipment are confined mainly to periods of active new investment, but changes in the location of actual production occur at all stages of the business cycle.

When capacity is seriously underutilized, the owners of all factors of production seek fuller utilization. For labor, this means a flight from industrial unemployment to makeshift rural "security"; for capital and enterprise, it means an accentuated search for locations where the labor supply is more amenable to changes of technique designed to reduce overhead. Real-estate owners and others with a large stake in fixed locations become more eager in depression periods to attract new or "substitute" industry to their localities in order to maintain the utilization and value of their own properties.[2]

---

[1] A. F. Burns and W. C. Mitchell, "Measuring Business Cycles," National Bureau of Economic Research, New York, 1946.

[2] The competitive subsidization of industrial migration by small towns came into full flower as a depression phenomenon. The first Mississippi Balance-Agriculture-With-Industry Act of 1936, under which municipalities were authorized to buy

Since transfer rates are cyclically less flexible than most other prices, the locational importance of procurement and distribution costs is enhanced in depression periods. Finally, the greater curtailment of output in durable goods lines, as compared with nondurable, changes the geographic pattern of total employment and consumer income, with obvious effects on market-oriented industries.

It is significant that these depression effects predominantly favor a decentralization of both employment and population. It has long been recognized that human migration between farm and city follows this cyclical pattern,[3] but there was a tendency in the 1930's to overlook the temporary cyclical character of some of the industrial decentralization which occurred.

SECULAR CHANGES OR TRENDS. These are gradual alterations in one direction, which persist for long periods and show no tendency to reverse or repeat themselves as cycles and the seasons do. The growth of population in a fairly stable and settled area, for example, follows such a trend, and the resulting trend of locational change can be analyzed. The depletion of an exhaustible resource with use is another example. One may perhaps without undue optimism include also a secular trend of technical progress, or increased efficiency in processing and transfer. The locational significance of all these developments will be discussed in the next two chapters.

STRUCTURAL CHANGES. Such changes revolutionize conditions or techniques and abruptly change the slopes or directions of trends. The distinctions among cyclical, secular, and structural are

---

or build industrial facilities for lease to new industries virtually rent-free, was allowed to expire in 1940; the general feeling in Mississippi was that it served its purpose as an "emergency" measure but did not need to be continued after general economic revival had set in. See E. J. Hopkins, "Mississippi's BAWI Plan, an Experiment in Industrial Subsidization," Federal Reserve Bank of Atlanta, 1944. Prosperity, however, has not damped the zeal of community and regional promoters. BAWI was revived in 1944 in a somewhat different form. See R. B. Highsaw, Two Years of the BAWI Program, University of Mississippi, Bureau of Business Research, Business Bulletin, vol. 4, No. 6, August, 1946.

[3] Since rural populations typically reproduce much faster than urban but the more rapid long-run growth of economic opportunity is in and around the cities, the flow of migration is almost always in the rural-urban direction, swelling in prosperous times and shrinking in slack times. Cf. Table 7·2.

obviously nebulous, depending largely upon the area of reference and upon the degree of continuity that the historian sees fit to impute to the march of events.[4]

9·2   *Differential Growth Rates and Relocation*

In referring to an "industry" we ordinarily have in mind the productive factors committed to it. "Migration" of the industry, however, does not necessarily entail migration of these factors. Land does not move at all; capital, enterprise, and labor may or may not. The well-known migration of most of the American cotton-textile industry from New England to the South involved some shift of enterprise and capital funds and even a considerable shipment of concrete capital goods (spindles and other machinery).[5] But in the main, the new Southern mills recruited a new labor supply; it was indeed primarily this opportunity which motivated the shift of the industry. On the other hand, the movement of fine textile production from the Low Countries and France to England in the sixteenth and seventeenth centuries involved primarily a movement of skilled workers.[6]

An industry can even change its pattern without any actual geographic shift of either persons or equipment. When the culture

[4] Thus Isard explains the long "cycles" of construction activity and locational change in the United States on the basis of certain epochal improvements in transportation, from canals and turnpikes to aircraft. The effects of such transport improvement might be viewed from a long perspective as part of a "secular" trend of reduction of transfer costs, yet the actual development clearly involved intermittent waves of investment which fit the "cyclical" pattern, while in particular areas the resultant reordering of economic relations was so radical as to merit the term "structural." Walter Isard, Transportation Development and Building Cycles, *Quarterly Journal of Economics,* vol. LVII, No. 1, November, 1942, pp. 90–112; Caroline and Walter Isard, Economic Implications of Aircraft, *Quarterly Journal of Economics,* vol. LIX, No. 2, February, 1945, pp. 145–169. See also Chap. 10 of this book.

[5] Enormously greater movements of capital goods have been carried out in Europe during the recent war and in connection with disarmament and reparations. In these cases, however, the incentive was much stronger than it normally is in peacetime—the alternative to movement was destruction, and the need was urgent at the points of destination.

[6] Laurent Dechesne, "La Localisation des diverses productions," pp. 116–118, Les Editions Comptables, Commerciales et Financières, Brussels, 1945.

of silk declined in China and increased in Japan, the geographical distribution of silk production was changed, and we should ordinarily speak of this change as a "redistribution," a "shift," or even a "migration" of the industry. Yet what happened is that in China some labor, capital, and land formerly devoted to silk culture were diverted to other uses while at the same time in Japan labor and capital and land were put into silk production, representing in part a net addition to total productive resources and in part a diversion from other uses.

It would seem that any of three things may happen to any of the factors involved in production, as a part of the process of changing the locational pattern of an industry. They may move, shift occupations, or pass into or out of productive use.

There are certain limitations, however, on this rather wide range of theoretical possibilities. Land and some of the heavier forms of capital equipment are for practical purposes immobile and can participate in locational change only by being shifted to new uses in the same place or by being newly brought into productive use or abandoned. Possibilities of shift to other uses are limited too. Some production factors (mineral sites and special-purpose machinery and structures) have no value in any kind of production save that for which they are designed. When the industry using such a factor moves away, the factor must be either taken along or abandoned.[7]

The third possible type of participation in locational shift (by net addition to or subtraction from the total amount of the factor in use) is also limited. Any production factor can be abandoned, but capital, labor, and enterprise increase slowly, and land, in so far as it is really "natural" resources, not at all. The existence of idle reserves of all types of factors most of the time gives, of course, some leeway for change.

---

[7] Even some types of labor find themselves in this position. A study of former cigar makers in a New England city found that a large proportion of the older workers failed to find any other employment at which they could make a living. D. B. Creamer and G. V. Swackhamer, "Cigar Makers—After the Lay-off," Works Progress Administration, National Research Project, Report No. L-1, Philadelphia, 1937 (processed). The relapse of the Amazonian Indians into their primeval state of self-sufficiency with the collapse of the wild rubber industry is another example of "stranded" production factors losing their place in the modern economic system.

The way in which any particular production factor participates in a readjustment is determined by its spatial mobility, its adaptability to alternative uses, and the availability of idle reserves or increased supply. The character and amount of the locational shift that actually occurs in response to a given stimulus depend on the mobility, adaptability, and elasticity of supply of all the factors concerned.

Chapter 11 will discuss some of the problems arising from the maladjustment of production factors to geographical shifts in the demand for them.

In practice, most shifts in the location of any specific industry are essentially geographic differentials in the rate of growth of the industry,[8] with the actual relocation of firms or plants playing a minor role [9] and the migration of labor usually occurring tardily or not at all.

[8] Thus, for example, D. B. Creamer defines interstate locational shift in a recent study as "a difference between the change in the number and distribution of wage jobs which actually occurred in a given industry in a given State and that change which would have resulted if this industry had grown or declined in the State at the same rate it did in the Nation." National Resources Planning Board, "Industrial Location and National Resources," Chap. 4, Shifts of Manufacturing Industries, Government Printing Office, Washington, 1943.

[9] D. B. Creamer's analysis of U. S. Census data for the period 1928 to 1933 disclosed that the "birth" and "death" rates for manufacturing jobs are of the ordei of 3 to 4 per cent per biennium; i.e., 3 to 4 per cent of the manufacturing employment at any time is in plants that did not exist two years earlier, and a roughly equal percentage is in plants that will go out of business during the next two years. This measure of turnover runs many times higher in the clothing industries and is higher still in trade but is much lower in the durable-goods industries as a group. The rate of plant relocation (in terms of wage jobs involved over a 2-year interval) seems to be only about one-tenth as great as the birth or death rate for manufacturing as a whole. D. B. Creamer, "Is Industry Decentralizing?", University of Pennsylvania Press, Philadelphia, 1935; Carter Goodrich and others, "Migration and Economic Opportunity," University of Pennsylvania Press, Philadelphia, 1936. A still earlier study based on independent inquiry is described in "Industrial Development in the United States and Canada, 1926 and 1927," National Electric Light Association and Metropolitan Life Insurance Co., undated. In that study, 1,934 cities reported a breakdown of their gains in industrial employment (56 per cent in new plants, 25 per cent in branch plants, 19 per cent in relocated plants) and their losses (65 per cent in plants gone out of business 35 per cent in plants—including branches—relocated).

Neither of the investigations cited attempts to measure the amount of locational shift in employment brought about by expansion and contraction of existing

Industries differ considerably in this respect, to be sure. In those where branch plants are common, an important part of any shift in the industry pattern is likely to be accounted for by openings and closings of branches, which involve relocation of factors at least to the extent of the upper management strata and some of the equipment. Other employees, often given an opportunity in such cases to retain jobs and seniority by moving, are more mobile than they would be if it were a question of looking for a new job with a new concern. General observation indicates, too, that branch plants are more responsive to change in locational advantage than independent plants under otherwise similar circumstances.

Because of the moderate skill requirements and the prevailing system of leasing rather than owning machinery, the shoe-manufacturing business is one in which physical transference of plant is easier than in most other industries.[10] Nevertheless, most of the actual change in the industry's location pattern appears to involve "births" and "deaths" of plants rather than relocation. Between 1929 and 1933, for instance, the proportion of United States shoe-factory employment located in the main and satellite cities of census industrial areas dropped from 32.7 to 26.1, which is equivalent to a shift of about 13,000 jobs (total employment in the industry was then in the neighborhood of 200,000). During the same period the net loss of shoe-factory employment in these cities by plant relocation was less than 1,300.[11]

9·3   Local Repercussions of Shifts of Industry

The effects of a lasting major locational change are almost never confined to a single industry. Even if the technical development or other "initiating" factor of change applies directly to only one industry, that industry's response will alter the basis of locational

---

plants. General observation would indicate that this is quite large, since plants may be quite small when first established and likewise may curtail employment drastically before finally liquidating or moving.

[10] Small-town subsidies to industry (in the northeastern and North Central states at any rate) have attracted shoe factories probably in greater number than any other type of business.

[11] Creamer, *op. cit.*, Table 24, p. 70, and Table 29, p. 89.

preference for several others. Their responses, if any, will do likewise, and a chain of locational repercussions is thus set in motion that may change the face of a continent.[12]

Locational repercussions in such a broad perspective as this, involving the whole process of the spread of settlement and economic development, will be discussed later, in Chap. 11. The present aim is more modest: to examine the more direct and immediate local effects of a change exemplified by the opening of a sizable industrial plant in a community.

The effects of such an occurrence may be envisaged in terms of the new demands and new supplies that the added productive activity brings to the community. It brings added demand for materials, land, labor, transfer services, and various local services. By adding directly and indirectly to the income of the community, it brings a rise in demand for consumer goods and services of all kinds. At the same time, the products of the new industry constitute an addition on the supply side.

The immediate economic effects on the community may then be summarized as follows: a tightening of the labor and real-estate markets, reflected perhaps in rising labor costs [13] and rents for other businesses; an enlarged local demand for all consumer goods and services and for any local materials the new or expanded industry uses; and finally a cheaper and more plentiful local supply of the products of that industry.

We should expect, then, that the stages of production which precede and follow the industry in question will find this community a better location than before. So will market-oriented in-

[12] For the most comprehensive discussion of the process of transmission of locational change, see August Lösch, "The Economics of Location," Chapters 19 and 20, Yale University Press, 1954.

[13] This explains why a chamber of commerce gets at best only lukewarm cooperation from the absentee management of a big firm with a branch plant in its city when it is a question of inducing other firms to locate plants there too. The "absentee" firm has no interest in the expansion of income or property values in the city itself, since its markets are much wider and the personal interests of its executives lie elsewhere. On the contrary, additional demand in the local labor market can hardly fail to raise labor costs and is therefore unwelcome. This is especially likely if the plants that might be brought in are of a sort offering higher or steadier wages or better working conditions than the plant already there.

dustries in general, *e.g.*, some new retail stores will probably open. The only adverse effects will be felt by other industries with which the new one competes for local materials, labor, local consumer markets, or desirable sites. On the whole, the adverse effects are of minor significance. Even market or labor competition can be an advantage to other local industries to the extent that it builds up the local commodity markets and labor market in size and variety and therefore in attractiveness to still other buyers and sellers.[14]

The aggregate of all these effects on other local industries is clearly so dependent on the particular situation in the area that little can be said by way of generalization. Much depends on the characteristics of the new industry, some possessing a good deal more of what we may call "locational leverage" than others. Plainly, an industry that pays out most of its costs locally, for pay roll or for materials in fairly elastic local supply, and that furnishes a product suitable for further processing at that point has a relatively high leverage. Coal mining is a good example.

Some attempts have been made to measure statistically the "geographic multiplier," meaning usually the effect on market-oriented industries resulting from local pay-roll and materials expenditure by a new industry and consequent local reexpenditure of part of the same flow of payments.

Michael Daly has found, for instance, a somewhat irregular relationship in various British areas between the increase in employment in "unfettered" industries, *i.e.*, those not closely market-

[14] Where concentration of sales is dictated by the buyers' insistence upon comparison, major shifts in location are infrequent because the whole industry is concentrated at just a few points; but at rare intervals when a migration to a new center gets under way, it may proceed with striking rapidity and lead perhaps to a complete replacement of the older center of concentration by the new. This phenomenon can sometimes be observed within large metropolitan cities where there are specialized districts devoted to particular trades catering to a fashion or "shopping" market. When for any reason a few leaders transfer themselves to a different district of the city, the rest will follow in a very short time. The New York City garment district has made several such jumps. In this case the repercussions of a locational change on the part of one important producer are that a large proportion of the other producers are impelled to move not away from him but as near as possible to his new location.

oriented, from 1921 to 1931, and the increase of employment in local market-oriented industry. He concludes:

> If, *e.g.*, 120,000 men are put to work in the unfettered industries of an area, probably not less than 162,000 new jobs in the localized (market-oriented) industries of the region will be created.[15]

Other approaches to local multiplier measurement by Barfod [16] and Vining [17] have attempted to trace the flow of increased local income and expenditure arising from an initial increase in spending. Barfod was concerned with evaluating the economic effects of a Danish oil works on its local community (Aarhus), while Vining's primary interest was in analyzing the way in which cyclical variations in investment and spending are transmitted from one local trading area to another, with certain areas in Arkansas as examples.

It should be noted that a measure based on the tracing of income and expenditure, *e.g.*, Barfod's, does not take account of all elements of "locational leverage." Price and cost effects are ignored.[18] Actually, the coming of a new establishment to a community tends to raise the price of land, labor, and whatever kinds of local materials it uses while lowering the price of things it produces. These changes in turn affect both the incomes and the locations of other industries.

9·4   *Some Major Developments in the Location of Population and Manufacturing in the United States*

This book makes no attempt to describe or analyze specific actual location patterns or their changes. For the sake of back-

---

15 M. C. Daly, An Approximation to a Geographical Multiplier, *Economic Journal*, vol. L, Nos. 198–199, June–September, 1940, p. 254.

16 Børge Barfod, "Local Economic Effects of a Large-scale Industrial Undertaking," Einar Munksgaard, Copenhagen, and Oxford University Press, New York, 1938.

17 Rutledge Vining, The Region as a Concept in Business-cycle Analysis, *Econometrica*, vol. 14, No. 3, July, 1946, pp. 201–218.

18 Lösch's theoretical approach takes in these effects. but he makes no attempt to incorporate them in a "multiplier" computation.

ground, however, it will be of interest to look briefly at some outstanding over-all shifts in the geographic distribution of industry and population in the United States. Three aspects of change will be considered: distribution by regions, degree of concentration in cities and metropolitan areas, and degree of similarity between the locational patterns of manufacturing and population. The next two chapters will throw some light on the causes of shifts and the nature of the adjustment problems they create.

TRENDS PRIOR TO 1940. A noteworthy feature of the national pattern of development for many decades prior to 1940 is the trend toward more equal interregional distribution. Population growth has been more rapid in the less densely settled regions, and the density of population has become steadily less unequal in different parts of the country.[19]

While population was spreading itself more evenly over the area of the country, manufacturing activity was spreading itself more evenly over the population. The degree of industrialization, as measured by the number of manufacturing wage earners per

[19] This trend has been measured, using states as the geographic units. In each decennial census year since 1850, the percentage breakdown of the area of the United States by states and territories was placed alongside the percentage breakdown of total United States population by states and territories. For each state or territory that accounted for a larger share of population than of area, the difference in percentage points was calculated, and these differences were summed to give the coefficient of concentration measuring the degree of discrepancy between the interstate distributions of area and of population. This coefficient shows a steady though slackening fall from 65.7 per cent in 1850 to 42.1 per cent in 1940. F. M. Hoover, Interstate Redistribution of Population, 1850–1940, *Journal of Economic History*, vol. I, No. 2, November, 1941, pp. 199–205. The same type of coefficient has been widely used in recent years to measure the degree of concentration or "localization" of individual industries with respect to area, to population, or to one another. See, for example, Political and Economic Planning, "The Location of Industry in Great Britain," Appendix II, London, 1939; National Resources Planning Board, "Industrial Location and National Resources," Chap. 4, Government Printing Office, Washington, 1943.

The reader should be warned that coefficients of this type based on different sets of geographical units are not comparable; *e.g.*, a coefficient calculated by counties will be larger than one based on the same data lumped together in state totals.

The best discussion of techniques of measurement for geographic distributions is John K. Wright, Some Measures of Distributions, *Annals of the Association of American Geographers*, December, 1937.

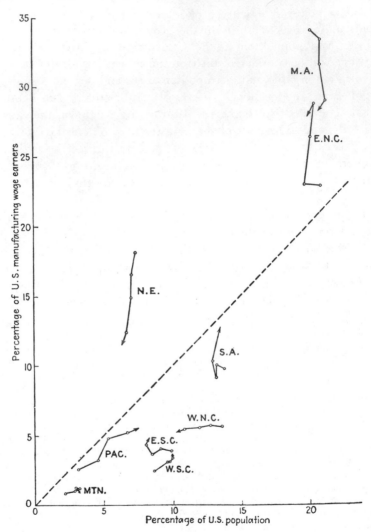

Fig. 9·1 Changes in the regional distribution of population and manufacturing employment in the United States, 1900 to 1940. The line plotted for each region represents data for 1900, 1910, 1920, 1930, and 1940 in chronological sequence (the arrow point standing for 1940). The diagonal dotted line represents equal percentages of total United States population and total United States manufacturing employment; regions shown above the dotted line had more than the national average number of manufactur-

1,000 population, shows decreasing interregional differences for at least several decades before 1940.[20]

This development can be seen in Fig. 9·1, which shows the distribution of population and of manufacturing wage earners by census geographic regions in the United States at 10-year intervals from 1900 to 1940. In each year each region is plotted as a point, with its position on the horizontal scale representing that region's share of the total population of the United States and its position on the vertical scale representing the region's share of the manufacturing wage earners of the United States. The five points for each region representing the five census dates covered are connected with lines, and an arrowhead is added at the 1940 end to show the direction of time. Finally, the diagonal line on the diagram represents *equal* percentages of population and of manufacturing. Points below or to the right of the diagonal represent regions "less industrialized" than the United States as a whole, and points above or to the left of the diagonal represent the "more industrialized" regions.

Figure 9·1 will repay careful study, as it presents a great deal of information. The most noteworthy points are

a. The steady decline of New England in relative importance with respect both to population and to manufacturing. The Middle Atlantic region likewise failed to keep pace with the rest of the country in manufacturing, and in the 1930's the East North Central region joined the laggard group.

[20] Changes in the degree of concentration of specific manufacturing industries with reference to population have been measured by the use of Lorenz curves. E. M. Hoover, The Measurement of Industrial Localization, *Review of Economic Statistics,* vol. XVIII, No. 4, November, 1936, pp. 162–171. Manufacturing activity as a whole shows also a trend toward more even distribution with reference to *area.* G. C. Smith, Jr., Lorenz Curve Analysis of Industrial Decentralization, *Journal of the American Statistical Association,* vol. XLII, No. 240, December, 1947, pp. 591–596.

ing wage earners per 1,000 population, whereas those shown below the dotted line had less than the national average. The manufacturing wage-earner data refer in each case to the Census of Manufactures of the year preceding the decennial Census of Population. (*Bureau of the Census and Bureau of Agricultural Economics, "Changes in Distribution of Manufacturing Wage Earners, 1899- 1939," Table 2, p. 25, and Table 4, p. 27, Washington, 1942.*)

b. The rapid and sustained advance of the Pacific region in relative importance.

c. The striking interchange of positions between the East South Central and West South Central regions.

d. The North-South shift between 1930 and 1940, which involved a reversal of previous trends in no less than four regions. In the 1930's all three northeastern regions lagged and the three southern regions forged ahead.

e. The trend toward greater equalization of manufacturing relative to population in the various regions, shown in the figure by the general tendency of the regional lines to head in toward the diagonal representing the national average relationship.[21]

However, while the population was distributing itself more uniformly over area on an interregional scale, it was steadily concentrating on a local scale. The proportion of the population living in "urban" places (2,500 population or more) has increased with every census. Mention has already been made of the persistent rural-urban migration which has effected this urbanization in the face of the notably lower fertility of urban populations.[22] Table 9·1 shows that the prewar trend was not only an increasing proportion of the population in cities and towns as a group but until 1930 a more rapidly increasing proportion in the larger places. Another manifestation of the trend of intraregional concentration is the fact that the rate of population increase in the 33 Census Industrial Areas [23] averaged 2.7 per cent annually be-

---

[21] The coefficient of concentration of manufacturing relative to population described above in footnote 19 on p. 155 could be calculated (on a regional basis) from the diagram by simply adding all the upward deviations of regional points from the diagonal in a given census year. The same total, incidentally, would be obtained by adding all the downward deviations or all deviations to the right or all deviations to the left. For the five census years shown in Fig. 9·1, the values of the coefficient are 26.3, 25.0, 24.5, 21.5, and 17.9 per cent. It will be noted that the decrease is particularly marked in the last decade, *i.e.*, the 1930's.

[22] Table 7·2 and the accompanying discussion.

[23] The census defines an Industrial Area as "an area having as its nucleus an important manufacturing city and comprising the county in which the city is located, together with any adjoining county or counties in which there is great concentration of manufacturing industry." The number of manufacturing wage earners employed in each area was at least 40,000 in 1929.

Table 9·1   Percentage of United States Population in Urban Places, by Size, and in Rural Nonfarm and Farm Territory, 1910–1946

	1910	1920	1930	1940	1944 *	1946 *
Total United States..............	100.0	100.0	100.0	100.0	100.0	100.0
Urban places, total †............	45.7	51.2	56.2	56.5	59.6	60.0
By size classes:						
500,000 and over...........	12.5	15.5	17.0	17.0⎫	31.0	‡
100,000–500,000..........	9.6	10.5	12.6	11.8⎭		
25,000–100,000..........	8.9	9.8	10.5	11.2⎫	28.6	‡
2,500– 25,000..........	14.7	15.5	16.0	16.5⎭		
Rural territory, total †..........	54.3	48.8	43.8	43.5	40.4	40.0
Nonfarm †..................	§	18.8	19.3	20.5	20.0	19.9
Farm †....................	§	30.0	24.6	22.9	20.4	20.1

* Percentages for 1944 and 1946 are estimates for civilian population only. For these two dates, areas are classified according to their 1940 urban or rural status and size. The percentages of civilian population in areas that would have been classified as urban in 1944 and 1946 would probably be larger than the figures shown.

† The 1940 census definitions of "urban," "rural nonfarm," and "rural farm" territory have been applied for all years. For this reason some of the percentages for the earlier years differ from the ones originally published for those years.

‡ Data not available.

§ Comparable data not available, owing to change in classification of places.

Sources: United States decennial census figures through 1940 and Census Bureau estimates for 1944, from "Statistical Abstract of the United States," 1938 and 1946 Census Bureau estimates for 1946 from census release, Series P-S, No. 19, Feb. 20, 1947.

tween 1870 and 1930 as compared with an average annual increase of only 1.9 per cent for the country as a whole.[24]

Interestingly enough, manufacturing industry did not join in this trend of intraregional concentration. The share of total manufacturing wage earners accounted for by the 33 Census Industrial Areas remained remarkably stable at about 55 per cent throughout the period 1869 to 1939.[25] Within the Industrial Areas,

[24] G. E. McLaughlin, "Growth of American Manufacturing Areas," Table 11, p. 45, Bureau of Business Research, University of Pittsburgh, 1938.

[25] McLaughlin, op. cit., Table 22, p. 100; Bureau of the Census and Bureau of Agricultural Economics, "Changes in Distribution of Manufacturing Wage Earners, 1899–1939," Table 10, p. 36, Washington, 1942; "Statistical Abstract of the United States," 1946, Table 934, p. 845.

manufacturing employment tended to shift from the principal city to the suburban fringe.[26]

Some results of this difference in local concentration tendencies of population and manufacturing are shown in Table 9·2. Noteworthy points are

Table 9·2   Concentration of Manufacturing Employment Relative to Population in Industrial Areas and in Cities by Size Classes, 1899–1937

Area or city size class	Number of manufacturing earners per 1,000 population *				Relative concentration of manufacturing †			
	1899	1919	1929	1937	1899	1919	1929	1937
United States....................	62	86	72	69	100	100	100	100
33 Census Industrial Areas........	126	151	112	106	203	176	156	154
Remainder of United States........	38	54	49	48	61	63	68	70
Cities, by size classes based on population in 1930:								
500,000 and over..............	125	136	105	97	201	158	146	141
100,000–500,000..............	125	142	108	98	201	165	150	142
25,000–100,000..............	130	157	121	122	210	183	168	177
Remainder of United States........	35	52	46	46	56	60	64	67

* Population based on nearest decennial census.

† Manufacturing wage earners per 1,000 population in area or size class, as percentage of number of manufacturing wage earners per 1,000 population in the United States as a whole.

Source: Bureau of the Census and Bureau of Agricultural Economics, "Changes in Distribution of Manufacturing Wage Earners, 1899–1939," Table 10, pp. 36–39, and Table 16, p. 50. The ratios in the last four columns have been calculated by the present author.

a. The consistent trend toward equalization of the degree of industrialization as among cities of different size groups and as

[26] A detailed analysis of this development by Daniel B. Creamer is in Carter Goodrich and others, "Migration and Economic Opportunity," Chap. VII, University of Pennsylvania Press, Philadelphia, 1936. McLaughlin, *op. cit.,* Table 26, p. 192, shows that most of the Census Industrial Areas had a decreasing proportion of their manufacturing employment within the "central city" in nearly every census from 1879 to 1935. Corresponding ratios on the basis of value added by manufacture are given in *ibid.,* Table 36, p. 187.

between the Census Industrial Areas and the rest of the country.[27]

b. The fact that cities of 25,000 to 100,000 population have been, at least for the last half century or so, the most heavily industrialized size group. As compared with larger places, this relative specialization has increased.

c. The fact that the peak of relative importance of manufactures as a source of employment was passed nearly a generation ago. Even in absolute numbers the trend of manufacturing employment in the United States now appears to be downward. This reflects, of course, the more rapid growth of "tertiary" (trade and service) occupations, a development that bears significant locational implications.[28] Most trade and service activities are more closely oriented to consumer markets than manufacturing industries as a class and are, perhaps, less likely to be "foot-loose."

DEVELOPMENTS SINCE 1940. The 1940's have seen an unprecedented expansion of manufacturing capacity and equally unprecedented displacements of population under abnormal conditions. In the absence of any general census of population or of manufactures since 1940 and 1939, it is impossible to evaluate precisely in terms of redistribution the direct effects of the war and the postwar boom, to say nothing of the ultimate effects. Some conclusions can be reached, however, in the light of information at hand.

The magnitude of the war-motivated expansion of industrial capacity is roughly gauged by the statement that its cost represented about one-third of the value of manufacturing facilities existing in 1940. In addition, nearly half the preexisting capacity was temporarily converted to war use.[29]

The regional distribution of the new investment in facilities is shown in Table 9·3, which also makes a comparison with the

---

[27] This may seem to conflict with an earlier statement that the share of the Industrial Areas in total manufacturing has remained constant. The explanation is that the Industrial Areas have acquired an increasing share of the country's population while failing to augment their share of manufacturing.

[28] Cf. Section 11·7.

[29] G. E. McLaughlin, Regional Problems of Industrialization (Chap. IX in "Economic Reconstruction," S. E. Harris, ed.), pp. 163–165, McGraw-Hill Book Company, Inc., New York, 1945. In evaluating the importance of wartime expansion of facilities in terms of capacity, the very high construction costs should be taken into account.

Table 9·3   Regional Distribution of 1939 Manufacturing Activity and Total and Privately Financed War Facilities Expenditures, 1940–1944

Region	Percentage of United States total value added by manufacture, 1939	Percentage of United States total war facilities expenditures approved June, 1940–June, 1944 *	
		Total	Privately financed
United States.................	100.0	100.0	100.0
East North Central..........	31.5	31.1	31.3
Middle Atlantic.............	29.8	19.1	22.7
New England...............	9.8	4.9	6.5
South Atlantic..............	9.1	6.9	7.9
Pacific.....................	6.5	9.2	11.0
West North Central.........	5.5	7.4	3.7
East South Central..........	3.4	6.2	5.4
West South Central..........	3.3	11.3	9.3
Mountain..................	1.1	3.9	2.2

* Exclusive of 3.5 per cent of the total of such expenditures, for which regional distribution is not available.

Source: Based on data in G. E. McLaughlin, Regional Problems of Industrialization, Table 3, p. 167 (Chap. IX in "Economic Reconstruction," S. E. Harris, ed.), McGraw-Hill Book Company, Inc., New York, 1945. Percentages in the second column have been adjusted upward to total 100.0; percentages in the last column have been calculated from data in McLaughlin's table.

prewar regional pattern of manufacturing activity. It is clear that the New England, Middle Atlantic, and South Atlantic regions received relatively small shares of the war facilities (less than 30 per cent in all) in comparison with their prewar importance in manufacturing (nearly 50 per cent of the national total of value added by manufacture in 1939). In part this regional redirection of investment was the result of an effort to locate plants away from the seaboard and in areas where surplus labor supplies existed; in part it was the result of the fact that the industries involved in war expansion were not a representative sample of peacetime industries.

To evaluate the lasting effect on regional development, account would have to be taken of the different degrees of reconvertibility of the types of war facilities established in different regions. A large proportion of the explosives and ammunition plants, shipyards, and aircraft factories, for example, have little prospect of peacetime use. A very rough measure of the degree to which the war industry of a region is reconvertible is the extent to which it was privately financed.[30] On the basis of this and other criteria it seems that the less industrialized regions in general did not receive such a disproportionate stimulus as the over-all distribution of war facilities might seem to indicate.

Even after allowance for this consideration, the pattern of wartime industrial investment conspicuously furthered the progress of three rather new industrial territories which had been growing rapidly before the war: the Gulf Southwest, California, and the Tennessee Valley.[31] In many individual metropolitan areas as well, the war boom introduced large-scale manufacturing for the first time. Atlanta, Oklahoma City, Denver, Omaha, and Phoenix are cited as cities that received their industrial "baptism" in the war period.[32]

Within regions, most types of new war facilities were placed in metropolitan areas.[33] This was true of virtually all the larger plants except those devoted to ammunition loading and explosives (including the atomic bomb). In the absence of over-all statistics, one may surmise that the percentage of total manufacturing concentrated in metropolitan areas rose to an all-time high in the war period.

Within metropolitan areas the prewar trend to the suburbs seems to have continued, though no comprehensive figures are available. Housing shortages in cities and the typical large size of the war plants combined to emphasize the advantages of suburban location.

---

[30] Nearly all the investment in aircraft, explosives, ammunition, and shipbuilding facilities came from public funds; by contrast, private investors supplied over half the capital needed for new facilities in the petroleum, coal, and machinery fields. McLaughlin, *op. cit.*, Table 2, p. 166.

[31] *Ibid.*, p. 176.

[32] *Ibid.*, p. 171.

[33] *Ibid.*, p. 176.

Population redistribution during the war was likewise unprecedented in extent, though not in direction. The Census Bureau has estimated that more than 15 million civilians migrated across county lines between Dec. 7, 1941, and March, 1945.[34] Much of this migration represented an acceleration of prewar migration currents, notably to the Pacific Coast and from farms to cities, and has therefore shown no substantial backflow after the war. By July, 1946, as Table 9·1 indicates, 60 per cent of our population was urban as compared with only 56.5 per cent in 1940. The proportion of civilian population residing in "metropolitan counties" (counties containing or adjoining major cities) rose from 50.8 per cent in April, 1940, to 53.4 per cent in March, 1943.[35] Fragmentary information indicates that the greater part of this growth occurred outside the corporate limits of the "central cities" of metropolitan areas.[36]

The wartime expansion of industrial facilities still left many industries with inadequate, obsolete, or poorly located capacity and is rapidly being overshadowed by private postwar expansion programs. No compiled information is yet at hand to indicate the locational impact of this postwar expansion in more than a very general way. But it is worth noting that industrial construction activity in 1946 showed a continuation of certain trends previously noted: relatively rapid growth on the Pacific Coast, in the Gulf Southwest, and in some sections of the Southeast, and relatively slow growth in the Northeast.[37]

[34] Bureau of the Census, Special Report, Series P-S, No. 5, Sept. 2, 1945.

[35] War Production Board, "Regional and Industry Impacts of War Production," Part B, Table 23, p. 43, Washington, 1944 (processed). The population in metropolitan counties grew faster than that outside of metropolitan counties in each state, with only four exceptions.

[36] In March to June, 1944, 10 congested war production areas were canvassed by the Census Bureau: Charleston, S. C., Detroit–Willow Run, Hampton Roads, Los Angeles, Mobile, Muskegon, Portland, Ore., Puget Sound, San Diego, and San Francisco Bay. In the 14 "central cities" (some of the areas had more than one), population had increased 17.3 per cent since the 1940 census. In the territory comprising the remainder of each Census Metropolitan District the increase was 42.8 per cent; while in the remainder of the still larger area designated for the survey, the increase was 46.2 per cent. In each of the 10 areas the rate of increase for the central city was less than that of either ot the other two parts of the area canvassed. Bureau of the Census release, Series CA-1, No. 11, Sept. 20, 1944.

[37] This statement is based on estimates by the Office of Economic Research, Federal Works Agency. A tabulation of the larger factory construction contracts from

SUMMARY

The initial causes of locational shift are seasonal variations in weather; cyclical fluctuations in investment, income distribution, factor utilization, and relative prices; the gradual growth of population and depletion of exhaustible resources; and the development of new resources and techniques.

"Migrations" of specific industries represent primarily geographic differentials in growth rates rather than physical transference of production factors to new locations. Branch plants are more easily involved in deliberate relocations than independent plants are.

A shift in one industry produces shifts in others, through various economic interrelations. The preceding and subsequent stages of production and market-oriented industries in general will move in the same direction as the original shift; other industries may be repelled by the higher costs of local materials, labor, and land at the place to which the shift was made.

The most noteworthy over-all trends in location in the United States have been in the direction of equalization of the interregional distributions of industry and population, equalization in the degree of "industrialization" of various regions, greater concentration of population in urban areas, and suburbanization of both population and manufacturing. The placing of new war industry facilities brought manufacturing development for the first time into many areas, but its permanent effect depends on the adaptability of the various kinds of war plants to postwar use.

May, 1945, through October, 1947, shows Texas and California as the leading states. Petroleum refining, chemicals, and iron and steel accounted for over 70 per cent of such construction in those two states and for over 40 per cent of the total in the United States as a whole. "Survey of Industrial Expansion," Territorial Information Department (a joint research and information agency of several utility corporations), Chicago, 1948 (processed).

CHAPTER 10

Technology and Locational Change

THE LAST CHAPTER mentioned three causes that produce relatively permanent structural or secular changes in locational patterns as distinguished from the more temporary swings based on seasonal and cyclical fluctuations. These three long-term causes are technological progress, population growth, and the discovery and depletion of resources.

The present chapter is devoted to the locational effects of technological development, including improved methods of transfer, labor utilization, materials utilization, and energy use. Chapter 11 will proceed to a consideration of locational adjustment and "problem areas," involving population and resource use as well.

10·1 Effect of Improved Transfer Service

Changes in transfer costs and services play a peculiarly significant part in locational evolution. Each innovation (turnpikes, canals, railroads, steamships, telegraph, telephone, electric transit, automobiles, radio, or aircraft) cheapens transfer and at the same time alters the whole structure of transfer costs and the locational significance of distance and volume. The consequent recasting of the over-all locational pattern makes some locations economically obsolete but opens up investment opportunities in new areas and is thus closely associated with variations in the total *amount* as well as the *location* of investment and economic activity.[1]

[1] See Walter Isard, Transportation Development and Building Cycles, *Quarterly Journal of Economics,* vol. LVII, No. 1, November, 1942, pp. 90–112, and The Transport-Building Cycle, *Review of Economic Statistics,* November, 1942; Caroline and Walter Isard, Economic Implications of Aircraft, *Quarterly Journal of Economics,* vol. LIX, No. 2, February, 1945, pp. 145–169. Isard ascribes six major waves of investment and locational change in the United States to transport innovations as follows: canals (beginning about 1830); railroads (1843, 1862, 1878); electric railways (1895); automobiles (1918); and foresees a comparable structural change coming from the development of aircraft in the immediate future. He is concerned

Let us first consider the effects of the general downward trend in transfer costs. Not only have rates fallen, but the quality of transportation and communication service has steadily improved.[2] In the absence of any other changes, the effect of all-round cheaper transfer is to give greater locational influence to differences in processing costs.[3]

Transfer costs link the production of consumers' goods and services to the pattern of consumer demand and link the earlier stages of processing to the pattern of extractive activity. In both cases, these costs have a decentralizing influence, since consumer markets and most kinds of extractive activity are relatively scattered. Exploitation of the advantages of concentrated processing is impeded by the necessity of keeping distribution and procurement costs down. In terms of the economy of areas, transfer costs encourage self-sufficiency by protecting local industries against outside competition.

Cheaper transfer means some relaxation of these constraints. Industries distributing to relatively scattered markets find they can now serve them just as well from a greater distance and concentrate their operations in fewer, larger, and more efficient processing units, each with a larger market area.[4] Correspondingly, industries collecting materials from relatively scattered sources

---

only with goods and passenger transport and does not consider the effects of innovations in communication apart from air mail.

[2] For further details see 79th Congress, 1st Session, Senate Document No. 76: Board of Investigation and Research, "Technological Trends in Transportation," 1944.

[3] This statement ignores possible changes in the *structure* of transfer costs, which are taken up in Section 10·2. It is also to be noted that the locational effects of improved transfer can be offset if processing-cost differentials are reduced at the same time by enhanced mobility of labor and capital or by technical developments favoring small-scale production.

[4] ". . . the general improvement in transportation service has operated to permit manufacturers to consolidate their warehouse stocks at the more important distribution centers. . . . The time on carload shipments [between Chicago and Minneapolis] has been reduced from 3 or 4 days to 36 hours. As a result in some lines it is no longer necessary to carry stocks of merchandise in both Chicago and the Twin Cities." R. S. Vaile and A. L. Nordstrom, "Public Merchandise Warehousing in the Twin Cities," University of Minnesota Studies in Economics and Business, *Bulletin 3*, p. 40, Minneapolis, 1932; quoted in National Resources Planning Board, *op. cit.*, p. 76n.

now find it possible to concentrate processing operations in fewer, larger, and more efficient units, each with a larger supply area.[5] Any particular community or region becomes less self-sufficient, and interregional trade grows on the basis of specialization according to processing advantages.[6]

10·2   *Effect of Changes in the Structure of Transfer Costs*

The level of transfer costs does not change simultaneously everywhere. Each advance in methods of transfer favors routes particularly well suited to the new techniques, and these routes may constitute a very limited network. Thus the introduction of canals in the United States in the early nineteenth century put increased emphasis on relative transfer advantages, favoring a small number of locations. The development of new means of

[5] "In the past it was the custom to establish cheese factories from 2 to 4 miles apart. This was no doubt due partially at least to the bad condition of roads over which milk had to be hauled in wagons. A short hauling distance was necessary in order that the farmer might deliver his milk to the factory in a suitable condition for cheese making. Under such conditions, the small factory may serve satisfactorily; but where roads have been improved and the automobile truck is extensively used, few and larger factories are being built. At present factories operate very successfully in warm climates and collect the milk in trucks within a radius of 20 to 25 miles of the factory." Points to Consider in Establishing a Cheese Factory, *U. S. Department of Agriculture Miscellaneous Publication* 42, Washington, 1928, p. 5. *Cf.* also the parallel case of sugar-beet collection, noted in the discussion of Fig. 3·2.

[6] For local industries previously sheltered from outside competition, this involves a sometimes painful readjustment. Danish wheat growers, for instance, converted to dairying when transport improvements brought cheap New World wheat to Europe in the latter nineteenth century. More recently, improvement of milk transport into United States cities has widened milksheds and forced some readjustments on the nearer dairymen, as the following quotation shows: "Decreased cost of transportation and preservation of good quality in milk shipped by tank car is opening up new areas of potential supply and developing competition such as the highly specialized dairymen in the most northern part of the state [Indiana] have never experienced before. . . . The identical milk market conditions that have caused many dairymen in extreme northern Indiana to become greatly discouraged and pessimistic concerning the outlook for the future have caused dairymen around Francesville and in similar grain producing areas to take a new lease on life." "What Is Happening to Agriculture in Northwestern Indiana?", *Purdue University Agricultural Experiment Station Bulletin* 321, p. 8, 1928.

transfer with different cost and rate structures alters cost relations between long and short hauls, between large and small shipments, and between different kinds of traffic. All these changes have important locational implications.

RAILROADS AND SHIPPING SERVICES. Their terminal costs are high, but line-haul costs are low, so that rates per ton-mile drop off sharply for longer hauls. The route networks, also, are much less dense than highway networks. Railroad and waterway transport development, as a result of these characteristics, has been especially significant for *interregional* specialization. Individual regions have been enabled to concentrate on certain branches of production, serving widespread markets and using materials gathered at a distance, but the *local* pattern of towns and cities and within small districts was not radically changed by the advent of these means of transport. Trains and ships are large transport units, particularly adapted to cheap transport in bulk; consequently they favor the concentration of production in large plants. Finally, their high proportion of costs other than those of line haul is the basis for a large latitude of discrimination in the rates on different classes of traffic. It has already been indicated in Section 3·5 that this discrimination usually runs in favor of materials as against their products, on account of the lower unit value of the materials and consequently greater elasticity of demand for transport. This discrimination, by inflating delivery costs relative to procurement costs, encourages orientation to markets.

AUTOMOBILE TRANSPORT. This has a higher proportion of costs varying with distance and therefore a more nearly proportional progression of costs with length of haul. The investment required for establishing a route is small. It is particularly adapted, then, to short hauls between a great number of points over a very dense network of routes.

Consequently the principal effect is not upon interregional specialization but upon the structure of metropolitan and other local areas. Retail shops can draw customers and factories can draw labor from greater distances; so both are enabled to expand in size. Still more important is the fact that necessary movements and contacts within the metropolitan area no longer call for such close crowding as before. A notable loosening, sometimes graphically described as "explosive" growth, has been observed in American cities in the past two or three decades. Residence has been greatly decentralized by the automobile; business establishments seeking the advantages of the local labor market or close contact with other local manufacturing, servicing, or distributing enterprises can retain these advantages with a more suburban location than before.

Some over-all statistics indicative of this "suburbanization" [7] tendency have been presented in Chap. 9, while Chap. 11 will take up some problems of adjustment that have arisen as a result. At this point, however, we may glance at some graphic evidence of the "explosive" character of the change. Figure 10·1 shows the built-up areas of Baltimore, Washington, and Chicago before and after (or during) the explosion. It will be observed that the outward extension has followed the radial pattern of main highways but has left interstitial areas vacant. Many gaps are caused by rapid settlement just outside municipal boundaries, to avoid taxes and building restrictions, before the territory within the city itself has been fully built up.

The effect upon agriculture in the zones immediately tributary to cities is complex. Direct trucking of produce to urban markets offers little or no cost reduction in the remoter parts of large supply areas where the long-haul advantages of railroads come into play.[8] For shorter hauls the use of trucks has tended to equalize distribution costs as between large and small producers and as between producers near railroad stations or processing plants and those more distant from such points. It seems likely, then, that a comprehensive examination of the development of local supply

---

[7] The term "suburbanization" is used here in order to avoid the much-abused word "decentralization," which as noted in Section 1·1 has at least three other distinct connotations.

[8] It was found some years ago that in the New York City milkshed, "tank trucks have a decided advantage over the railroads on short-haul traffic, but the advantage decreases with distance. Apparently truck costs are about equal to rail rates at 200 miles. Beyond that, rail transportation usually is cheaper." H. R. Varney, *Transportation of Milk and Cream to the New York Market, Cornell University Agricultural Experiment Station Bulletin* 655, p. 40, Ithaca, N. Y., 1936.

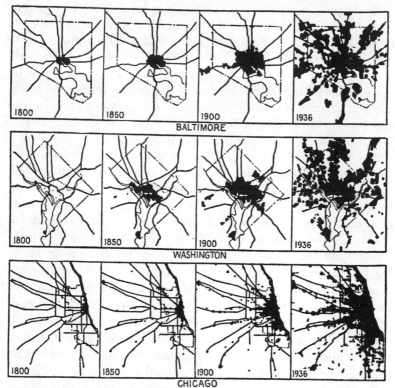

FIG. 10·1 Expansion of the built-up areas of Baltimore, Washington, and Chicago. The main highways that appear in the series of diagrams for each city have been unchanged in location throughout the period covered. Different scales have been used in mapping the three cities. (*Reproduced from Interregional Highways, message from the President transmitting report of National Interregional Highway Committee, Fig. 26, p. 55, 78th Congress, 2d Session, House Document No. 379, Washington, 1944.*)

areas around cities in the past few decades would show an increasing correspondence to actual distance from the city, with particular kinds of production such as fluid milk developing more and more coherent doughnut-shaped production zones.[9]

[9] R. D. McKenzie, in "The Metropolitan Community," p. 80, McGraw-Hill Book Company, Inc., New York, 1933, envisaged a trend toward more compact local agricultural supply areas. The greater emphasis on perishable products (milk and

AIR TRANSPORT.[10] This method too has characteristic economic features that determine its locational effect. Advantages are high speed, low costs of route establishment and maintenance, small unit of movement, *i.e.*, the capacity of a single plane as compared with that of a train or a ship, and almost complete freedom of movement in direct lines regardless of terrain. Its handicaps, which are being reduced, are high line-haul costs, extensive terminal-space requirements, dependence on weather, and the dangers and difficulties of use by nonprofessional pilots.

The high line-haul costs seem likely to prevent air freight from competing with existing rail and water carriers on anything but valuable and urgent express shipments during the foreseeable future. No direct effect upon the location of heavy manufactures or the most important branches of extractive industry is to be anticipated.[11] Indirectly, however, air transport is already greatly accelerating the industrialization of undeveloped areas by carrying key personnel, equipment, and supplies as well as some compact materials and products and providing that contact with industrialized areas which seems to be necessary to boost backward regions over the threshold of industrialization.[12] The great advantages of air transport in such areas are its disregard of surface barriers and the low capital requirements for establishing routes. Indirectly, then, air transport may pave the way to an earlier development of the surface-transport facilities necessary to exploit

---

fresh vegetables) and rapid direct marketing does work in that direction, offsetting to some extent the reduction in transfer costs for any given haul.

[10] For further details see the informative and stimulating article by Caroline and Walter Isard, Economic Implications of Aircraft, *Quarterly Journal of Economics,* vol. LIX, No. 2, February, 1945, pp. 145–169, and W. F. Ogburn, "The Social Effects of Aviation," Houghton Mifflin Company, Boston, 1945.

[11] In terms of tonnage, air-freight traffic is still negligible. Only about 0.01 per cent of the total intercity commodity traffic in the United States in 1946 was carried by air (*Cf.* Table 2·1). The relative significance of air freight is, of course, much greater in countries where surface transport is less well developed. In 1938 the top five countries in air-freight tonnage were the USSR, New Guinea, Canada, Honduras, and Colombia (Isard, *op. cit.*). For long-distance passenger transport the air lines are already competing advantageously with railroads and ships. For analyses of the potential market for air transport see Air Transport of Agricultural Perishables, *U. S. Department of Agriculture Miscellaneous Publication* 585, 1946. and Ogburn, *op. cit.*, Chap. 8 and *passim.*

[12] Such problems of regional transition are discussed in the next chapter.

the bulkier resources of undeveloped areas like the interiors of China and Brazil.

As an improved means of maintaining personal contacts over long distances, the airplane will thus speed the integration of backward regions into the more advanced industrial economy. Within and between more developed regions as well, it facilitates the extension of control over branch plants and the maintenance of contacts with distant suppliers or customers. Some further expansion of market and supply areas, then, should result even in cases where the materials or products involved are not themselves shipped by air. The mobility of capital and enterprise is being rapidly increased. Without air transport for key personnel, it seems doubtful that so many industrial firms could have been induced in the period 1940 to 1944 to take on the operation of new war plants making unfamiliar products at great distances from the center of operations of the firm.

The design of cities must, of course, make provision for airports and their connection with the local surface-traffic system. Whether or not air transport will really revolutionize metropolitan structure, as Isard and others have suggested,[13] seems to depend on the extent to which present handicaps of runway requirements and difficulty of nonprofessional operation can be overcome. If the family helicopter becomes a reality, it will have just as revolutionary locational effects as the family automobile. Effects upon metropolitan structure analogous to those of the automobile, but greatly magnified in distance terms, are to be expected. Residence and some services, light industry, and trade may decentralize explosively. Industrial centers with some tributary resident population will remain, as will likewise the principal centers of finance, administration, and specialized trade. Particular significance will attach to the points or zones of connection between air and ground transport—perhaps a ring of air stations and parking spaces surrounding the city centers.

MEANS OF COMMUNICATION. The concept of "transfer," of course, includes more than just the transportation of goods. Personal contact is a vital part of many commercial relations and

13 Isard, *op. cit.,* and references there cited.

involves passenger transport by any or all of the agencies already discussed. Those offering the greatest speed and frequency of service (associated with small units of traffic movement) naturally are of the greatest importance in facilitating contact at a distance, which accounts for the fact that automobile and air transport have already attained preeminence in this regard out of all proportion to their relative importance as carriers of tonnage freight.

Contact is also effected by the transmission of messages alone, which likewise puts a premium on speed rather than low tonnage rates. The fastest medium of carriage, aircraft, seems about to take over completely the job of carrying nonlocal letters. Instantaneous communication by telegraph, telephone, radio, and television has progressively made easier the coordination of economic activity and the standardization of tastes, which in turn facilitate both the spread and the specialization of industries.

10·3 Technical Maturing of Industries

Changes in labor requirements, generally as the result of a modification of processes, exert profound effects on the locational patterns of industries. As indicated in earlier chapters, an industry requiring specialized or highly trained labor generally has a concentrated and rather stable pattern, clustering at points where such a labor supply has gradually developed. But eventually the processes of almost any industry become routinized, through technical and managerial improvements, so that ordinary labor without special training can be used.[14] The normal result is that the industry spreads or moves to other areas, its dispersion from the original centers being sped by the relatively high wages and inflexible conditions that have become established there by the skilled elite.[15] Some technical changes involve so much mechanization as to make labor supply an inconsequential factor, in

---

[14] "Routinization" means merely the standardization and simplification of the individual worker's task so as to make less demand on his skill. But once a process has been resolved into repetitive operations, it becomes possible to do most or all of those operations by machinery. Routinization thus normally leads in practice to a considerable degree of mechanization.

[15] Cf. Section 7·4.

which case the industry may reorient itself in relation to whatever other considerations were next in importance.

The locational histories of individual industries have very often —one may almost say "typically"—involved an early stage of increasing concentration followed by a later stage of redispersion.[16] This sequence can be explained largely on the basis of the supply of labor and management personnel. When an industry is young and its problems unfamiliar, it prospers best in those few places which provide the combination of appropriate basic skills (generally developed in preexistent similar industries), together with experienced managers and some venturesome enterprisers and financial backers. The product is then perfected and standardized, the best methods of cheap large-scale manufacturing are worked out in those places, and the economies of mass production and geographical concentration assert themselves. The rise of Detroit to preeminence in automobile manufacturing is an example.

Ultimately the industry and its main production center "mature," in the sense that the rate of growth of market has slackened off, the fundamental questions of product design have been settled, and the necessary specialized machinery has been devised. It is then that a dispersion phase often sets in. When the technical uncertainties of production and the commercial uncertainties of market development are reduced to a point where other locations may successfully cope with them, independent outside competition may arise. Even before that, however, the labor skill requirements may have been so reduced that established firms in the main center of the industry are free to consider branch plants in areas of lower labor cost or closer to market and in extreme cases, e.g., the New England cotton-textile industry, may gradually move the bulk of their operations elsewhere.

This common association of decentralization with maturity does not by any means imply, however, that industry *as a whole* will or should progressively decentralize. New industries are continually being born. In their early stages, before they become fully mechanized, these are especially likely to be dependent on versatile

[16] This historical pattern was stressed by Malcolm Keir in "Manufacturing," The Ronald Press Company, New York, 1928.

labor and venturesome capital. It is found that the larger and better established industrial centers play a leading part as germinating grounds for new industries.[17] Some evidence on this point is provided by D. B. Creamer's analysis of census data:

> In view of the abundant evidence of an ever-decreasing share of wage jobs located in the principal cities [of industrial areas], it is of interest that the highest birth rates in both durable and semidurable goods industries have been in the principal cities. On the other hand, despite the relative growth in manufacturing importance of the industrial peripheries, these communities have a relatively low [industrial] birth rate. The data on relocated establishments suggest that the periphery towns have grown chiefly by the immigration of manufacturing plants and their expansion subsequent to relocation. . . .
>
> Another result that seems very clear is that the bulk of the loss of wage jobs due to relocated establishments has been sustained by the principal cities of the industrial areas. . . . This loss has been shared to a lesser extent and with exception of 1930–1931 by the large satellite cities (B) of the industrial areas. The chief recipient of the gains in each case has been the industrial peripheries (C). The next largest gains were in the communities in the "All the rest" category (G) with the exception of 1928–1929 when the second largest share of the gains was received by the important industrial counties (F).[18]

10·4 *Changes in Material Requirements*

Improvements of processing methods have altered the balance of advantage between market and material orientation in specific lines of production. The locational effect of a technical change

---

[17] There is food for thought in the contrast shown here between the behavior of industrial enterprises and that of people. Human beings seem to reproduce more bountifully in a rural than an urban environment, which gives rise to a characteristic current of cityward migration. New businesses, on the other hand, spring up in the more densely settled areas in greater numbers, and such migration as occurs is more often outward.

[18] Carter Goodrich and others, "Migration and Economic Opportunity," pp. 334, 340–341. University of Pennsylvania Press, Philadelphia, 1936.

increasing the yield of products relative to materials is, of course, generally an enhanced attraction toward markets. Thus in the coke industry, the replacement of beehive ovens by by-product ovens has shifted most of the industry from the coal towns to the vicinity of the iron- and steelworks where the coke and by-product gas are used. The bulkiness of the chief additional product, gas, is the principal reason for this shift.

In cases where one material is substituted for another, the locational effect depends on the importance and sources of the materials involved. The substitution of extracts and synthetic tanning agents for crude bark and other vegetable materials in the leather industry has freed tanneries from dependence on nearness to forests and allowed them to concentrate at points better located in relation to hide supply and markets. Where the bark supplies themselves are close to hides and markets, however, they are still a basis for tannery location.[19]

Another important basis of change in material requirements and in location is the fact that large-scale production or concentrated and specialized production in general calls for materials that can be supplied in large quantities and over long periods to a single processing point. Wood charcoal and bog iron ore are adequate materials for isolated local ironworks operating on a small scale, but output equal to that of a large blast furnace would quickly exhaust local supplies of this character. The replacement of extensively produced by intensively produced materials is reflected in a greater concentration of the industries oriented to those materials.

The third major change in process requirements is a very rapid increase in the use of nonhuman energy. It would seem that this must increase the locational importance of energy sources, but that has not always been the case. The changing locational significance of energy use is important and complex enough to warrant discussion in a separate section which follows.

---

[19] See E. M. Hoover, "Location Theory and the Shoe and Leather Industries," Chap. IX, Harvard Economic Studies, vol. LV, Harvard University Press, Cambridge, Mass., 1937, and L. C. Brown, S.J., "Union Policies in the Leather Industry," Harvard University Press, Cambridge, Mass., 1947.

10·5   *Energy Utilization and Transmission*

New techniques of energy utilization and transmission always affect the location patterns of at least some industries. Not only are costs of energy lowered, but the newer forms have generally been more transportable than the old and either more or less adaptable to the needs of small users. Thus the whole pattern of costs with reference to location and scale is changed for each industry.

Although the consumption of energy in production has rapidly increased, energy sources have not necessarily become a more important factor of location. In some periods the contrary has been true. Energy has become steadily cheaper; moreover, it has become progressively easier to transport fuels and electricity, which means that geographic differences in energy costs have diminished. No two new developments in energy have had quite the same effect on the over-all locational pattern.

WATER WHEELS. These were the first device used on a considerable scale for the conversion of nonhuman energy and naturally attracted industries to natural water-power sites. As long as the energy secured was nontransportable, the plants concerned had to concentrate at the site itself. The early growth of textile manufacturing along the streams of New England is well known, the largest developments being those at Lowell, Manchester, Lawrence, Holyoke, and Lewiston before the Civil War.[20]

STEAM ENGINES. This form of power provided a means for converting fuel into mechanical energy and could be set up wherever fuel was obtainable. Since in this case the material (though not the energy itself) was transportable, the locational effect was more elastic. Energy costs reflected primarily the costs of transporting coal from the mines.

This pattern of energy costs contrasted sharply with that set

[20] T. R. Smith, "The Cotton Textile Industry of Fall River, Massachusetts—A Study of Industrial Localizations," Table 8, p. 42, King's Crown Press, New York, 1944 (processed).

by water power. Especially before the coming of the railroad, coal was cheapest along navigable water rather than in the back-country locations where small and easily exploited water-power sites abounded. The locational effect was to concentrate industry on navigable water as well as in the coal regions themselves. To refer again to the history of the New England textile industry, the application of steam power to cotton spinning and weaving led to the rapid growth of the industry in the Fall River—New Bedford area after the middle of the nineteenth century.[21] In the same period, a rapid growth of heavy industry occurred near the Pennsylvania coal mines. Steam also provided an indefinitely expansible energy source, permitting manufacturing agglomerations much larger than could have been sustained by direct use of water power. Steam power and its application to transport in the railroad locomotive were the principal factors in the revolutionary concentration and urbanization of industry that occurred in the nineteenth century in Europe and North America.

It should be noted, though, that continued improvement in the utilization and transport of fuel has reduced the importance of nearness to fuel sources, so that only certain groups of industries (notably ferrous metallurgy, heavy chemicals, cement, ceramics, glass and primary metal processing) are still influenced significantly by geographic differences in fuel costs.[22]

[21] "Fall River's rise to the position of the leading textile center in New England was the beginning of the shift of the locational center of gravity in the industry toward the southern coast of New England. This was in large measure made possible by the changing competitive position of coal and water as sources of power for the expanding industry. . . . Competitive equality between the two as sources of power for new plants had been reached before 1870. This was the result of two closely related developments which took place during the 20 years prior to the Civil War. The first of these was the increasing scarcity of large, easily developed, conveniently located water privileges upon which such an important part of the textile capacity of 1850 had been based. The second was the improvement of the steam engine and its more successful adaptation to the power requirements of the textile industry." Smith, *op. cit.*, pp. 40–41. Still a third reason, less important, was the higher atmospheric humidity of the coastal district.

[22] For further discussion see National Resources Planning Board, "Industrial Location and National Resources," Chap. 7, Government Printing Office, Washington. 1943.

ELECTRICITY.[23] The conversion of mechanical energy into electricity (and perhaps even more important, the development of transmission in high-voltage alternating currents) has likewise had important locational effects, though less revolutionary than those of steam. Energy transmission in the form of electricity over distances of as much as 300 miles gives added flexibility of location in relation to both water-power and fuel resources. In the case of water power, which would otherwise not be transportable at all, this advantage is very important and has restored some of the locational attraction of water-power sites. Hydroelectric power generated at the best sites and used in the immediate vicinity is sold to continuous users at rates less than those for any other form of energy, and this type of location has consequently attracted those processes which need the largest amounts of energy relative to other requirements.[24] These include some operations involving electrolysis (as in aluminum reduction) and some involving heat (as in ferroalloys and special steels and abrasives). No processes are attracted to such sites for savings in costs of mechanical energy.

[23] Nearly a decade ago it was estimated that the use of nonhuman energy in the United States was equivalent to the continuous utilization of about 33 horse power per person. This came from the following primary sources:

Source	Per Cent
Bituminous coal	48
Petroleum	32
Natural gas	10
Anthracite coal	6
Water power	4

National Resources Committee, "Energy Resources and National Policy," pp. 8-9, Government Printing Office, Washington, 1939. These primary sources of energy are used to some extent directly (the fuels in combustion and other chemical reactions, the water power as physical energy). But nearly all the water power is converted into electricity first. About an eighth of the coal is used in generating electricity for sale, and manufacturing and mining establishments supplement their purchases of electricity by generating over half as much themselves for their own use. The mechanical energy used in manufacturing in the United States is now provided mainly from electric motors.

[24] Cf. Federal Power Commission, "Power Requirements in Electrochemical, Electrometallurgical and Allied Industries," Washington, 1938. Further information on electric energy requirements in specific manufacturing industries is given in National Resources Planning Board, "Industrial Location and National Resources," Chap. 7, Washington, 1943.

In the meantime, changes in fuel-burning equipment have steadily increased the energy yield (in terms of mechanical and electrical energy) of fuels. The average amount of coal burned to produce 1 kilowatt-hour of electrical energy in the United States in 1902 was 6.4 pounds. By 1920 this had fallen to 3.4 pounds and by 1944 to 1.3 pounds,[25] while in large plants built in recent years it runs well under a pound. Where fuel is cheap, such plants can produce electricity at costs comparable to those of large hydroelectric developments.

It is certain that the rate of energy yield from coal and oil will continue to improve as already proved devices such as the gas turbine are put into wider use. Locationally, the effect is to diminish the importance of nearness to fuel sources but at the same time to encourage production techniques and products that call for large amounts of energy.

Many persons have thought that the availability of electricity in small or large quantities anywhere on the distribution system [26] would produce a general scattering of industry to small rural plants or even back into workers' homes.[27] No such shift has occurred or seems likely. Energy rates are considerably lower for large users and are a significant element in location for only a few large-scale chemical and metallurgical processes.

One significant locational effect has arisen, however, from the easier transmissibility of energy *within industrial plants* when electricity is used. The nineteenth-century large factory building was a blocky structure several stories high, built in this fashion partly in order to minimize the distance over which power had to be transmitted by belts and shafting from the steam engine or water wheel. By contrast, large modern factories using electric

[25] "Statistical Abstract of the United States," 1946, Table 531, p. 475. Fuel oil and gas consumed have been converted into coal equivalent, accounting in 1944 for about 19 per cent of the total electric energy generated. Similar economies have been recorded in cement making, metallurgy, and other direct heat-using processes.

[26] General practice of utility companies is to change a uniform rate over a wide area, the only concession to near-by customers being an occasional special rate to large continuous users who take off their power at the generating site before it is stepped up to transmission voltage.

[27] For a rather extreme view on this point see Laurent Dechesne, "La Localisation des diverses productions," pp. 81–82, Les Editions Comptables, Commerciales et Financières, Brussels, 1945.

motors can be low and extensive, since power travels on wires. Frequently they are only one story high. This change in plant design has played a part in the choice of more suburban locations for new industrial plants—though motor transport of materials, products, and workers has probably been a still more important cause.

ATOMIC ENERGY. Controlled nuclear disintegration in atomic piles is a new source of heat energy, the importance of which it is difficult to assess in the light of the scanty information thus far available. A few general observations, however, may be ventured.[28]

Piles of present types operate at moderate temperatures. The principal use of the heat is envisaged as the raising of steam for generation of electricity in conventional power plants, and there is no indication that the high temperatures needed in metallurgical processes can be economically developed under suitable conditions. We shall assume, then, that atomic energy means essentially a new fuel for steam power stations.

Heat will probably be developed and converted into electricity at two kinds of pile installations, apparently of roughly equal importance in terms of potential electrical energy output. These are "primary" units using purified uranium and "secondary" units using plutonium produced by the primary units. In both cases the weight of transported materials required is negligible: a 500,000-kilowatt primary pile unit would consume only about 5 tons of purified uranium in a year.

The use of primary units is subject to two probable limitations: They can more easily make explosives and are thus likely to be under more stringent control than the secondary units; their

[28] These comments are based primarily on the following sources: H. DeW. Smyth, "A General Account of the Development of Methods for Using Atomic Energy for Military Purposes under the Auspices of the United States Government, 1940–1945," Government Printing Office, Washington, 1945; Atomic Energy: Its Future in Power Production, *Chemical Engineering*, October, 1946; reprinted with an appended summary of the report transmitted to the United Nations Atomic Energy Commission by the United States representative on Sept. 7, 1946; S. H. Schurr, Economic Aspects of Atomic Energy as a Source of Power, *Bulletin of the Atomic Scientists*, April–May, 1947; Walter Isard, "Some Economic Implications of Atomic Energy," *Quarterly Journal of Economics*, vol. LXII, No. 2, February, 1948, pp. 202–228.

efficiency depends on very large size. Cost estimates have been made for capacities on the order of 500,000 kilowatts for the primary units [29] and 20,000 to 100,000 kilowatts for the secondary.

The prospective costs of electric power generated from atomic heat are difficult to estimate, since they depend to a considerable extent on how much of the total cost of the plant is charged to military purposes and how much to the production of radioactive "tracer" isotopes. This is the same problem of cost allocation that confronts any multiple-use energy development but is particularly full of uncertainties in the present stage. The consensus is, however, that in a few decades secondary-pile installations will become competitive with ordinary coal-burning power stations except in areas where coal is unusually cheap, while the more efficient primary units will match the costs of the cheapest coal-burning power stations and all but the cheapest hydroelectric plants.

The outlook, then, is that almost any region on earth may soon be able to generate electric energy from secondary-pile units at costs comparable to present costs in those regions of the United States which must bring coal considerable distances by rail. Any region in which there is a sufficiently concentrated potential demand to use, say, 500,000 kilowatts of new capacity from a single source can (if regulatory authorities permit a primary unit) get electricity at a generation cost lower than that of present coal-burning stations but still not so low as the best hydroelectric sites.[30]

[29] To visualize this size, it may be helpful to know that 500,000 kilowatts represents about 0.8 per cent of the total electric generating capacity in the United States, including both utility and industrial installations. It is roughly equal to the capacity of public-utility generating plants alone in any one of the following states: Kansas, Florida, Kentucky, Louisiana, or Oklahoma.

[30] The report printed in *Chemical Engineering (loc. cit.)* concludes that this restricts the use of primary units to a few of the largest metropolitan areas of the world. This may be going too far. It should be remembered that electricity is being transmitted as far as 300 miles. A circle of even 200 miles radius has an area of more than 125,000 square miles; for such an area, a primary pile capacity of 500,000 kilowatts would be equivalent to only 4 kilowatts per square mile. Taking the United States as a whole, we now have about five times that much generating capacity per square mile. Each of the nine census regions of the United

Atomic energy does not seem to portend, then, any revolutionary locational changes. It will be as if every country on earth were to be endowed, at the possible discretion of an international authority, with coal resources similar to those of the United States, subject to the important qualification that this coal could be used only in large electric power plants. The new source of power will not significantly affect transport costs (except possibly those of water transport, which are already extremely low). It will have little effect on the retail cost of electric power to domestic and other small users, where the main item is distribution cost. It is unlikely to replace good hydroelectric sites. Direct use of atomic heat in metallurgical processes does not appear imminent. Apart from metallurgy and the electroprocess industries now oriented to superior hydroelectric sites, *e.g.*, aluminum, magnesium, and artificial abrasives, most manufacturing industries are not greatly affected in their locations by energy-cost differentials, since those costs are small in proportion to other items of procurement, distribution, and processing costs.

SUMMARY

Technological improvements have affected locational patterns through changes in transfer costs, labor requirements, materials requirements, and energy costs.

Cheaper transfer has enlarged market areas and supply areas, allowing further concentration of market-oriented and material-oriented industries but at the same time a loosening of the structure of metropolitan communities. Each new transfer medium developed has had a different effect on location, reflecting its own characteristic of cost structure.

In individual industries, technical "maturity" makes labor requirements less specialized and exacting and permits a spread or

---

States has at least 3 kilowatts of capacity to the square mile; only the Mountain region is below 7 kilowatts. The total potential demand of any of a great many regions, then, would probably absorb the output of such a plant, although many years might elapse before full utilization could be attained. Experience in such areas as the Tennessee Valley shows that the long-run elasticity of demand for electric energy is very large.

decentralization to new centers of production after the initial concentration phase.

Technical improvements which increase product yields lessen the attraction of material sources; but for modern large-scale industry, size and permanence of a materials source are increasingly important.

The vastly increased use of nonhuman energy in production has been offset by improved techniques that make energy cheaper and more transmissible and tend to equalize the advantages of various locations in respect to energy cost. Atomic energy development, as now foreseen, is unlikely to produce radical locational changes. It can lower electricity costs in areas where they are now high but probably cannot compete with the best hydroelectric sites. The lowest cost atomic power is likely to be available only in areas of fairly concentrated demand, and its location and development may be primarily dictated by strategic and political considerations.

CHAPTER 11

Locational Adjustment and Problem Areas

THIS BOOK does not attempt to prescribe for specific practical situations or even to discuss them in detail. It is concerned only with laying a groundwork of understanding of the economic forces with which the administrator (either in business or in government) must reckon.

Nonetheless, it is essential to indicate where the major problems lie. Locational change, some of the causes of which were discussed in the two preceding chapters, produces a variety of stresses and maladjustments. When a whole local or regional economy is seriously involved, we have a "problem area."

Most problem areas are included in these three categories:

a. "Backward" areas, which have failed to keep up with the trend of economic progress
b. "Stranded" areas, which have experienced a net loss of productive employment through "emigration of industry"
c. Urban "blighted" areas

This chapter will first explore the locational aspects of economic progress, with emphasis on circumstances that may arrest development in specific regions temporarily or permanently. Then it will take up the problem of the adjustment of smaller areas to loss of industry and will present very briefly some case histories illustrating both types of problem. The final section will describe and analyze the development of blighted areas within cities.

Diagnosis, not prescription, is still our main concern in this chapter. Discussion of appropriate policies for palliation, cure, or prevention of locational ailments will be found in Part Four.

A

PROBLEMS OF ECONOMIC PROGRESS

11·1 *Necessary Conditions for Regional Economic Development*

Economic progress is measured by a rising standard of consumption of goods and services, which involves changes in the character and also the location of production. Different regions do not advance at the same rate, and serious locational problems are raised by these differences.

In a primitive region, the high costs of transport prevent the development of much specialization of production and require that each locality produce nearly the whole range of commodities it consumes. Local self-sufficiency is the rule, and the only known ways to live on this basis are by hunting, fishing, grazing, or cultivation of the soil. Products not essential to existence have little place in such primitive economies.[1]

An advance to higher living standards requires more trade. Such trade permits each locality to share, to some extent, the production advantages of other localities and to attain a better consumption standard by concentrating on the lines of production in which it has the greatest relative advantage. The essentials for

[1] For more detailed materials on the process of economic development and industrialization of backward countries, the reader is referred to

A. J. Brown, "Industrialization and Trade," Royal Institute of International Affairs, London, 1943. Brown stresses the adjustment required in the United Kingdom as the result of industrialization of backward countries.

T. W. Schultz, "Agriculture in an Unstable Economy," McGraw-Hill Book Company, Inc., New York, 1946. This stresses the readjustment of American agriculture.

Kurt Mandelbaum, "The Industrialization of Backward Areas," Oxford Institute of Statistics, Monograph No. 2, Oxford University Press, New York, 1945. This stresses the problem of industrialization of the overpopulated and backward areas of southeastern Europe.

Colin Clark, "The Conditions of Economic Progress," Macmillan and Co., Ltd., London, 1940; and "The Economics of 1960," The Macmillan Company, New York, 1942.

League of Nations, "Industrialization and Foreign Trade," 1945.

increasing trade are reduction of transfer costs and increased specialization of production, involving shifts of resources to new uses.

To secure a continually larger income from the same area, there must be continually increasing intensity of land use. Gradations of intensity in agriculture run from range grazing through cereals and other extensive crops through fruit and dairy farming to poultry keeping and truck gardening.[2] A few fortunately situated agricultural countries like Denmark have kept increasing populations well abreast of advancing world standards of living by following this sequence of increasingly intensive forms of agriculture.

Much more generally, however—for large regions, one may say "always"—economic progress depends eventually on industrialization, *i.e.*, the development of manufacturing. This is a commonly accepted generalization, though the reasons behind it are not well understood. The next two sections will examine the basis of advantage for industrialized areas.

11·2 *Increased Relative Demand for Manufactures As Incomes Rise*

One important advantage of industrial regions as against agricultural regions is based on "Engel's law." As people become better off, they increase their expenditures on food much less than proportionally.[3] The expenditures of the well to do embody a greater proportion of payment for services and for manufacturing operations and a smaller proportion of payments going ultimately to agriculture than do the expenditures of the poor.[4]

[2] *Cf.* Laurent Dechesne, "La Localisation des diverses productions," pp. 148–161, Les Editions Comptables, Commerciales et Financières, Brussels, 1945.

[3] In economists' jargon, the "income elasticity of demand for food" is less than unity. This elasticity is the ratio of the percentage increase in food expenditure to the percentage increase in income with which it is associated. Under present conditions the income elasticity of demand for all farm products appears to be only about 0.25 in the United States. See Schultz, *op. cit.*, pp. 60–70. For certain luxury foods, of course, and for some nonfood farm products, the elasticity is greater than unity.

[4] Not only do the well to do spend a greater part of their incomes on manufactured goods and services, but they buy more expensive goods, the extra cost representing additional processing expense rather than additional materials.

This means that as world living standards improve, the growth in demand for farm products does not keep pace with the rise in income and falls far behind the rise in demand for manufactured goods and for commercial and other services. Even if technical progress went on at exactly the same rate in agriculture as in manufacturing, then, the growth of economic opportunity in agricultural regions would be much slower.

11·3 Industrialization and Population Pressure

Another major factor that hampers the economic progress of nonindustrialized areas is the way in which population development responds to environment. Areas devoted to the more extensive land uses nearly always develop a "population pressure" which retards progress and may lead to a vicious circle of economic stagnation and poverty.

It has been mentioned in Chap. 7 that rural populations reproduce much more rapidly than urban. As population growth outruns the growth of economic opportunity, a population pressure

Table 11·1 Percentage Age Distributions of United States Civilian Migrants * and Nonmigrants Fourteen Years Old and Over, 1935–1940 and 1941–1945

Age group	1935–1940		1941–1945	
	Migrants	Nonmigrants	Migrants	Nonmigrants
All ages 14 and over...	100.0	100.0	100.0	100.0
14–19..............	12.7	14.9	12.3	13.2
20–44..............	64.9	48.5	64.1	43.9
45 and over........	22.5	36.7	23.6	43.0

* Migrants for 1941 to 1945 include persons living in a different county in 1945 than they did on Dec. 7, 1941. Migrants for 1935 to 1940 include persons living in a different county in 1940 than they did in 1935, plus about 1,500,000 who moved into or out of a city of 100,000 population or more during this period but remained in the same county.

SOURCE. Bureau of the Census, "Civilian Migration in the United States: December, 1941, to March, 1945," Special Report, Series P-S, No. 5, Table 6, p. 6, Washington, Sept. 2, 1945.

develops that is reflected in emigration but never enough emigration to equalize living standards. Chapter 7 also pointed out that low levels of income seem to lead to high birth rates, so that population pressure is all too likely to build up in cumulative fashion. Progress is further hampered in population pressure areas by the resulting quality of the population. Low standards of nutrition, medical care, general education, and vocational training do not produce enough of the kind of employees or employers who can rapidly increase efficiency. The very fact of emigration weakens the population economically, as the emigrants are predominantly in the most vigorous and productive age groups. Table 11·1 shows this. Those left behind include a high proportion of dependent older people and children, which means a greater burden on the productive workers who stay behind. It is still a matter of controversy whether or not, within any given age group, the migrants are more intelligent and capable than the nonmigrants; [5] if that is the case, the area of emigration has a still further handicap to its economic progress.

Only in a somewhat industrialized region, it seems, is the population sufficiently urbanized to emancipate it from the vicious Malthusian circle of population growth and pressure. Once a region gets to this stage, however, it may dismiss the bogey of long-run overpopulation and commence worrying instead about the much less serious problems of eventual population decline.[6]

[5] See, for example, the discussion in National Resources Committee, "The Problems of a Changing Population," pp. 111–112, Government Printing Office, Washington, 1938. A pertinent investigation is reported by A. A. Gessner in Selective Factors in Migration from a New York Rural Community, *Cornell University Agricultural Experiment Station Bulletin* 736, Ithaca, N. Y., 1940. On the basis of a survey of 339 ex-students of an academy, Miss Gessner found that "52 per cent of the migrants and 44 per cent of the nonmigrants came from the upper halves of their classes. . . . If the selective process which has affected the migration of the older members of the group continues to operate in the same way upon the younger members, the selection of migrants on the basis of scholastic ability will eventually be much greater . . . 10 years hence, at least 65 per cent of all those who were in the upper halves of their classes when in high school will have migrated, but only 46 per cent of those from the lower halves will have left." Selectivity appeared still more prominently when the migrants *to cities* were compared with nonmigrants in this investigation.

[6] These include the transitional problem of age distribution (a larger proportion of dependent old people to be supported, which is partially offset by the diminished

It is well to note that the population pressure of *some* agricultural areas makes it more difficult for agriculture *anywhere* to provide a high income. The relative prices of farm products and manufactured goods—and the terms of trade between nonindustrialized and industrialized countries—reflect the low bargaining power of the nonindustrial worker and the obstacles to transfer from agricultural to industrial employment.[7]

11·4 Impediments to Industrialization

Though industrialization often represents a threshold to new opportunity, it is not an easy threshold to cross. The difficulties involved are similar to those involved in progress from subsistence agriculture to more specialized and intensive forms, but these difficulties loom particularly large at the outset of industrialization.

The location of manufactures depends on facilities for bringing in off-site materials, which are generally a very minor factor in agriculture and other extractive industries. For large and efficient plants which can compete with those of more industrialized areas,

---

proportion of children), and the long-run problem of military power and political prestige. The first of these problems may not be serious as long as the middle age brackets are receiving reinforcements through inward migration. Professor Alvin Hansen and others have stressed the difficulty of maintaining full employment in an economy in which a principal basis of new investment opportunity—the increase of population—is shrinking.

[7] Colin Clark refers to this in terms of the lower average productivity of labor in "primary" activities (agriculture, forestry, and fishing) as compared with "secondary" activities (manufacturing and mining). "The Conditions of Economic Progress," Macmillan & Co., Ltd., London, 1940, especially Chap. X and the table on p. 342. He observes, "From Sir William Petty's day to the present time the transfer of working population from primary production to secondary and tertiary has been continuing, and perhaps will continue for as many centuries more. This is clear evidence that world economic equilibrium has not yet been obtained, and indeed that the world is still within a very long distance of obtaining it. In other words, certain agricultural countries and regions must be regarded as being 'overpopulated.' This word is not used in the sense that they are in any way unable to support their present populations, but simply in the economic sense of the term, namely that their inhabitants could earn considerably higher average real incomes per head in other industries or territories, and, if actuated by economic motives, will in the course of time do so." *Ibid.*, p. 341.

good transfer facilities are therefore necessary in order to amass enough materials at one point.

The capital requirements for manufacturing are large relative to those of agriculture, and new and different kinds of skills and enterprise are called for. In this respect the rate of industrialization of new regions is dependent to a considerable extent on the mobility of capital,[8] enterprise, and sometimes skilled labor from regions where industry is already well developed.

Despite the almost infinite diversity of resources and conditions in different regions, the process of industrialization generally follows certain predictable lines. What has just been said regarding the chief difficulties of the transition from an agricultural to an industrial economy will indicate which types of manufacturing are easiest to inaugurate in nonindustrial territory and therefore usually lead the way. A region on the threshold of industrialization is presumably short on capital and capital goods (other than those embodied in the land), has a relatively undeveloped transport and communication system and probably a more scattered, poorer, and less educated population than the already industrialized regions.

11·5 Typical First Steps in Industrialization

Food processing, wood products, and the preparation of textile fibers are based directly on the products of agriculture and forestry and supply elementary human needs for food, shelter, and clothing. No unusual skills are required for the simpler grades of product. These are commonly the first steps, therefore, in the industrialization of a region previously specialized along extensive extractive lines.[9]

---

8 The advances of capital ordinarily are represented by shipments of industrial and transport equipment.

9 The improvement of transportation to a low-standard *self-sufficient* area often makes it temporarily, at least, more exclusively agricultural than ever. Domestic industries and other high-cost local manufactures are driven out of existence by cheap mass-produced imports from the more industrialized regions. Thus in the early part of the nineteenth century, much of the southeastern United States became more and more agricultural. Something similar happened in parts of southern

But the primary processing of materials already extensively produced within the region does not greatly ease the pressure of population upon the land. It merely makes the previous products more transportable and more valuable in external exchange. Major increases in the capacity of a region to provide for an increasing population are contingent upon

a. The exploitation of intensively produced domestic materials, by industries oriented to whatever minerals and energy sources the region possesses

b. The processing of imported materials, by stages of production that are far enough advanced so that transfer costs are unimportant relative to processing-cost advantages which the region possesses

The mineral and energy resources of the region and its transfer development thus assume decisive importance for the support of dense populations at a high income standard. Much the most important resources, at the present state of technology, are energy sources and metallic ores and especially coal and iron ore. These two commodities alone account for well over half the carload rail tonnage hauled in the United States. Fuels, ores, primary metals, and electric power cannot be transported very far without doubling their cost; the importance of having these basic materials close at hand is evident.

As a second stage of industrialization, then, we see (in the regions possessing economically usable mineral resources) such industries as the smelting, refining, and processing of metals; oil refining; chemical industries based mainly on coal, petroleum, potash, salt, and other minerals; and glass and ceramics industries. Where cheap hydroelectric power is available, industries requiring large amounts of cheap power (nonferrous metals refining, ferroalloys and special steels, artificial abrasives, etc.) are possible, as in Norway, Switzerland, the Tennessee Valley, and the Columbia River Valley.

England and in India where charcoal iron furnaces, small textile manufactures, and other small industries were destroyed by competition of the newly industrialized areas in the middle and north of England.

11·6   *Industries Based on Imported Materials*

For industries based on imported materials or on materials in which the region has no special advantage, the only possible basis is a favorable processing-cost differential. The overpopulation of regions in which industrialization has for any reason been delayed yields a competitive advantage manifested in low wages. Among the types of industry with which such regions may successfully lead off are those requiring a great deal of labor but not much skill and in which transfer costs over long distances are small in proportion to production costs. The simpler sorts of textile, garment, and shoe manufacturing fulfill these requirements. Any region new to these industries, *e.g.*, Japan, India, and the southeastern part of the United States in the past few decades, must begin with the simplest and cheapest grades of product and work up gradually to the grades requiring more skill.[10] The places that previously supplied textiles, shoes, and clothing to such regions, *e.g.*, England and New England, can survive the cheap-labor competition only by specializing more intensely in the finer grades in which they still have an advantage.

11·7   *Tertiary Activities*

Specialization in the so-called "secondary industries" (manufacturing and mining) is not the final stage of regional or national economic development. With higher incomes an increasing proportion of expenditure is devoted to commercial, transport, administrative, professional, and personal services. These service activities are often called "tertiary." In the more advanced "industrial" countries of the world, such as the United States and Great Britain, the percentage of the population engaged in tertiary activities has been increasing for some decades already, while employment in secondary activities has been decreasing relatively and even absolutely. Table 9·2 indicated the downward trend

---

[10] *Cf.* the discussion of "productions faciles et difficiles" in Dechesne, *op. cit.*, pp. 83–84.

in the ratio of manufacturing wage earners to population in the United States since 1919.[11]

The tertiary group of activities is quite heterogeneous in locational orientation. Clark's statement that tertiary producers are "by the nature of their work automatically excluded from international or interregional trade" [12] certainly goes too far. Some types of service, such as recreation on Florida beaches or on Broadway, bring the consumer to the producer. The same holds true of education and other types of specialized professional service. Transfer services are by their nature highly transferable and have constituted a substantial credit item on the international payment balances of maritime nations. Insurance, administrative, and investment services (including the passive services of the inactive investor) require only communications and a moderate amount of personal travel, which becomes increasingly easy and effective as means of communication and passenger transport improve. There is considerable scope, then, for a mature industrial region, with the surplus capital, business and professional ability, and good transfer connections that diversified secondary industries encourage, to shift into a greater emphasis on tertiary activities for export as well as for domestic consumption. For intensively developed areas that have lost some of their original competitive advantages in manufacturing or mining, such as Great Britain and

---

[11] For an exposition of the relation of primary, secondary, and tertiary activities to economic progress, see Clark, *op. cit.*, especially Chap. X. In a later work, "The Economics of 1960," pp. 70–71 and Appendix, The Macmillan Company, New York, 1942, Clark demonstrates a high correlation, by countries, between per capita income and ratio of tertiary employment to total employment. A similar correlation has been discovered among the states of the United States in 1939 by L. H. Bean, Industrialization and Per Capita Income, in National Bureau of Economic Research, "Studies in Income and Wealth," vol. 8, pp. 126–128, New York, 1946. Both investigations are cited by S. E. Harris, New England's Decline in the American Economy, *Harvard Business Review*, vol. XXV, No. 3, Spring, 1947, p. 352.

These correlations are sometimes cited as an argument that development of tertiary production *causes* higher income levels. The mere existence of correlation, of course, proves nothing as to cause and effect, and it might be more accurate to say that higher incomes cause a greater relative development of tertiary industries. This is to some extent a case of mutual causation.

[12] "The Conditions of Economic Progress," p. 339.

New England, fostering of this type of external trade [13] is just as logical an objective as the effort to keep a step ahead of newer regions in specialized lines of manufacturing.

B

STRANDED AREAS

11·8 Origins of Stranded Areas

Previous sections of this chapter have pointed out some of the hurdles encountered on the road of economic progress. It is particularly noteworthy that where the development of more intensive and efficient production has been arrested, the disability may easily become chronic. Low productivity and population pressure, in a backward economy, join in a vicious circle hard to break. The present plight of China and India—to mention only the two largest examples—illustrates what may happen when a region falls far behind in economic development.

Some of the same difficulties and other kinds as well are experienced in "stranded" areas or communities. This descriptive term is usually applied to smaller areas than the regions of arrested development that have been discussed above. It often refers, in fact, to individual cities or towns. The distinctive feature of a stranded area is that it has suffered a rather rapid absolute curtailment of local economic opportunity, posing the problem of adjustment to at least temporarily lowered incomes.

Stranding arises most frequently as a result of depletion of resources. Such depletion may be preventable, as in the case of soil, grass cover, forests, or fisheries; it may be inevitable but slow, as in the case of large mineral deposits like the Appalachian coal fields; or it may be both inevitable and rapid, as in the case of natural gas and oil fields and many mineral deposits which occur in small and scattered form.

Much the same effect is produced, without any physical change in local resources, by any drop in the demand for the area's prod-

[13] This is recommended for New England by S. E. Harris, *loc. cit.*

ucts. Such a drop may reflect falling incomes in the markets supplied, obsolescence of the product itself, new trade restrictions, or increasing competition from producers of the same or rival goods elsewhere. Often it is difficult to separate the causes of local distress. Thus, the difficulties of Michigan copper mines are due both to physical depletion and to the competition of newer and more productive mines in western United States and the Belgian Congo. Unemployment in the Pennsylvania anthracite region in recent years has been due partly to working-out of coal deposits and partly to the replacement ·of anthracite by other fuels, *e.g.,* by fuel oil for domestic heating.

11·9 *Difficulties of Adjustment in Stranded Areas*

Whatever the cause, an area where income has been curtailed by loss of industry faces readjustment. As explained in Chap. 9, factors of production can participate in migrations of industry by actual migration, by conversion to other uses *in situ,* or by abandonment. Not many communities can imitate Shevlin, Ore., which has moved "lock, stock, and barrel" five times in the last 26 years to stay with the sawmill that provides its livelihood.[14]

There is, of course, the possibility that a threatened loss of industry may be forestalled by some timely increase in efficiency which cuts costs and restores the competitive position of the location in question. Actual instances, however, are rare. If anyone has cost-reducing improvements up his sleeve, he is unlikely to wait until he is forced into installing them by the threat of serious loss. Moreover, the rescue of a jeopardized location by an increase in efficiency would imply that the same increase in efficiency could not be obtained equally well somewhere else.

The principal instances of this type of reaction appear to be those in which the threat of a shutdown breaks down previous resistance to laborsaving changes that were known to be possible. During the 1920's and 1930's, for example, many New England cotton mills managed to stave off liquidation or migration for a

[14] Associated Press news item, June 16, 1947.

while by getting their employees to agree to tend more looms, by having state laws on working hours and conditions relaxed, and by other similar expedients. But on the whole this type of recourse seems adequate only for fighting delaying actions.

Conversion of labor, capital, and land to alternative uses at the same location is on the whole the most hopeful course where some local diversity of production advantage exists and where the production factors themselves are not too narrowly specialized in character. It may even happen that the "substitute" industry turns out to be more of a local asset than the old one or that one large defunct industry may be succeeded by an assortment of activities whose very diversity brings local benefits.[15] It was on such grounds that a Southern town once erected a monument to honor the boll weevil, which had forced local farmers out of one-crop cotton farming into a diversified agriculture that turned out to be better after all. Similarly, New Bedford rejoiced in many decades of textile prosperity after the decline of her original specialty, whaling, had forced local capitalists to seek a substitute outlet for their resources in the cotton business.[16]

Manchester, N. H., presents a case of reasonably successful adjustment by conversion under strong local leadership. This city of 80,000 had grown up in the course of a century around the giant textile mills of the Amoskeag Manufacturing Company, which ranked among the world's largest. At the peak of its activity, Amoskeag employed a force of 18,000. Southern competition and two destructive floods brought about the final liquidation of the concern in 1935.

Local interests (chiefly utility, banking, and insurance) promptly incorporated under the name of Amoskeag Industries to buy the properties for $5,000,000 and try to put them to use. In 1946 the buildings were occupied by an assortment of 102 firms, employing in all 12,000 to 13,000 persons. The founders of Amoskeag In-

---

15 For an extended discussion of the possible benefits of local business diversifica tion, see Chap. 17.

16 Most of the cotton mills have, in turn, left New Bedford, but it would be premature to say that New Bedford rejoices over this loss and the influx of cheap garment factories that ensued.

dustries had been repaid 100 per cent in dividends and still had assets equal to the original investment in value.[17]

Conditions in stranded areas are normally, however, such as to make increases of efficiency or successful conversion to substitute industries quite difficult. The local atmosphere is unfavorable to quick and easy adjustment. Increases in efficiency that might restore the competitive position of the ailing industry generally require new capital for modernization of equipment, plus imaginative, venturesome management. Both are scarce in stranded areas.

Another handicap is the fact that local public services must continue to be supported on a smaller tax base if an important industry liquidates. In such cases it may be difficult to avoid a rise in tax rates, which makes the location still less attractive to other businesses that might be sought as substitutes.[18]

Still another disadvantage is the usually run-down state of public services, streets, buildings, and the like, in a depressed area. Such conditions make an unattractive setting for any new industry.

Finally, there is the factor of selective migration, mentioned earlier in this chapter. The most active and productive workers (at least as far as age is concerned) are the ones likely to move away first in case of distress. An inferior population is left behind to hinder economic recovery.

In view of the difficulties just discussed, the stranded factors of production usually can find employment only by accepting lower returns or by moving elsewhere. For land and immobile equipment, of course, the only possibility is a reduction of returns, but this bitter pill is often not swallowed in time.

Curtailed returns may be accepted by landowners, capital investors, enterprisers, employees, or taxing authorities if any of these parties feels sufficiently impelled to make a sacrifice in order

[17] The above account is based on information supplied by the Manchester field office of the U. S. Department of Commerce in December, 1946. Extensive background on the Amoskeag case is given by D. B. Creamer and C. W. Coulter in "Labor and the Shutdown of the Amoskeag Textile Mills," Work Projects Administration, National Research Project, Report No. L-5, Philadelphia, 1939 (processed).

[18] This situation is often met by special tax exemptions offered to new industry.

to avoid the threatened locational shift. Each would naturally prefer that the owners of some other production factor make the sacrifice instead, but sometimes it is possible to reach a satisfactory agreement that reduces costs [19] sufficiently to let the affected industry continue.

This flexibility has important social advantages. It eases the adjustment for the community at large, by avoiding or at any rate postponing a catastrophic fall of income; yet it gives the owners of all production factors a warning and a continuing incentive to look for a more permanent adjustment. Employees who have taken a wage cut under threat of permanent loss of their jobs in the community will certainly begin to consider, if they had not already, a move to some other place where standard wages are paid and the prospects for advancement look better. Owners of equipment and land, too, will devote thought to alternative uses that might yield a better return in the long run or, failing that, will be cautious about making long-standing commitments for maintenance or replacement. Thus gradually the way is paved for a migration of mobile factors, a conversion of convertible factors, and a junking of immobile inconvertible factors, which in the interests of efficiency should eventually occur.

C

PRINCIPAL UNITED STATES PROBLEM AREAS

11·10   Four Major Areas

To illustrate actual problem-area situations of the types discussed so far, brief attention will be given to the four principal areas of population pressure in the United States as they appeared in 1936 to the "Study of Population Redistribution." [20] These

---

[19] This type of cost reduction involves getting production factors cheaper; the cost reduction mentioned earlier as an "increase of efficiency" involves getting more output from a given input of production factors.

[20] These were not by any means the only areas of locational maladjustment in the United States in 1936, but they were perhaps the largest and most important. Cf. the report of the study: Carter Goodrich and others, "Migration and Economic Opportunity," Chaps. I–V, University of Pennsylvania Press, Philadelphia, 1936.

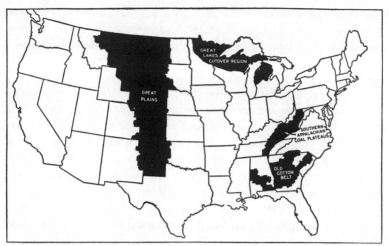

FIG. 11·1 The four principal areas of population pressure discussed in the report of the Study of Population Redistribution ("Migration and Economic Opportunity"), 1936. The "Old Cotton Belt" as here shown includes only the specialized cotton-producing areas with declining production in Georgia, South Carolina, and Alabama that are described in the report (*ibid.*, p. 142) as the "core" of the problem zone. (*Based on maps and statements in Carter Goodrich and others, "Migration and Economic Opportunity," pp. 203, 230, 164, 139, 142, and 55, University of Pennsylvania Press, Philadelphia, 1936.*)

areas, shown on the accompanying map (Fig. 11·1), were designated as follows:

a. The Great Lakes Cutover Region
b. The Great Plains
c. The Old Cotton Belt
d. The Southern Appalachian Coal Plateaus

Conditions have changed in some respects in the decade since these areas were examined for the "Study of Population Redistribution" and will change further in the future. Nevertheless, the maladjustments evident in these areas are so deep-seated that they will be problems of national concern for a long time.

THE GREAT LAKES CUTOVER REGION. This has become a problem area because of depletion of forests and minerals and the poor quality of the soil. Over the area as a whole, lumber output has fallen to a small fraction of what it was a generation or two ago; the copper and iron mines of Michigan are all but extinct as a result of depletion and the competition of better deposits elsewhere.

In this region distress was greatly aggravated by misguided agricultural settlement on what turned out to be poor, rocky, and stumpy soil. Not only was the land incapable of supporting most of the would-be farmers, but the population never became dense or wealthy enough to support the elaborate structure of local government that was set up on the assumption that settlement would follow the patterns established farther south. During the depression years of the 1930's a great influx of refugees from urban unemployment put further burdens on local productive and fiscal resources.

THE GREAT PLAINS. The basic difficulties of the Great Plains are vulnerability to drought and to wind erosion, which operated in disastrous conjunction in the dust storms of the dry 1930's. Agricultural settlement in the area has failed to evaluate adequately the risks of crop failure through drought and has provoked destructive wind erosion by plowing up the original grass cover. In this region the 1930's were marked by very large emigration, primarily to other agricultural areas.

THE OLD COTTON BELT. This has been a substandard region of the United States for generations, but its difficulties were accentuated by new developments in the 1920's and 1930's. The principal factors were a reduction in export markets for cotton, crop destruction by boll weevils (to which this part of the cotton belt is particularly vulnerable), competition from lower cost producers farther west, and soil depletion and erosion. The prevailing sharecropper system, together with the low quality of farm labor in this region due to its poverty, and the special problem of interracial relations have aggravated the destruction and misuse of soil resources. In the face of declining opportunity, the natural increase of the rural population has been high. Increased mechanization of cotton farming (weeding with flame throwers and picking by machine) will further reduce labor needs on the plantations and at the same time hurt the competitive position of this southeastern area whose only advantage is cheap labor.

THE SOUTHERN APPALACHIAN COAL PLATEAUS. Here farming and mining are of roughly equal importance as sources of employment. The poor and hilly agricultural lands have been badly overcrowded by continued natural increase of population in communities relatively isolated from the outside world. As a result, farms are too small to provide an adequate living, and too much sloping land has been plowed and its soil carried off by erosion. Authorities are agreed that a large reduction in the farm population and cultivated acreage in this region are essential to any great improvement in living standards. During the depression years of the 1930's, as in the Great Lakes Cutover Region, temporary migrants from cities and towns increased the pressure on local land resources.

Employment in the coal, oil, and gas industries appeared even in the 1930's to be past its peak. In the case of oil and gas, resources have been depleted; the coal deposits of this region are enormous and of high quality, but the market for coal now shows no long-run trend of increase, and some of the original competitive advantages of this area in coal mining have been lost by equalization of wages and working conditions with other producing areas farther north. The surplus farm population, then, finds no outlet in local mining activity.

All four of these problem areas showed the usual symptoms of population pressure: high unemployment, low income levels, emigration, and high rates of natural increase of the population.[21]

In some respects conditions in these areas have improved during the last decade. More adequate rainfall and improved soil-control practices in the Great Plains, the regrowth of some timber and the development of a flourishing tourist trade in the cutover country, some industrialization in the cotton belt, and most important of all the effects of several years of war prosperity have increased incomes and drained off some surplus population. Some of these effects, however, are temporary. It is to be feared that a succession of humid years in the Great Plains, for example, will

---

[21] High fertility has been least in evidence in the Great Plains—perhaps because the distress there was of relatively recent occurrence.

lead to a repetition of the cycle of oversettlement, too intensive cultivation, and destructive erosion when drought returns.

11·11   Other Problem Areas

To illustrate the complications involved in any demarcation of "problem areas," three other maps are included which were based on somewhat different criteria.

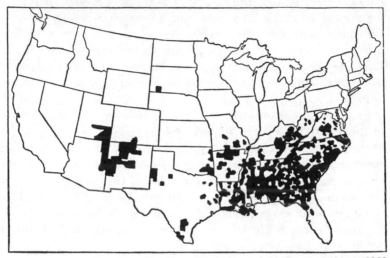

Fig. 11·2   Counties with lowest "plane of living" index in 1928 to 1929. The index is based on per capita income tax returns, residence telephones, and radios, each as a percentage of the national average. The three percentages for each county are averaged with equal weights to obtain the 'plane of living" index. (*Redrawn by permission from a map in Carter Goodrich and others, "Migration and Economic Opportunity," Plate I, University of Pennsylvania Press, Philadelphia, 1936.*)

Figure 11·2, likewise taken from the Goodrich report, shows in black those counties rated lowest in the United States in terms of a specially constructed "plane-of-living" index based on the number of telephones, radios, and income tax returns per capita in 1928 and 1929. The rural South stands out solidly on this map as the area most deficient in these attributes of a modern standard of life; most of the gaps in that region represent urban areas.

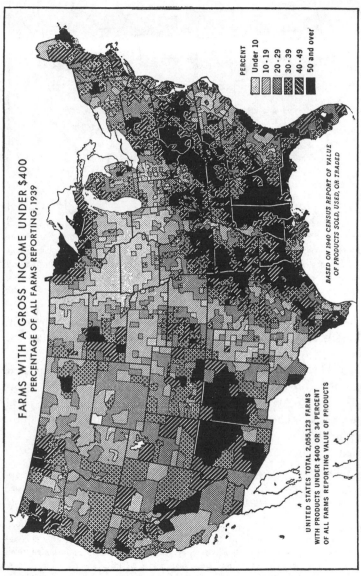

FARMS WITH A GROSS INCOME UNDER $400
PERCENTAGE OF ALL FARMS REPORTING, 1939

PERCENT
Under 10
10 · 19
20 · 29
30 · 39
40 · 49
50 and over

BASED ON 1940 CENSUS REPORT OF VALUE
OF PRODUCTS SOLD, USED, OR TRADED

UNITED STATES TOTAL 2,055,123 FARMS
WITH PRODUCTS UNDER $400 OR 34 PERCENT
OF ALL FARMS REPORTING VALUE OF PRODUCTS

FIG. 11·3 Farms with gross income under $400 as percentage of all farms reporting, 1939, by counties. (*Bureau of Agricultural Economics, U. S. Department of Agriculture.*)

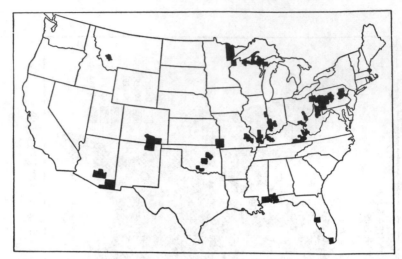

Fig. 11·4 "Problem areas" in the United States, based primarily on relief loads in 1934 to 1935 and unemployment in 1940. Predominantly agricultural areas with very low population densities have been excluded. *(Drawn by permission on the basis of a list prepared by Marion Hayes of the Occupational Outlook Division, U. S. Bureau of Labor Statistics.)*

Another very poor region in the arid Southwest, with a population largely Indian, likewise appears on this map but is far less significant in terms of the number of people involved.

Figure 11·3 refers only to farms, showing by shadings the percentage of farms in each county that yielded less than $400 gross income in 1939. Here again the relative poverty of the rural Southeast is evident, but large areas in the middle Appalachian, intermountain, Great Plains, and northern cutover regions likewise make a poor showing.[22]

[22] M. J. Hagood of the Bureau of Agricultural Economics has prepared maps showing geographic variations in the rural farm and nonfarm "level of living" by counties in 1940. Individual county data and maps appear in "Rural Level of Living Indexes for Counties of the United States, 1940," Bureau of Agricultural Economics, Washington, October, 1943 (mimeographed). The geographic pattern shown is not significantly different from that of Fig. 11·3, although the Hagood maps are based on more comprehensive criteria. For the rural-farm index of level of living, the component series and their respective weights are as follows: percentage of occupied dwelling units with fewer than 1.51 persons per room, 0.467; percentage of dwelling units with radios, 0.281; percentage of farms with gross

Figure 11·4 presents a radically different picture, being based not on living standards or income but on unemployment and relief loads.[23] Population pressure in farming areas is not so likely to take these forms, and the "solid South" is conspicuously missing from the map. Most of the areas shown in black on Fig. 11·4 depended largely on mining activities, which for various reasons (depletion, technical changes, and competition of other areas) had not maintained the former level of employment. Appalachian coal areas figure prominently here and are joined by other depressed coal-mining districts in eastern Pennsylvania (anthracite), Ohio, Illinois, Indiana, and Colorado. The oil industry is represented in Oklahoma. Zinc and lead mining in the tristate area of Kansas, Missouri, and Oklahoma; copper mining in Michigan, Montana, and Arizona; and iron mining in Michigan, Wisconsin, and Minnesota all give rise to local "problem areas" by the criteria used. In a few areas on the map, manufacturing industries are important factors: steel in Ohio, railroad shops in Altoona, Pa., cigars in Tampa, and textiles and shoes in eastern Massachusetts.

D

URBAN BLIGHT

11·12 *Peripheral Growth and Internal Decay*

The basic structure of urban areas has already been discussed in Chap. 8, and its close dependence on means of transfer has been indicated. We turn now to a brief examination of the prob-

---

income of more than $600, 0.226; percentage of farms reporting automobiles of 1936 or later models, 0.403; median grade of school completed by persons twenty-five years of age and over, 4.351. The above weights were determined mathematically "in such a way as to ensure that counties receiving the same index value will be as similar as possible with respect to each of the items included." *Op. cit.,* p. 2.

[23] Figure 11·4 is based by permission on an abridged list of prewar depressed areas prepared for discussion purposes by Marion Hayes of the Occupational Outlook Division of the U. S. Bureau of Labor Statistics. The criteria used include percentage unemployed in 1940, percentage on relief in 1934 to 1935, and other factors including "judgment and general knowledge." Predominantly agricultural areas with very low population densities have been excluded.

lems of structural reorganization created by the growth of the cities themselves and by changes in the means of local transit and communication.

The growth of urban areas in recent generations has been spectacular and seems everywhere to have exceeded the growth of rural areas. In the United States 5 per cent of the population was urban in 1790, 28 per cent in 1880, 56 per cent in 1940, and 60 per cent in 1946.[24] As has been indicated already, the progressive urbanization of populations in all parts of the world is due entirely to migration, since cities have much lower rates of natural increase than rural areas of the same regions.

City growth has involved an outward extension of the various zones of urban and suburban land use. The most intensive "downtown" uses have made room for themselves partly by expanding upward into taller buildings and partly by displacing residential and other uses in the zone surrounding the city center.

It is in the inner transition zones that the conspicuous and arresting problem of "urban blight" has appeared. In most of our large cities the transition has been marked by blighted areas where property values have fallen, many buildings are in disrepair or vacant, housing and social conditions are notably unsatisfactory, and tax delinquency is high.

Some of the explanation of this phenomenon lies in growth itself or perhaps more accurately in changes in the rate of growth. As more and more people go daily in and out of the "central core" of the city to do business, the desirability of sites on the borders of that core, for relatively intensive "downtown" uses, increases. There is thus a demand for a certain amount of land for conversion to these more intensive uses. On the other hand, the increased traffic makes the intermediate transition zone *less* desirable for residence and therefore for the trade and service establishments doing a "neighborhood" business. This creates a supply of land available for the reconversion indicated. If the demand and the supply can be equated at the existing prices for land, con-

[24] Table 9·1, and Bureau of the Census, "Urban and Rural Population Growth from 1790 to 1940," Nov. 15, 1941. The census defines as "urban" all incorporated places of 2,500 population or more.

version may proceed smoothly with no inordinate vacancy or dilapidation and no fall in property values.

While cities were growing very rapidly and the agencies of public passenger transit to the downtown area (streetcars, rapid transit, and later busses) were being rapidly improved, the more or less automatic conversion just described seemed to be the rule.[25]

But it appears that in most of our larger cities during the past few decades the supply of land rendered less valuable in existing uses in the areas surrounding the central core of the city has been in excess of the demand for conversion for expansion of the central core. This condition of acute blight has directed attention forcibly to the problem on both economic and social grounds.

11·13   Basic Causes of Urban Blight

There are at least three reasons for the aggravation of blight in such areas. One is the vertical diversion of expansion in the urban core, ascribable to improved elevators, better methods of skyscraper construction, and the prestige value of the skyscraper as such. These enhanced possibilities of vertical growth naturally diminish the demand for land for lateral extension of the core.

A second reason is the slackening in the growth rate of cities as a whole, in keeping with the slackening growth rate of populations in industrialized countries. The rate of percentage increase diminished, as shown in Table 11·2. This slackening of population growth converted a relative decline of property values in the areas surrounding the city core into an absolute decline.

It should be noted, however, that the experience of the 1930's gives an exaggerated impression of the decline in urban growth rates, due to the poor industrial employment situation prevailing during most of the decade and the consequent retarding of rural-

---

[25] The development of electric transit stopped the rise of land values in the zone just outside the Loop in Chicago, for example, around 1900 but does not seem to have been the basis of any considerable actual decrease in values. The population of the city as a whole was still growing rapidly in the early decades of this century, and the peculiar effects of automobile transport (which will be described) did not come till much later. See Homer Hoyt, "One Hundred Years of Land Values in Chicago," University of Chicago Press, Chicago, 1933, Chap. VI, The Relation between the Growth of Chicago and the Rise of Its Land Values, especially Figs. 88 and 89 on pp. 362 and 363.

Table 11·2   *Average Annual Rate of Increase of Population in the United States, in Urban Places, and in Cities of 100,000 Population and Over, 1910–1946*

Period	Average (geometric mean) percentage rate of population increase per year		
	United States	All urban places	Cities of 100,000 or over
1910–1920	1.4	2.6	3.1
1920–1930	1.5	2.4	2.8
1930–1940	0.7	0.8	0.4
1940–1946 *	0.8	1.7	†

* Rates of increase shown for the period 1940 to 1946 are for civilian population only and are thus not comparable to those shown for earlier periods.

† Data not available.

Sources: Calculated from data for 1910 to 1940 in "Statistical Abstract of the United States, 1946," Table 11, p. 13, and data for 1940 and 1946 in Bureau of the Census, "Urban and Rural Population of the United States, by Age and Sex: 1946, 1945, and 1940," Series P-S, No. 19, Washington, Feb. 20, 1947.

urban migration.[26] As Table 11·2 suggests, the population growth of American cities in the 1940's may be much larger than in the 1930's.

The third and probably the most important factor explaining urban blight in the last generation is the development of automobile transport, already mentioned in Chap. 10. The great flexibility of this new means of freight and passenger transport gave businesses of all kinds more latitude in their location relative to materials, markets, and labor supply. An increased proportion of manufacturing and distributing enterprises were freed from direct dependence on rail connections and no longer needed to seek locations in the crowded trackage and water-front zones. Suburban locations have become more popular as a greater percentage of the labor force is prepared to drive to work.[27]

[26] Cf. Table 7·2.

[27] At the same time (as noted in Section 10·5) the progressive electrification of manufacturing called for a new type of factory design. The older multistory

The automobile thus opened up large new areas in the outer parts of cities to business and residence use. At the same time, it directly injured the congested downtown districts by making people dependent on a vehicle that takes up vastly more street space per passenger than public vehicles do, to say nothing of parking space. The streets in central parts of our cities were never designed to carry an important part of the daily traffic flow in private vehicles.

The natural result has been a rapid growth of suburbs at the expense of the whole congested inner part of the city, including the commercial "core." Lateral expansion of the core to take over more of the land ruined for other purposes by congestion was still further checked, and blight in the zone surrounding the core was aggravated.[28]

Redevelopment of slum and blighted areas in American cities has been delayed primarily by the high cost of land acquisition and by reluctance to use public powers of eminent domain to the extent that would be needed. Inflated land prices in many neighborhoods reflect only false hopes based on overzoning for commerce and industry.[29]

factories, which were made compact in order to facilitate the transmission of power by belts and shafting within the plant, gave way to lower and more extensive plants employing many separate electric motors to produce their mechanical energy. This necessitated more spacious sites and contributed substantially to the oft-noted suburbanization of industry.

[28] An interesting map published by the Chicago Plan Commission shows the residential areas considered as "blighted or near blighted" in Chicago, lying in a fairly continuous belt around the central business district. The area is roughly coterminous with that shown in the lowest rental classification in Fig. 8·8 above and was delimited on the basis of criteria laid down in the Illinois Neighborhood Redevelopment Law of July 9, 1941: ". . . those urban districts in which the major portion of the housing is detrimental to the health, safety, morality, or welfare of the inhabitants by reason of age, dilapidation, overcrowding, faulty arrangement, lack of ventilation, light, or sanitary facilities, or any combination of these factors." For a detailed statement of the measures applied, see Chicago Plan Commission, "Master Plan of Residential Land Use of Chicago," Table 17, p. 72, Chicago, 1943. The map in question appears as Fig. 109, p. 86, but is not reproduced here, since it is in process of revision.

[29] A current and comprehensive discussion of urban blight and an analysis of redevelopment proposals is to be found in J. F. Dewhurst and associates, "America's Needs and Resources," Chap. 18, pp. 411–430, by L. N. Bloomberg, H. G. Brunsman, and A. B. Handler, The Twentieth Century Fund, Inc., New York, 1947.

SUMMARY

For sustained economic progress, a region needs improved transfer facilities and a shift to more and more intensive forms of production. Manufacturing ordinarily begins in a region as the processing of local materials for local needs; further industrialization can be based either on exploitation of minerals and energy sources or on processing of imported materials with cheap labor.

At any stage in economic progress and particularly at the threshold of industrialization, development may be arrested for lack of necessary resources, transport development, capital, skill, or enterprise. Arrested development, particularly in regions not far advanced, usually leads to cumulative population pressure and low income standards.

Resource depletion, technological change, and other causes often produce a net loss of employment in specific "stranded areas." Such areas face handicaps in recovering their economic position. Where conversion of the unemployed production factors to substitute uses proves impossible, the adjustment is less painful if factor prices are not too inflexible.

Four major problem areas in the United States illustrate features of arrested development and emigration of industry.

As cities grow, the central commercial core expands to take over some land from less central uses. The development of tall buildings, the use of automobiles, and the slackening of city growth have all interfered with this transition in recent decades, producing a zone of blight or economic obsolescence where land values have fallen.

Part Three

The Locational Significance
of Boundaries

CHAPTER 12

Political Boundaries as Trade Barriers

TRADITIONALLY, great stress has been placed upon the differences between international and domestic trade, while their many similarities have been too often ignored. Statesmen and businessmen have favored in the international sphere many policies—such as protective tariffs and restriction of exchanges—that they would dismiss as absurd for domestic application. Economic theorists must accept a share of the blame for this common failure to realize the resemblances between interregional and international trade, for most of them have until quite recently analyzed international problems on a framework of assumptions quite unrelated to their ideas of domestic trade and industrial location.[1]

This seems quite unjustifiable when it is realized that the only difference between the locational relations within a country and those applying between countries is that in the latter case political boundaries lie athwart the path of commerce. This book treats political boundaries as one of the many factors influencing locational patterns, currents of trade, and the activities and welfare of communities. In previous chapters the principal other locational considerations have been set forth in sufficient detail to explain the character of the pattern without reference to boundaries. The task of the remaining chapters is to put the theory in as realistic a light as possible by taking account of the effects of boundaries that divide the earth's surface into different political jurisdictions.

---

[1] The usual assumptions in simplified expositions of international trade theory have been that factors of production are fully mobile within a country but immobile between countries and that transfer costs are nonexistent, at least domestically. In effect this treats each country as a single geographic location. The most noteworthy attempts to integrate the theories of location and international trade, with more realistic assumptions, are Bertil Ohlin, "Interregional and International Trade," Harvard University Press, Cambridge, Mass., 1933, and August Lösch, "The Economics of Location," Yale University Press, 1954.

The sharpest boundaries are generally those between nations; so it is appropriate to give primary attention to questions raised by national policies and international boundaries. Many of the aspects of international boundaries, however, apply also to boundaries between provinces, federated states, or even smaller administrative units such as municipalities. Their difference in significance is largely a matter of degree; though in some respects, such as that of monetary standards, the international boundary is the only important kind.

Any political unit can, of course, follow a policy designed to affect in some manner the location of activities within its territory or as between it and the rest of the world. For instance, a city administration may forbid the operation of slaughterhouses within the city limits or may zone the whole area of the city for various categories of use, while a nation may adopt a long-range policy of protective tariffs designed to foster manufactures.

The ends and means appropriate to such policies are the subject of later chapters. However, even in the absence of any locational policy, there are certain locational effects that almost inevitably follow from the mere existence of a boundary. It is these which are here at issue. The present chapter will discuss only the direct effects of boundaries as hindrances to trade. Other important locational effects of boundaries will be taken up in the following chapter.

12·1   How Boundaries Obstruct Trade

A political boundary hinders trade in a variety of ways. Most obvious, of course, are barriers deliberately erected as a part of public policy. Internationally we have not only tariffs (usually on imports but occasionally on exports) but a variety of exchange controls and quota systems. Our state governments, constitutionally forbidden to interfere with interstate commerce by levying tariffs, have managed to evade the intent of the Constitution by an impressive array of devices.[2] These include preference to home-

---

[2] There is a voluminous literature on the subject of United States interstate trade barriers. Some major contributions are the following: F. E. Melder, *State and Local Barriers to Interstate Commerce in the United States—A Study in*

state suppliers in purchasing by state institutions; discriminatory taxes, inspection requirements, and labeling requirements on such out-of-state products as milk and oleomargarine; and discrimination against interstate motor carriers. Semiofficial and unofficial "Buy at Home" campaigns are designed to have a similar repressive effect on trade.

Even in the absence of tariffs or other intentional restrictions, boundaries would constitute barriers to trade. In the case of international frontiers there is the expense and time required for filling out extra forms and arranging the transaction. Special packing is often stipulated for export trade as well. Interstate highway transport is made more expensive by the wide variety of limitations and stipulations that the various states place upon trucks.[3]

Trade across boundaries is also hindered by the differences in tastes, customs, and language between the two jurisdictions. Even in trade between countries with such similar conditions as the United States and Canada, it is often found that special pains have to be taken to adapt the product to the export market. Where differences are greater, it may be necessary to make completely different lines of goods for export purposes, and much of the advantage of concentrated production is thereby lost. Thus if one country has a different language from the other, all labels, instructions, advertising, correspondence, and the like must be translated; if the two countries use different systems of weights,

Economic Sectionalism, University of Maine Studies, Second Series, No. 43, *The Maine Bulletin*, vol. XL, No. 4, November, 1937; Works Progress Administration, "Comparative Charts of State Statutes Illustrating Barriers to Trade between States," Government Printing Office, Washington, 1939; Council of State Governments, *Trade Barrier Research Bulletin Series*, Chicago, 1939; U. S. Department of Agriculture, "Barriers to Internal Trade in Farm Products," Government Printing Office, Washington, 1939; U. S. Department of Commerce, Marketing Laws Survey, "Interstate Trade Barriers—Outlines of Studies," Government Printing Office, Washington, 1942; Board of Investigation and Research, "Interstate Trade Barriers Affecting Motor-vehicle Transportation," 79th Congress, 1st Session, Senate Document No. 81, Government Printing Office, Washington, 1945.

[3] Some state motor-vehicle laws appear to be aimed at the interstate truck in particular, but the mere fact that different states impose different rules as to lights, loads, dimensions, etc., also hampers interstate operations. Some of these differences in requirements are defensible in view of the differences in highway construction standards; others could be eliminated without lasting hardship.

measures, and engineering standards, the dimensions of the article, including even the gauges and threadings of nuts and bolts,[4] must be differentiated for the export trade. In some cases religious practices impose restrictions. Exporters to India or Pakistan, for instance, must avoid using beef or pork fat in their products.

A still less obvious characteristic of trade across customs or inspection barriers is its circuity. A frontier station costs some-

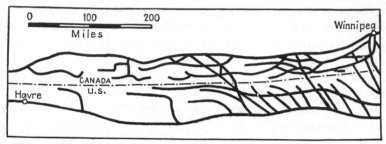

Fig. 12·1   Railroad lines near the United States–Canadian border between Winnipeg, Man., and Havre, Mont. (*From August Lösch, "Die räumliche Ordnung der Wirtschaft," Fig. 80, p. 292, Gustav Fischer Verlag, Jena, 1940. All rights reserved. Copyright vested in the Attorney General of the United States, pursuant to law. This figure is reproduced here by permission of the Attorney General in the public interest under License No. JA-1219.*)

thing to maintain, just as a bridge across a river does; so frontiers like rivers are provided with crossings only at intervals. When the traffic across the frontier is light, the crossing points may be few and far between. Since all legal traffic must pass through one of these scarce bottlenecks, it is obvious that on a large proportion of international shipments the trip is made more circuitous and hence slower and more expensive, entirely apart from any extra time and expense involved in the actual crossing of the frontier.

Even on the peaceful and inconspicuous border between the United States and Canada, this situation has some importance. The accompanying map (Fig. 12·1) shows that most of the north-south railroad lines in the 600-mile stretch of prairie country west of Winnipeg stop short of the frontier.

---

[4] Not until 1948, in fact, did the British, Canadian and United States screw-thread associations agree on a common standard for the shapes of such threads.

12·2 Conformity of Trade-area Boundaries with Political Boundaries

A trade barrier produces an abrupt upward jog in transfer-cost gradients at that point, which distorts the pattern of market areas

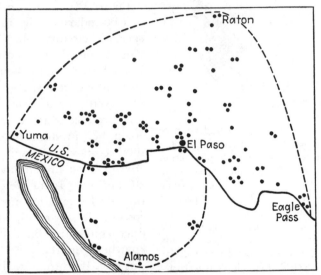

FIG. 12·2 The financial sphere of influence of El Paso, Tex., on both sides of the United States–Mexican border. Each dot represents one bank keeping an account at an El Paso bank. (*From August Lösch, "Die räumliche Ordnung der Wirtschaft," Fig. 81, p. 293, Gustav Fischer Verlag, Jena, 1940. All rights reserved. Copyright vested in the Attorney General of the United States, pursuant to law. This figure is reproduced here by permission of the Attorney General in the public interest under License No. JA-1219.*)

and supply areas. Parts of such areas that would otherwise project across the boundary are reduced in size if not altogether elimi-nated. The higher the barrier in cost terms the more nearly will the boundaries of such economic areas coincide with the political boundary. Where all of them coincide exactly, no trade passes the border.

This effect appears in Fig. 12·2, which shows the locations of all banks maintaining deposit relations with banks in El Paso,

Tex. That portion of the El Paso "financial area" lying in Mexico is notably more restricted than the part lying in the United States. The same general picture would hold true for most lines of commodity trade as well and with respect to both market and supply areas.

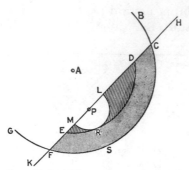

FIG. 12·3   Effects of a trade barrier and port-of-entry restriction upon the distribution area of a production center. The production center is located at *A*. In the absence of trade barriers or restrictions, the product can be sold as far as the arc *GFSCB*. With a trade barrier along the line *KH* but crossing permitted at any point, the product can be sold as far as *GFERDCB*—the stippled territory has been lost. With the further restriction that all transborder traffic must pass through *P*, the product can be sold only as far as *GFMRLCB*—the shaded territory also has been lost.

Figure 12·3 shows the effects of a boundary barrier plus the special "circuity effect" previously noted. Producers are located at *A*, and a boundary runs along the straight line *HK*. Within the home country, producers at *A* can lay down their product at the same total cost—say $2 per unit—anywhere on the circular arcs *BC* and *FG*.[5] If transfer across the border entailed no extra costs or circuity at all, the product could also be delivered anywhere on the arc *CSF* at this cost. If crossing the border does entail some extra costs but can be effected at any desired point, producers at *A* can sell only as far as the arc *DRE* in the foreign country. The stippled area in the figure represents the loss of distribution range due to the barrier effect of the boundary. If it be further stipulated that all transboundary traffic must pass through the port of entry *P*, the limit of $2 delivery shrinks to *GFMRLCB*. The further loss of distribution range due to circuity, *i.e.*, to the funneling of traffic through *P*, is indicated by the shaded area in the figure.

The effect of trade barriers is, of course, not uniform in degree for different types of goods. Some commodities and services, as

---

[5] A line of this sort is sometimes called an "isotim" (line of equal price).

explained earlier, have very small market areas because the importance of nearness to a scattered market outweighs any opposing factors of procurement or processing cost. The locational pattern of such industries consists of a very fine-meshed network of market areas, each served by a different production center. The distorting effect of the boundary will in such cases be felt by only that small fraction of market areas which happens to touch the boundary, while for the rest of the country the distribution of the industry is unaffected. International trade in such commodities and services is unimportant relative to domestic trade save in the smallest countries. Similarly, industries like cotton gins or grain elevators have a fine-meshed network of supply areas, only the outmost of which are affected at all by the boundary.

By contrast, the effect of boundaries as trade barriers may be great indeed in the case of concentrated industries that draw materials from long distances or serve widespread markets. In such cases the boundary is likely to cut off a sizable part of the market area or supply area or both for most of the possible locations within a country and thus to make these locations less advantageous and to work a considerable change in the whole national pattern of the industry and those related to it. In some cases an industry is dependent on international trade for the whole of its market or material supply.

The general effect upon the domestic pattern of location is not hard to picture. Trade barriers at the boundary decrease the accessibility of outside material sources and markets and therefore increase the dependence of the industry upon domestic markets and sources, if any. A concentrated industry located primarily with reference to distribution costs, *i.e.,* one that tends to locate at the strategic distribution points for its product, will be led by the barrier to move nearer the point of minimum distribution cost to *domestic* markets—a point that is usually more central than a location selected with an eye to serving both domestic and export markets. Production points near the boundary will suffer under the disadvantage of greater average distribution costs or smaller scale production or very likely both. Similarly, a concentrated industry located at strategic procurement centers will be led by the barrier to move nearer the optimum procurement point for domestic materials. In either case, locations near the boundary are at a disadvantage as processing centers.[6]

12·3   Creation of Protected Trade Areas and Production Centers

Reduction of the size of market areas entails, of course, an increase in their number, *i.e.*, a greater dispersion of processing points over the whole market territory. The purpose of "protective" import duties (in direct or disguised forms) is to acquire or retain for the protected home producers a separate market area that would otherwise not exist. Export duties on raw materials or power are likewise designed to keep such materials at home for further processing, *i.e.*, to carve out a protected supply area for home processors.

Figure 12·4 presents a relatively simple case of protection in which only processing costs and distribution costs are assumed to vary locationally. This might apply to mining or other extractive industries which make relatively little use of transported materials. The jagged line at the top of the figure represents the pattern of processing costs for points along a route passing through *A*, *X*, *B*, and *C*. The smoother sloping gradients show the variation in total delivered cost of the product at different markets when it is produced at *A*, *X*, *B*, or *C*.

In the absence of trade barriers, it is evident (following the lowest sloping line) that *A* can serve all markets more cheaply than any alternative processing point can. All processing will be concentrated at *A*.

But if there is a trade barrier at *X*, with added costs amounting to *DE* on shipments from the *A*-country into the *BC*-country, *C* will be shielded from foreign competition sufficiently to command a market extending as far as *H* and *N*.[7] If the trade barrier is raised to a height of *DF*, the delivered-cost gradient on goods im-

---

[6] *Cf.* Lösch's discussion of the characteristic "border wasteland," *op. cit.*, pp. 203–206.

[7] Under these circumstances the total delivered cost of *A*'s product in the *BC*-country is shown by the gradient *EH*, which intersects *C*'s gradient at *H* and *N*.

ported from *A* rises to the position *FL* and both *B* and *C* can compete. *C* will ship as far as *K;* *B* will dominate the markets between *K* and *L;* and goods imported from *A* will continue to be sold in the markets between *L* and the border. Finally, the barrier is raised to a height exceeding *DG;* goods from *A* will not cross the border at all. A fourth production center located immediately

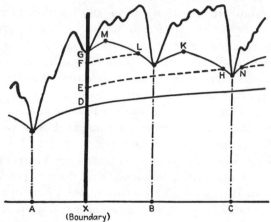

FIG. 12·4   Diagram illustrating the protective effect of a trade barrier (at *X*) upon high-cost processing locations (at *X, B,* and *C*) in competition with lower cost producers at *A.*

to the right of the boundary will serve the territory between it and *M,* while *B*'s market area will extend now from *M* to *K.*

In this case it is evident that the imposition of a barrier to importation may permit development of one or more domestic production centers, depending on the height of the barrier. This is, of course, at the immediate expense of the consumers of the product in the "protected" country, all of whom now pay more for the product.

12·4   *Advantages of Border Locations for Protected Industries*

In Section 12·2 it was indicated that producers are likely to shun the territory near a trade barrier which would curtail their market or supply areas. Producers on the other side of the barrier, however, who are protected by it, are likely to choose a location near the barrier.[8]

For example, a country that has been importing some manufactured commodity may decide to import the materials instead and do the processing itself. The process in question may be material-oriented (which would account for its previous absence from the country in question). If so, the location of minimum transfer costs for the new protected industry is at the port of entry for the materials, *i.e.,* as close to the material supply as it is possible to be while still remaining within the protected market area. Even if the protected industry is not definitely material-oriented, ports of entry may be ideal locations because they are transshipment and junction points and also usually the centers of important local markets. The transfer advantages of such points were described in Sections 3·7, 3·8, and 8·3.

As an illustration, cane-sugar refineries are nearly always located in port cities in the countries that do not produce their own cane.[9] In this particular case there are often two kinds of protection: a tariff or quota on refined sugar to protect the cane-sugar refiners and a tariff or quota on raw sugar to protect the domestic beet-sugar producers from the domestic cane refiners.[10]

Location of a protected industry at border points is also likely if the new industry has been created by imposing an export restriction on a domestic material that was formerly exported in unprocessed form. If the export restriction was really necessary in order to bring the processing operation into the country where the material originates, this may indicate a market orientation of

[8] Anyone can see an example of both tendencies by crossing a boundary between two states with different rates of gasoline or liquor taxation. Gasoline or liquor stores will be clustered thickly on the low-tax side of the boundary and will be notably remote on the high-tax side.

[9] The first stage of processing—crushing the cane and extracting raw sugar—is always performed on the plantations, because the cane is bulky and subject to rapid deterioration once cut. The American Sugar Refining Corporation operates two "centrals" (crushing plants) on its Cuban plantations and has refineries at Boston, New York, Philadelphia, and Baltimore and near New Orleans.

[10] The United States levies both duties in addition to operating a preferential import quota system. Until 1913 duties were higher on the refined product; since then the same rate per pound has applied to both raw and refined sugar.

the processing operation. In that case, production for export will take place as near the point of export as possible. If the process is neither strongly material-oriented nor strongly market-oriented, the point of export will still present special transfer advantages as a junction and transshipment point.

SUMMARY

Trade barriers of various sorts are often erected at political boundaries as part of an effort to influence location. Even in the absence of such policies, however, trade across boundaries is ordinarily slower, more complicated, more roundabout, and therefore more costly.

Trade barriers tend to bring the boundaries of supply and market areas into conformity with political boundaries. Discouragement of external trade brings the existing industries of a "protected" country into closer proximity to home markets and resources; but if new industries are created by the imposition of a trade barrier, they are quite likely to be located at border points.

CHAPTER 13

Political Boundaries as Barriers to Factor Movement, Payments, and Coordinated Area Administration

IN THE PREVIOUS CHAPTER, one important locational aspect of boundaries was considered, namely, the fact that they act as trade barriers and thus impede the expansion and amalgamation of market and supply areas. The present chapter will examine the locational significance of some other usual characteristics of boundaries.

Boundaries hinder the migration of labor, capital, and enterprise much as they hinder trade. Some of the obstacles to crossing the frontier are deliberately erected as a part of national, state, or local policy; others merely reflect the inevitable difficulties of passing from the jurisdiction of one set of laws and customs to that of another.

International transactions generally involve conversion from one monetary unit to another. This raises at least a possibility of locational effects, which must be explored.

Finally, political boundaries frequently cut across areas that are essentially economic units and inevitably hinder the efficient development and administration of such areas.

13·1 Boundaries as Barriers to Mobility of Factors of Production

Boundaries characteristically impose an additional obstacle to the migration of labor and capital. Whether or not imposed as a matter of policy, such restrictions cannot fail to have locational effects.

Laws and taxes directly restricting such migration are an important type of barrier. The control or outright prohibition of international human immigration has become increasingly prevalent within the past generation,[1] even in some countries formerly regarded as "underpopulated." One important country, the USSR, forbids emigration as well. High visa fees and taxes on immigrants or the stipulation that emigrants must leave their property behind are only somewhat less complete bars. The international flow of capital and enterprise, too, is often retarded by special laws or taxes in both the lending and the borrowing countries.

Such restrictions have existed even in the most peaceful times, and in periods of international tension or war they practically eliminate the international mobility of production factors. On the other hand, subsidies to encourage migration of labor, capital, and enterprise across boundaries have not been unknown in the past. Special travel rates or cheap land for new settlers or advantageous concessions to tempt foreign capital constitute a "negative barrier" at the boundary, which may help to offset certain hindrances to factor migration.

Even in the absence of deliberate controls, the migration of labor, capital, or enterprise across a boundary presents special difficulties. This is particularly the case with international boundaries, since an international frontier usually separates people of different traditions, customs, and language. Powerful historical forces work toward the adaptation of political boundaries to cultural-linguistic boundaries and vice versa.[2] In any event, areas under separate political control develop different systems of laws, regulations, and taxes and customs relating to business.

Boundaries between federated states or local-government areas are much less significant as barriers to the migration of production factors. Some state and local governments in the United States, however, did undertake to restrict immigration during

---

[1] The United States quota system of limitation dates from 1921.

[2] There are, of course, exceptions. Throughout most of the republics of Latin America a single language is current, whereas Switzerland, Finland, and Eire are examples of states with more than one language but a strong national feeling. In other cases the divergence between cultural-linguistic frontiers and political frontiers is more conspicuous, e.g., in Canada, Belgium, and Spain, all of which have had serious separatist movements.

the 1930's. California, for example, imposed a property qualification on would-be immigrants. Also relevant here are local residence requirements to establish eligibility for public relief or unemployment compensation. To the extent that security depends on length of residence within a particular jurisdiction, migration between such jurisdictions is discouraged. In more than half the states residents have priority in public-works employment.[3]

13·2 Interregional Factor Movements and Trade as Alternatives

The effect of all these boundary obstacles to migration of labor, capital, and enterprise is to enlarge and perpetuate differentials in wages, interest, and profits between political jurisdiction areas and to make the supply of labor, capital, and enterprise a more significant element in locational advantage.[4]

The effect of barriers to factor migration upon the industrial specialization of an area may best be visualized by a simplified hypothetical case. Suppose that in Country A wage and interest rates are such that a man can be hired at the same expense as $50,000 of capital,[5] whereas in Country B a man of equal abilities can be hired at the same cost as $10,000 of capital.

In the absence of restrictions to the contrary, it is evident that this situation would lead to migration of labor or capital (or

[3] Indiana goes so far as to stipulate that unskilled laborers employed in construction of state highways and bridges must be residents of the *county* in which the work is being done. For a survey of this type of state laws, see Works Progress Administration, Marketing Laws Survey, "Comparative Charts of State Statutes Illustrating Barriers to Trade between States," Washington, 1939.

[4] Boundaries also generally mark abrupt differences in factor productivity. If, for instance, the laws of one state are such as to make night work in a particular industry inordinately expensive, a larger capital investment will be required to turn out a given amount of product in that state than in another state where more lenient laws make possible a fuller utilization of equipment through night shifts.

[5] For instance, wages may be $1,500 a year and the interest rate 3 per cent. In that case, the interest on $50,000 will equal the wages of one man. In any specific enterprise in either country, the combination of labor and capital is presumably so adjusted as to equate the marginal product per equivalent amount of capital ($50,000 in A or $10,000 in B).

both), which would bring the relative returns of these factors into closer correspondence in the two countries.

But if the wage and interest differentials are prevented from being equalized through factor migration, it is evident that Country *A* will find it profitable to specialize in products, such as automobiles, that require a large amount of capital per man; whereas Country *B* will find it profitable to specialize in clothing manufacture and other lines requiring less capital in proportion to labor.

This specialization can be carried much further if international trade is easy and cheap, for in that case *A* can import all its clothing from *B* and use its scarce man power to better advantage in making cars for export, while *B* can import all its cars and make its scarce capital resources go further in the clothing industry.

It appears then that external trade will raise the productivity of (hence the demand for) the more plentiful production factor in each country. *A*'s relatively plentiful capital and *B*'s relatively plentiful labor are more useful and more in demand if such trade exists.

The effect of this trade upon factor prices is to raise interest relative to wages in *A* and to raise wages relative to interest in *B*. In other words, the original disparity between relative returns of the two factors in the two countries is reduced by trade just as it might have been reduced by labor or capital migration.

Even land, despite its immobility, participates in this indirect equalization of factor prices through trade. Whichever country has the relatively more abundant supply of land (as measured by low rents in relation to the prices of the other factors) will find it profitable to specialize in the more extensive types of production. The freer the trade the further this specialization can go. This means a greater demand for land in the low-rent country and a tendency to push rents up. At the same time, trade permits the other country to curtail its extensive lines of production and concentrate on those requiring less space; this allows rents to fall relative to other factor prices.

Commodity movements and factor movements, then, are somewhat substitutable for each other. Differentials in wages, interest, profits, or rent are reduced by the exchange of products on the basis of production-cost differentials.

This means that if a political boundary impedes migration of capital, enterprise, and labor, the relative production costs of different types of goods on the two sides of the boundary are kept further out of line, so that the possible gains from exchange of goods across the boundary are increased. In other words, if factor migration is prevented, there is more of an economic incentive to use its substitute, trade.

Conversely, of course, a trade barrier is likely to increase the disparity of factor prices on the two sides of the border and to increase the incentives to migration of capital, enterprise, and labor.

If a reduction in this inequality be accepted as a criterion of over-all efficiency or sound policy—as it quite generally is in domestic location—then it may be laid down as a general principle that a heightening of either sort of barrier (trade or factor) increases the need for a reduction of the other sort. For instance, if a nonindustrial country that is relatively short of capital adopts a policy of protective tariffs on manufactures, designed to build up domestic manufacturing industry, its needs for capital become all the greater and can logically be relieved by a reduction in the barriers impeding inflow of foreign capital. Again, if a country erects barriers against immigration, a logical complement to this policy is the freer admission of products of cheap-labor industries in other countries. Furthermore, an area of population pressure may raise its real wage level by encouraging either emigration or the exchange of exports embodying mainly labor for imports embodying mainly other factors.

But here we begin to depart from the realm of strictly economic criteria. A particular policy or type of barrier may increase the returns to one factor in a given country, say labor, but at the same time reduce the returns to another factor, say land. A policy designed to maximize the income per wage earner will not be the same as a policy designed to maximize the income per dollar of investment or per acre of land. There are no a priori grounds for determining the desirability of either course; the ultimate welfare of the country in question, to say nothing of that of the world as a whole, is weighed in terms of social values.

13·3   Exchange between Different Monetary Systems

We must now inquire if significant locational effects arise from the fact that boundaries between nations are also generally boundaries between different monetary systems. In order to attack that question, however, we must first look a little more closely into the part played by money payment balances between different areas under a single monetary system, e.g., between Ohio and Kentucky or between a city and its rural "umland."

Any area that is not completely self-sufficient exchanges products and services with the outside world. For its "exports," its inhabitants receive claims to payment from individuals and firms elsewhere; on the other hand, its "imports" must be paid for by remittances to other areas. The banking system provides a means of offsetting these inward and outward payments against each other and avoiding the constant crosshauling of currency that would otherwise be necessary. In a farmers' market town, for example, the proprietor of the local grain elevator, as an "exporter," receives credits for the sale of grain in outside markets. He leaves these as a balance in a local bank and signs over some of them from time to time to local grain growers. They, in turn, use these funds to buy supplies from a local retailer, who as "importer" uses these credits to pay outsiders for the merchandise he buys. The net external clearing balance of the local banks indicates whether the inward or the outward payments total is larger in any given period.

When an area begins to export, say, an increased amount of some one product, e.g., a newly discovered mineral or the product of an improved manufacturing process, it receives increased payments from other areas. Some of this increased income will be spent outside, thus increasing imports and directly tending to bring the external accounts back into balance. A considerable part, however, is spent locally.[6] This has a less direct effect in the

---

[6] The "local multiplier" discussed in Section 9·3 measures the total increase in local incomes in relation to the initial added inflow of funds.

same direction. The increased local expenditures mean more demand for transported materials and imperfectly mobile production factors; rents, wages, living costs, and materials prices tend to rise, and through the far-reaching local interdependence of prices the whole structure of prices in the area is pushed up along with the level of income and expenditure. This means both an increased market for imports and a relative cost handicap for exports, both of which lead to eventual reversal of the temporary excess of incoming money payments.

Meanwhile, opposite reactions have been occurring in competing areas where the original shift meant a shortage of inpayments: their incomes and price levels having fallen, these areas are in a position to export more and import less. Thus the flow of payments, impinging on imperfectly mobile supplies of production factors, produces reactions that tend to stabilize the payment balances between areas. An initial excess of exports produces effects that ultimately discourage exports and stimulate imports.

If factors of production were completely immobile between areas, the whole cycle of adjustment would merely mean some shifts of factors to different uses in each area and offsetting "migrations" of different industries in opposite directions. In each area, increased employment in the stimulated industries would be just offset by reduced employment in other industries from which the stimulated ones had bid away part of the inelastic supply of capital, land, enterprise, and labor.

The discussion of "locational leverage" in Section 9·3 more realistically assumed some mobility of production factors between areas. In that case the area experiencing the initial increase in income is likely to arrive at the new equilibrium position with increased aggregate productive capacity. Growth in the stimulated industries will have more than offset the decline in industries adversely affected by the change in circumstances.

Permanent investments of personal or business capital are, of course, quite different in character from the short-run fluctuations of credit accounts which help to clear the day-to-day balance of payments. The long-term investor has in mind not so much the recovery of his principal as the establishment of a permanent source of income. Long-term investment may even take the form of an actual transfer of the owner of the productive factor; *i.e.*, the capitalist, enterpriser, or worker may migrate to the new area and enjoy the fruits of his investment or effort there as he becomes a part of the area's economic structure. The balance of payments of such an area would include an inward item of capital flow representing property and funds brought in by "immigrant" investors, enterprisers, or employees.

How is all this altered when a national boundary intervenes? Such boundaries generally require conversion of all payments from one monetary system into another. The basic equilibratory tendencies already mentioned are still present under these circumstances,[7] but the situation is less simple.

The processes of adjustment are likely to include an additional variable: fluctuations in the exchange rate. If so, speculation on future movements of such rates enters the picture with results possibly fatal to stability.

A more fundamental consideration is that each monetary system is controlled by a separate authority which can manipulate money supply, interest rates, prices, foreign investment, the volume and kind of imports and exports, and the exchange rate, all with an eye presumably to the maximization and stabilization of income in its own economy rather than internationally. What is always to be feared, of course, is that the immediately conflicting interests and policies of different countries will force a resort to further restrictions of trade and exchange so that the basic tendencies toward equilibrium are thoroughly submerged and much of the possible gain of international specialization and orderly development is lost.

All this adds up essentially to a restriction on the international mobility of long-term investment. Within the sphere of a single monetary system, a region with an "excess of imports" may continue on that basis for a long time by gradually mortgaging itself

---

[7] For a discussion of the effects of different currency standards and exchange arrangements, gold standards, managed currencies, etc., on the speed and character of trade adjustments, see August Lösch, "The Economics of Location," pp. 276–300, Yale University Press, 1954.

to outsiders or by depleting its capital. A considerable portion of the farm assets of some Middle Western states passed into the hands of Eastern financial institutions in the depression of the 1930's, for example. The domestic mobility of investment is encouraged by confidence that no new barriers to retransfer of funds will be imposed by the government and by the absence of any uncertainties about exchange rates. In the Victorian free-exchange era, international investment was nearly as uninhibited. But in latter day international investment, a risk premium reflecting greater sacrifice of liquidity and a wider range of uncertainties discourages the long-term commitment of funds both by *rentiers* and by "direct" investors who expect to control their investment. International participation in the development of backward areas, with the all-round benefits that this brings, is thus discouraged.

It remains to be seen how far this picture will be modified by the operations of the International Monetary Fund and Bank and the International Trade Organization.

13·4　*Boundaries as Hindrances to Coordinated Development and Administration*

The relation of one land use to others in the same vicinity is often so close as to call for some coordinated resource development and administration. In the metropolitan complex of land uses, for example, there is such close interrelation of advantages that any control of one use is certain to have effects on others as well. Exclusion of factories from certain neighborhoods will drive them to others and affect residential and other property value there; relief of downtown congestion by street or transit improvements alters the relative advantages of outlying locations; the location of a new "farmers' market" is of interest to farmers and urban buyers alike.

When political boundaries (municipal, county, state, or even national) cut through such a metropolitan area, efficient administration of functions covering the whole area is obviously much harder to secure. In some cases a solution has been sought in terms of a superimposed metropolitan authority, *e.g.*, the Port of New York Authority or the Boston Metropolitan District Commission, to which the various local governments delegate powers in specified fields. In other cases an attempt has been made to enlarge city boundaries and to combine city and county administration so as to encompass the area of the major problems. It is fair to say, however, that no generally adequate solution of the problem of metropolitan administration has been reached. The rapid areal expansion of metropolitan settlement in recent decades and the increasing scope of public responsibility have made this boundary problem increasingly acute.

Attention has already been invited in Sections 9·4, 10·2, and 11·12 to the rapid extension of areas of urban-suburban settlement, which have generally overrun municipal boundaries. "Overleaped" might be a more accurate term, since there is frequently a clustering of settlement just outside the city limits while land just inside is still vacant on account of higher taxes or building restrictions.[8]

Another important case of the cutting of natural areas of development and administration by political boundaries occurs in connection with the control of water resources for power, irrigation, navigation, flood control, fisheries, and other uses. Major watersheds are large areas. Where they extend into two or more states or countries, or where the "natural" market area for the power or irrigation water would in the absence of restrictions extend over a border, a host of suspicions and jealousies are usually added to the difficulties and delays involved in the extra for-

---

[8] An interesting recent study in this field is Walter Firey, Social Aspects to Land Use Planning in the Country-city Fringe: The Case of Flint, Michigan, *Michigan State College Agricultural Experiment Station Special Bulletin* 339, East Lansing, Mich., June, 1946. This study is not unique but is cited as a sample from a voluminous literature to which sociologists, political scientists, planners, economists, geographers, and other specialists have contributed.

A striking example of the clustering of settlement just outside city boundaries occurs along Eight Mile Road, a section of the northern boundary of Detroit. An almost solid front of small new factories, backed by residence development, occupies the north side; on the south side, within the city of Detroit, there is scarcely a building of any kind to be seen.

malities of coordinating different authorities. The Hoover Dam development on the Colorado River was held up for years by interstate disputes over water rights, and similar conflicts still block the comprehensive development of the water resources of the Missouri. The St. Lawrence navigation and power project has been the subject of negotiations between the United States and Canada for more than three-quarters of a century. Coordinated development of the resources of the Danube Valley, which could bring backward southeastern Europe into the march of economic progress, is still a dream. Russian domination over a major part of the stream's length removes one previous obstacle but appears to create others.[9]

Such complications are an important reason—though not the only reason—why political geographers disapprove of rivers as boundaries. Boundaries do least damage when they coincide with watershed development limits and with the limits of natural market and supply areas.[10]

SUMMARY

Any political boundary serves as a barrier to the migration of labor, capital, and enterprise. In the case of international frontiers, the inevitable obstacles of different laws, customs, and language are especially great and most likely to be reinforced by deliberate restrictions upon factor migration.

The effect of reducing factor mobility is to accentuate differences in the relative availability of production factors in different jurisdictions and thus to increase the economic incentives to trade. Trade developed on the basis of such processing-cost differentials has the effect of utilizing production factors where they are relatively cheapest and partially equalizing their returns in different places. Such trade thus serves as a partial substitute for migration of factors. Conversely, barriers to trade increase the economic incentive to factor migration.

[9] *Cf.* George Kiss, TVA on the Danube?, *Geographical Review*, vol. XXXVII, No. 2, 1947, pp. 274–302.

[10] For a nontechnical discussion of desirable and undesirable boundary features, see Roderick Peattie, "Look to the Frontiers," Harper & Brothers, New York, 1944.

International boundaries usually require conversion of payments from one currency medium to another. Independent national currency policies introduce additional risk and lead to general restriction of international investment.

All types of boundaries interfere with effective development and administration of land use when they divide areas (such as metropolitan communities or river basins) in which local economic interrelations are especially important.

Part Four

Locational Objectives and Public Policy

CHAPTER 14

The Sphere of Public Responsibility and Control

UP TO THIS POINT we have considered the locations of enterprises, industries, and populations primarily as determined by the decisions of the individual persons or firms involved, acting in their own interests as they see them. It is evident, however, that these decisions themselves are made in a framework of conditions established in part by the decisions of public administrators. In the chapters on the effects of political boundaries, certain aspects of the locational significance of public action have already come to light. But that is only a small part of the story. Almost any conceivable action by government, however dissociated it may be from any conscious policy aimed at affecting locations, does, in fact, influence the geographic pattern of locational advantages. This will be made plain in the next chapter by consideration of such fields of governmental action as fiscal operations; control of transport, communications, and trade; control of the prices and use of production factors; promotion of technical progress; and control of commodity prices and pricing policies. The present chapter is concerned with the scope and aims of locational policy in general and its proper timing and direction.

14·1 Increasing Importance of Conscious Locational Policy

The power of public control over location is rapidly increasing. Governments assume jurisdiction over a larger part of economic life, and their budgets are larger relative to aggregate private incomes and expenditures. For some types of activities, moreover, the enhanced mobility of goods and production factors reduces the importance of "natural" locational advantages and gives wider scope for locational choice.[1]

Not only is the influence of government upon location growing, but so also is the influence of location upon government. Public authorities have an ever-growing stake in the locational pattern in the form of fixed investments and commitments which lose some of their value if locational changes take an unexpected turn. In addition to public investments in buildings and other fixed structures, there is the public responsibility for relief of local unemployment and distress brought about by locational maladjustments. This is a responsibility increasingly recognized and assumed by the central governments of most countries. Since the taxpayers of the country as a whole defray more and more of the costs of local unemployment, it is only logical that these taxpayers and their government should take a greater interest in minimizing locational maladjustment.

Although governments have a large stake in the results of locational development, great power to influence that development, and a correspondingly heavy responsibility for influencing it in socially desirable directions, few governments have ever followed any coherent policy in regard to location. Even in the international sphere, where the influence of a tariff or an export subsidy is fairly simple and obvious, policy has often been the aimless resultant of pressures of special interests urging the protection of this or that industry or the development of this or that local resource. It is not statesmanship on a truly national level, to say nothing of a world level. In the domestic sphere matters are more complicated and clear directions of policy quite generally lacking.

Usually the locational effect of public action upon location has come as an unexpected by-product of policies devoted to other ends. Even when various policies have been undertaken with a strictly locational aim in view, e.g., the encouragement of settle-

[1] It would seem that recent trends of technical progress, particularly in chemistry, often enlarge the locational alternatives by widening the range of alternative materials and processes available for filling a specific need. Thus, the development of synthetics made from common and widespread materials has broken down the former exclusive advantages of areas producing natural nitrates, rubber, liquid fuels, silk, and quinine, to mention only a few examples.

ment in an area by provision of cheaper transportation, there has all too often been an aimless conflict of diverse policies of different individual government agencies.

14·2   Basic Aims of Locational Policy

There is no single ultimate criterion of the desirability of an economic policy, be it locational or other. Few policies have unmixed effects for good or evil—the usual result of any action by public authorities is to aid some parties or areas at the expense of others. In order to measure the over-all benefit or detriment, we should have to set off the individual gains and losses against each other and strike a balance. In this sphere, however, arithmetic commands little confidence, for there is no unit in which to compare the satisfactions of different persons. Only where there is a clear preponderance of benefits over injuries will a socially minded consensus call a policy "good." If a project entails certain damages or costs that can be compensated with funds levied from the beneficiaries, and if the assessments and compensations can be so arranged that all concerned feel themselves better off than before, the project would appear sound. With locational policies, however, it particularly often happens that costs cannot be directly offset against benefits because so many of the costs as well as the benefits are indirect.[2] Some locational policies, then, will be accepted as sound and desirable under one concept of the social good, while by a different set of ultimate values they would be rejected.

As a starting point, there are some generally accepted ultimate social aims. Nearly everyone favors the full and continuous use of production factors, good all-round living and working conditions, individual economic security, variety of individual economic opportunity, national solidarity, security and power, and rapid economic progress. Unfortunately it is also clear that we cannot head full speed for all these goals at the same time but

[2] For a discussion of the problems of assessment of such gains and losses see the British Ministry of Works and Planning, "Final Report of the Expert Committee on Compensation and Betterment" (known as the "Uthwatt Report"). Cmd. 6386, His Majesty's Stationery Office, London, 1942.

must compromise. Differences in the evaluation of specific locational policies mean that communities and nations attach different priority to the indicated aims.

Locational controls can be directed either toward reducing frictions and lags in the process of locational adjustment or toward improving the long-run distribution of employment and population. In the former case the main goal is the reduction of individual insecurity and waste of productive resources; in the latter case the goal is to provide for a locational pattern conducive to rapid technical progress and national security and capable of quasi-automatic adjustment to necessary change. More detailed attention will be given to these various lines of attack in later chapters.

14·3 Timing of Locational Policy Measures

The effectiveness of location-control measures depends to a large extent on the phase of the business cycle in which they are applied. Some such measures make sense only in periods of increasing employment and active capital investment; others are suited to the depression phase. The proper timing of controls, then, is a vital aspect of locational policy and planning.

It has already been pointed out that "migrations of industry" involve not so much the actual moving of equipment as differential rates of new investment in different areas. During depressions the location of facilities "marks time." [3] Long-range measures aimed at a better distribution of employment opportunities in private business, then, will be effective only at times when much new private investment is going forward.

On the other hand, if a program of countercyclical public works is followed, the government's views on desirable trends in

---

[3] The location patterns of *production and employment* in individual industries are, of course, shifting all the time. There is some evidence, however, that such shifts during depression periods are in directions opposite to or at least different from the long-run location trend of the industry; they are, so to speak, eddies in the stream. For a discussion of cyclical and secular changes in the relative advantages of small and large firms, an important aspect of this problem, see Joseph Steindl, "Small and Big Business," Oxford Institute of Statistics, Monograph No. 1, Oxford University Press, New York, 1945.

the location of *public* facilities will be translated into action mainly in the depression phases of the cycle when such works are being built. Some of the public-works construction, of course, will help to locate the private investment of the succeeding boom period. Water-power developments and improvements in transport and terminal facilities are especially significant in this connection.

Human migration goes on all the time but varies greatly in character and direction in boom and depression periods. The long-run migration trend in all progressive economies is from farm to city,[4] but this flow is not steady. It varies mainly according to the state of urban employment, reaching a maximum in periods of peak industrial activity. Unemployment (primarily an urban phenomenon) checks cityward migration and if severe enough may even lead to a temporary retreat to the land, as was the case in the United States in 1932.[5]

Locational policies that involve the shaping of future population distribution by guiding the flow of migration, then, are most effective in periods of high or at least increasing employment, when the migrant's risks are at a minimum and when the distribution of employment opportunities is staking out lines of future evolution. Migration in depression periods is essentially a search for temporary havens, characteristically found in marginal and submarginal farm areas. A policy that might seek to direct migration to areas offering the most favorable long-term agricultural prospects would overlook the fact that development of such areas requires settlers with capital, training, and the intention of making a career out of farming.[6]

---

[4] This trend is traceable to two factors, as previously indicated: the higher reproduction rates of rural populations and the fact that as per capita real incomes rise, the demand for farm products increases more slowly than that for urban products. Further determinants not discussed here include the relative gain in man-hour productivity in rural and urban production and the response of demand to changes in the price relation between rural and urban products. See T. W. Schultz, "Agriculture in an Unstable Economy," Chap. III, McGraw-Hill Book Company, Inc., New York, 1945.

[5] *Cf.* Table 7·2.

[6] See Carter Goodrich and others, "Migration and Economic Opportunity," Part Two, University of Pennsylvania Press, Philadelphia, 1936.

The conclusion must be that public control of location will produce results mainly during periods of business prosperity. Depression periods are appropriate for implementing such policies through countercyclical public works as well as for frankly palliative measures to offset depression maladjustments.

14·4 Selection of Industries for Purposes of Locational Policy

Locational policy should be carefully selective in its application to different industries. No locational policy can be intelligently implemented unless its effects on different types of industry are taken into account in advance. Different industries vary widely in their locational responsiveness to possible controls and in the leverage they exert by passing on the effects of locational change to still other industries. If the aim of a policy is to increase or stabilize employment in a specific area, concentration of effort on a carefully chosen group of industries may be essential to success.

Certain types of mining, agriculture, and material-oriented manufactures, especially those with great economies of scale or concentration, offer little latitude for choice or control of their geographic patterns without excessive cost. At the other extreme, such "residentiary" activities as retail trade and local services quasi-automatically follow shifts in the distribution of population and income as a whole and are likewise not good points of attack. On the same basis one may eliminate any industry that is locationally "ancillary," i.e., closely dependent on another. On the other hand, industries with a high proportion of pay-roll to total costs give a relatively large leverage effect on consumer incomes and hence on residentiary industries in their vicinity. Growing industries are obviously better objects of a policy of locational shift than are declining industries.[7]

[7] Cf. Section 3·5. A useful classification of industries according to determining locational factor and character of markets is presented by G. C. Means and G. W. Knott in National Resources Committee, "The Structure of the American Economy," Part I, Chap. IV and Appendix 8, Government Printing Office, Washington, 1939.

The above considerations lead to the conclusion that the most promising objects of attention for locational policy in general are likely to be rapidly growing small- or medium-scale manufacturing industries of a nonresidentiary and nonancillary character which employ a good deal of not too highly specialized labor.[8] For specific lines of policy, such as diversification, the field is further narrowed by considerations peculiar to the specific objective. For instance, for a diversification program in a particular community it is necessary first to determine the local profit prospects of specific industries of the types indicated. Then their contribution to the economic stability or other expected benefits not reflected in this profit calculation must be assessed to determine the extent to which public control is necessary or desirable.

14·5 Examples of Selective Promotion Plans

Two recent plans for selective community industrial promotion may be cited by way of illustration:

WORCESTER, ENGLAND. A planning survey made for the City Council by a research team from the University of Birmingham

(cf. also the maps in Appendix 15). A broad breakdown into occupational categories called "Located close to resources," "Located close to consumer," and "Relatively foot-loose" is also shown (op. cit., Table I, p. 36). It is the "Relatively foot-loose" category which in general affords the best points for public policy to influence the development of the over-all locational pattern.

8 This is only a sweeping generalization and fails to take into account cases such as tourist recreational development, often highly responsive to public stimulus in areas not suited to much else. The importance of land ownership and stream control is a special factor in this instance.

The manufacture of the cheaper grades of clothing and especially shoes has figured very largely in industrial promotions by small towns without much previous industrial experience. The relevant characteristics of this type of industry seem to be small scale of operations, low capital requirements (particularly true of the shoe industry, which leases most of its machinery), use of a large proportion of unskilled and female labor, adaptability to almost any kind of building, rapid turnover of firms, and a high ratio of labor cost to total cost (see also Section 11·6). For a recent and unusually thorough study of local industrial promotion see W. D. Knight, "Subsidization of Industry in Forty Selected Cities in Wisconsin, 1930–1946," Wisconsin Commerce Series, vol. I, No. 2, University of Wisconsin, Madison, Wis., 1947.

presented eight tests of suitability to be applied to possible new industries to be encouraged in Worcester: [9]

a. Employment of an especially large percentage of women (to help absorb the local surplus of female labor)

b. Employment of an especially small percentage of juveniles (juvenile labor being scarce in the Worcester area)

c. Good prospects of long-run growth, based on prewar experience and an appraisal of future trends

d. Cyclical stability of employment

e. Peak seasonal employment in the winter rather than the summer months (to offset the existing fluctuation in total local employment)

f. No nuisance features such as smoke or smell which might jeopardize the health and recreational resort business of the area

g. Assistance to existing local industries by furnishing an improved market for their products or an improved source of materials or supplies

h. Present concentration of the industry in question in Greater London (since British national policy is to reduce concentration in London)

It is worth noting that three of these criteria (long-run growth prospects, cyclical stability, and absence of nuisance features) would be applicable in almost any community, and one other (concentration in London) is presumably applicable at present in any small or moderate-sized British community. The remaining four criteria are tailored to Worcester's labor market and business pattern.

CINCINNATI. A somewhat similar problem was attacked by the Cincinnati Planning Commission in a recent "master plan" study.[10] Industries were rated as to suitability for a selective promotion program according to the following criteria:

[9] Janet Glaisyer, Tom Brennan, Walter Ritchie, and P. Sargant Florence, "County Town," pp. 84–87, John Murray, London, 1946.

[10] City Planning Commission of Cincinnati, "The Economy of the Cincinnati Metropolitan Area," pp. 64–69 and Appendix J, pp. 98–102, Cincinnati, 1946. A

a. High median annual wages or salaries
b. High proportion of employees receiving $2,500 or more per year
c. Seasonal stability
d. Cyclical stability
e. Employment of a high proportion of skilled workers
f. Employment of a high proportion of older workers
g. Employment of a high proportion of women
h. Employment of a high proportion of Negroes

The first four of the criteria listed are applicable in most communities, while the last four are designed for the specific local needs of Cincinnati. Rankings of major business activity groups according to the four generally applicable criteria (a to d) are as follows: [11]

Activity Group	Rating
1. Communication	11
2. Finance, insurance, and real estate	11
3. Utilities	11
4. Government	10
5. Wholesale trade	8
6. Transportation	6
7. Amusement, recreation, and related services	5
8. Manufacturing	5
9. Professional and related services	5
10. Business and repair services	4
11. Agriculture, forestry, and fishery	3
12. Personal services	3
13. Retail trade	3
14. Mining	2
15. Construction	1

The low rating of manufacturing as a group is noteworthy, in view of the tendency of local promotional groups to think of new factories as the economic panacea. It must also be recognized,

condensed discussion is given in Victor Roterus, Suitability of Economic Activities in Relation to the Local Economy, *Journal of the American Institute of Planners,* vol. XIII, No. 1, Winter, 1947, pp. 29–31.

[11] On each criterion each industry was assigned a rating ranging from zero to 3, and the ratings were added to give a total numerical score. The maximum score on the basis of four criteria was 12 points. In addition to the 15 major business activity groups listed above, 109 specific lines of business were rated with respect to all eight of the criteria.

however, that much of the employment in the groups rated more highly is not really "foot-loose" enough to be a good object of promotional effort.

SUMMARY

Governments have increasing power over location and increasing responsibilities for the use of their controls to reduce the wastes of locational maladjustment and to establish patterns of industry and population conducive to both security and progress. Public policy and planning must take into account the fact that the evolution of locational patterns proceeds mainly during cyclical upswings and that some industries are much more responsive to public locational control than others.

CHAPTER 15

The Tools of Public Policy[1]

A TOTALITARIAN GOVERNMENT can use all methods, military as well as economic, to accomplish its ends directly. For democratic governments there are definite limitations. Only to a moderate degree can the location of economic activities and the distribution of population be directly shaped by governmental activities. Governmental establishments are only one part of the total pattern, and relatively few governmental establishments are of a sort that can be freely located or relocated in pursuit of a chosen locational policy.

Apart from public institutions, the actual decision as to locations rests in the hands of the business executive. The factors of prospective profit which sway his decision, however, are inevitably influenced by the actions of public authorities, whether or not the latter proceed upon the basis of any clearly defined locational policy. It is this indirect (and frequently unintentional and aimless) determination of the conditions under which private business makes its decisions that constitutes the chief sphere of public locational policy in the United States.

The present chapter is devoted to a brief survey of the ways in which public authorities can and sometimes do influence location. All these methods can be consciously applied as tools of locational policy. It will be helpful to keep in mind the fact that the intentional influencing of location may involve any of four types of immediate objective with reference to the territory over which the governmental unit in question has jurisdiction:

a. Increasing the total productive activity or total income of the area. Indiscriminate promotional campaigns to "bring in pay rolls" have this simple objective.

[1] A somewhat more detailed treatment of this topic will be found in National Resources Planning Board, "Industrial Location and National Resources," Chap. 19, Governmental and Community Influences, by H. M. Oliver, Jr., and M. L. Forth, Government Printing Office, Washington, 1943.

b. Producing a more desirable combination of activities in the area. An example of this is the selective encouragement of new industries which will employ previously underemployed groups of the labor force.

c. Improvement of spatial arrangements within the area. Metropolitan zoning plans belong in this category.

d. Improving the processes of locational selection and adjustment to locational change. Provision of information about sites and job opportunities serves this function.

15·1 *Influence of Taxes and Public Expenditures*

A very considerable portion of incomes passes through public treasuries and is subject to redistribution in ways that affect the pattern of locational advantages for consumers and producers. In 1860 taxes in the United States accounted for $1 in every $25 of income; in 1945, for $1 in every $3.[2] Local governments rely almost exclusively on the general property tax, while the principal sources of state revenue are gasoline and motor vehicle, sales, and income taxes, and the Federal government relies most heavily on income and excise taxes.[3]

The process of public collection and expenditure of funds acts directly on the relative expendable incomes of people in different areas, for the geographical incidence of a tax or expenditure is generally uneven. For instance, a progressive income tax falls more heavily on the more prosperous areas, while a gasoline tax falls more heavily on those areas with many automobiles and with long distances of transport. An oleomargarine tax helps the dairy regions. A program of building up coast defenses adds to the incomes of the coastal regions and also those of the regions manufacturing the necessary armaments and materials. Thus governments, being frequently the largest "businesses" in their territories, cannot avoid exerting an important direct effect on the

[2] S. E. Harris, New England's Decline in the American Economy, *Harvard Business Review,* vol. XXV, No. 3, Spring, 1947, p. 363.

[3] Further details are presented in Bureau of the Census, "Financing Federal, State, and Local Governments: 1941," State and Local Government Special Study No. 20, Washington, September, 1942 (processed).

relative incomes of different areas and thus upon the locations of all market-oriented industries.

Governments must also decide on the location of new or expanded public facilities and in this way play a direct part in shaping the geographic pattern of capital investment and income. Such important cities as Madrid, Washington, and Leningrad trace their growth to arbitrary selection of an all but unpopulated spot as the site for a new national capital. Had the choice been otherwise, those sites might not have cities on them today. On a smaller scale, public authorities affect the geographic pattern every time they locate a new arsenal, warehouse, mint, hospital, post office, or other public establishment.

All levels of government allocate expenditures in ways that bear no close relation to the geographic pattern of tax collections and thereby redistribute large amounts of income among localities.[4]

This redistribution directly affects the locational preferences of those who bear the taxes or receive the payments. Conspicuous evidence of the results appears in the concentration of corporation offices in Delaware, the concentration of business establishments just outside the municipal limits of many cities, and the oft-voiced threat of the New York Stock Exchange to flee across the Hudson. The locational effect of a tax depends not only on the rate but also on the form of tax used. If there were such a thing as a tax on pure "land" in the sense of immobile, permanent, and non-reproducible property, it would have no locational effect at all. The general-property tax in practice applies to values based largely on decisions to maintain or develop structures and other improvements, and high property-tax rates will discourage such maintenance and development. An income tax is not usually considered a "cost" in quite the same sense as a property, processing, or license tax; yet it cuts into returns that are a necessary in-

---

[4] This is illustrated by a tabulation prepared by the Social Security Board in 1940, comparing the regional breakdown of Federal tax collections and Federal aid expenditures. The Middle Atlantic states, for example, paid 32 per cent of the taxes and received only 21 per cent of the Federal aid, while the East South Central states paid 3 per cent of the taxes and received 6 per cent of the Federal aid. This is, of course, not necessarily inequitable. National Resources Planning Board, *op. cit.*, p. 322.

centive to enterprise, and can affect the location of business ventures if the rates are high.

Even without geographic differentials in rates, taxes would have an influence on the relative advantages of different production locations. A tax that becomes a fixed cost regardless of rate of output, *e.g.*, a general property tax, has about the same effect as a higher interest rate: it penalizes localities where plant and equipment are less fully utilized and sharpens the producer's incentive to find a location where less capital investment is required per unit of output. Thus a combination of tight restrictions on overtime work, night work, and speed-up procedures with a large degree of reliance on general property taxes for local revenues can be doubly burdensome to industry. General property taxes are likewise a threat to solvency in periods of poor business and may contribute to a cumulative weakening of a producer's competitive position.[5]

Ingenious attempts have been made to measure the taxpaying capacity of counties and states and the extent to which this capacity is exploited by current taxes. One important purpose is to investigate the possibility of scientifically allocating Federal grants to states and state grants to local governments in accordance with need and "ability to pay." [6] The effects of taxes and aids on the location of production, however, are not necessarily closely related to such measures. A particular tax may take only a very small percentage of "capacity" in the sense of wealth or income, yet it may be decisive in precipitating the migration of an industry. Analysis of the probable locational effects of any given fiscal policy must weigh the factors of geographic competition in the industries in question.

[5] An interesting and relevant discussion of the burdensomeness of the Massachusetts state and local tax structure is to be found in Harris, *op. cit.*, pp. 364–365. In 1938 to 1939, 64.5 per cent of all state and local revenues in Massachusetts were raised by the general property tax. In ratio of property taxes to property values in 1938 to 1939, Massachusetts was exceeded only by Maine and Idaho, while Virginia, Georgia, and West Virginia showed the lowest ratios. Social Security Board, Bureau of Research and Statistics, "The Measurement of State and Local Tax Effort," Bureau Memorandum No. 58, Table 7, p. 34, Washington, 1944 (processed).

[6] See, for example, Social Security Board, *op. cit.*, and also "Measurement of Variations in State Economic and Fiscal Capacity," Bureau Memorandum No. 50, Washington, 1943.

15·2 *Influence on Transfer Costs and Services*

Public authorities have a powerful influence on location through their control of transfer costs. This control, in turn, rests on the role played by such authorities in the construction, subsidy, taxation, and regulation of carriers and means of communication.

Facilities for water, road, and air transport have been provided in most places at public expense. Although American railroads and communication systems have been privately built for the most part, government authorization has been necessary for the establishment of routes, and the early construction of our railroad net was made possible by large land grants and other subsidies.[7]

Public authorities have been largely responsible for the basic decisions about the layout of routes and the speed of development of our principal means of transport and communication. The levels of rates and the relative part played by different competing means of transfer have been influenced by tax policies; *e.g.,* railroads have complained that highway and waterway transport are being favored in this regard at the expense of the railroads.

Public authorities regulate rates and service standards directly and thus help to determine the level and the structure of transfer costs and the location of all kinds of economic activities. The relative rates on different classes of traffic, on different lengths of haul, and on different sizes of shipment are locationally significant in ways already pointed out in Chaps. 3 and 4, and all these relationships are subject to public control. The recent decision of the Interstate Commerce Commission to work toward uniformity of railroad freight classifications and class-rate levels in the various rate territories of the United States involves a major alteration of the rate structure and of the conditions of interregional competition.

National and state governments also shape the pattern of transfer costs by setting up trade barriers at their borders, generally

---

[7] See, for example, the reports of the Federal Coordinator of Transportation, "Public Aids to Transportation," 1938, and National Resources Planning Board, "Transportation and National Policy," 1942; also the reports of the Board of Investigation and Research, Transportation Act of 1940, 79th Congress, 1st Session, Senate Documents Nos. 78*ff.*

in order to protect home industry from outside competition. The methods used and their effects have already been discussed in Chap. 12.

15·3 Influence on Mobility of Capital

In two important ways, governments increase the mobility of investment capital and thus facilitate the development of industry in places where other considerations are favorable. Coordination and support of a national credit system and standardization and control of corporate financing procedures remove some of the obstacles to investment in previously undeveloped and remote areas. Regional and local differences in interest rates have notably diminished in the United States by the Federal Reserve banking system and the national systems of insurance of bank deposits and real-estate mortgages.

A somewhat similar effect can be ascribed to the publication of a wide variety of marketing and business statistics by Federal and state Departments of Commerce, Labor, and Agriculture. The availability of such data makes it possible for private investors to locate somewhat less blindly and reduces the locational disadvantage of areas that are relatively unfamiliar.

Promotional activity is practiced by all levels of government to attract private investment. Tangible assistance to incoming industry, however, usually involves either the provision of relevant information or some sort of subsidy.

Subsidies to new industry are practiced by governments at all levels. The British government and the Bank of England supported private investment in certain chronically depressed areas during the 1930's, with the avowed policy of diverting more industry into those areas and away from the relatively prosperous southeast. The Distribution of Industry Act of 1945 [8] empowers the Board of Trade and the Treasury to stimulate industry in what are now restyled "Development Areas" by condemnation of land, erection of buildings, improvement of public services, and loan or gift of public funds. Advance notice of the private con-

[8] This act (8 & 9 Geo. 6, Ch. 36) supplanted the Special Areas Acts of 1934 and 1937.

struction of any considerable new industrial plant or expansion must be given to the Board of Trade.

Our Federal government has no such broad powers, but some states and local governments have gone quite far. The unusual North Dakota constitution, which defines public welfare in terms of the state's "wheat economy," has allowed the state to build and operate such enterprises as grain elevators and flour mills. The Mississippi BAWI Act of 1936 allowed municipalities, with the consent of the state industrial commission, to bond themselves in order to provide buildings for new industries at nominal rent.[9] Tax exemptions and provision of buildings at low cost are standard baits to industry used by American towns and cities.

15·4 *Influence on Wages and Labor Mobility*

Government controls and attitudes in the labor market have important locational effects. Most obvious is the effect of direct control of labor standards (minimum wages, maximum hours, and working conditions) and conditions of labor bargaining, including recognition of unions and the status of mediation and arbitration.

Imposition of any uniform set of labor standards has the initial effect of raising labor costs in substandard areas. From the standpoint of location, Federal labor-standards legislation of recent years has aided the high-wage urban production areas as against the low-wage rural areas and the North as against the South.[10] This holds true not only of minimum wages but also of legisla-

[9] Municipalities could even request permission to operate plants themselves, but none did so during the four years' life of the original BAWI Plan. E. J. Hopkins, "Mississippi's BAWI Plan, An Experiment in Industrial Subsidization," Federal Reserve Bank of Atlanta, 1944. See also (on the revival of BAWI in 1944) R. B. Highsaw, Two Years of the BAWI Program, University of Mississippi, Bureau of Business Research, *Business Bulletin,* vol. 4, No. 6, August, 1946.

[10] Industry codes under the National Industrial Recovery Act of 1933 generally provided for wage differentials with lower minima in the South and in small towns, but the differentials were considerably smaller than those previously current. The Public Contracts (Walsh-Healy) Act of 1936, regulating wages paid under public contracts, specifies local "prevailing" wages as the standard, and this has sometimes been taken to mean local union standards of wages. The Fair Labor Standards Act of 1938 specifically prohibits any geographical differentials in minimum wages established under the act.

tion upholding collective bargaining, recognition of unions, closed shops, maximum hours, and conditions of work, since in all these respects labor's position is generally better in Northern and urban labor markets.

The locational effect described is what seems to happen in the short run. Ultimate effects, however, may be quite different. A rise in lowest bracket wages strengthens the employers' incentive to provide training and to use labor more efficiently and with more capital. It thus fosters an eventual improvement of the labor force in skill as well as physical stamina. Some have even suggested that the day will come when Southern citizens will erect alongside the monument to the boll weevil [11] another monument to the champions of uniform national labor standards.

State and national governments have also aided the equalization of labor opportunity and labor costs in a different and more neutral way. Public operation of employment exchanges, giving a wider dissemination of information about jobs and available man power and some standardization of job specifications, has notably eased the locational and occupational adjustment of labor. Provision of training and educational opportunities also increases mobility. When stress is laid on acquainting all persons with a broad range of basic knowledge and useful skills, the barriers of ignorance, inertia, and unadaptability are reduced and more rapid migration responses occur.

Not all public action, of course, works in the direction of increasing labor mobility. In the administration of relief and public-works employment, local residence requirements have sometimes been laid down that substantially discourage migration. On the international level, deliberate restrictions of migration are characteristic, and encouragements (usually for seasonal labor but sometimes for permanent settlers) play a smaller part.

15·5 Negative Controls on Land Use

Direct public control of private land use is usually negative in character. That is, certain uses are *proscribed* in specified places,

[11] *Cf.* Section 11·9.

without any other uses being specifically *prescribed*. Private interests are left free to discover and develop acceptable alternative uses.

The outstanding example of this kind of control is zoning, as practiced commonly by cities and in a few states by counties. The usual city zoning ordinance restricts inferior types of residence development in better class residential areas, prohibits commercial activities over a wider area, limits industrial plants still more drastically, and restricts certain particularly objectionable activities, *e.g.*, slaughterhouses, to relatively few places. In addition, the height, site coverage, setback, and other features of downtown buildings are limited by building codes.

A major purpose, though not the only purpose, of all these restrictions is to protect the value of certain types of sites, *e.g.*, residential property, from the depreciating influence of other uses that bring objectionable smells, sounds, sights, or traffic with them. Reduction of traffic congestion, in the interests of the whole urban economy, is also an important objective. Finally, economy in the utilization of public services calls for a more orderly parceling-out of different use types than might otherwise occur.

In rural zoning two purposes are uppermost: to discourage misguided agricultural settlement on what is known to be unsuitable land and to concentrate the pattern of settlement in such a way as to reduce public outlay for roads, schools, and other public services. In this type of zoning some areas are barred to agriculture and others to any type of permanent use at all.

Controls akin to zoning, though not usually known by that name, are applied also by state and national governments. In this country an important conservation function is served by the various state and national forests, game preserves, mineral reserves, parks, and monuments. These differ from local-government zoning controls in that the land is publicly owned, being acquired by purchase or tax reversion or simply retained in the original public domain. Quite generally there is a conflict between the immediate interest of a local population in cashing in its resources and the longer run public interest. Public authority, being in principle immortal and also in practice able to borrow at lower interest rates than private parties, is logically the guardian of the long-run interest of the community as a whole.

In addition to protecting users of a later date, land-use controls protect users at other places. In particular, the spread of injury to other areas by wind and water (involving smoke, fumes, wind erosion and deposition, stream pollution, floods, water erosion, and silting) is reduced or prevented by control of farm, forest, and industrial practices.

National governments have used zoning controls to keep vital industries out of areas subject to military attack. For security as well as other reasons, many national governments have been concerned about the heavy concentration of industry and population in their chief metropolitan areas and have had under consideration the restrictive zoning of such areas.[12]

15·6 River-basin Developments

Most governments aid or control the development of natural resources in ways that have a direct bearing upon location. Because of the multiplicity of interests involved, the use of public lands, and the necessity of large-scale and long-range planning, projects of multipurpose stream development are particularly common and logical types of public works. The various uses involved, including irrigation, water power, navigation, flood control, drainage, and fisheries, are in partial conflict with one another, and some compromise is necessary. For example, regularity of hydroelectric power production is best assured by keeping reservoirs full as much of the time as possible, whereas effective flood control calls for keeping them empty as much of the time as possible. The government's decisions on such conflicts, its choice of the particular river basins to be developed, and its allocation of the benefits and costs obviously operate with rather wide latitude for expression of public policy.

When several important uses are involved, the possibilities are

---

[12] The Distribution of Industry Bill as debated in the British parliament in 1945 contained an enabling provision (Clause 9) for this type of control; the clause was stricken out before passage of the bill. The curbing of London's growth is commonly accepted, however, as being British national policy.

especially varied. Someone must then determine how much of the total costs of the dams and other works shall be allocated to power and how much to flood control, irrigation, navigation, or other uses; the decision on this point, which is necessarily somewhat arbitrary, controls the levels of rates on electric power and the other services sold. Then there is the question of whether the costs of navigation improvement should be recovered from the users of the waterway in the form of tolls or should be spread over the whole country in the form of taxes, thus constituting a national subsidy to the region involved. The indirect benefits of cheap transportation are so difficult to trace and evaluate that either of these policies might plausibly be justified in a particular instance.

There is also the question of the structure of electric-power rates. The governmental authority may simply sell the power to the highest private bidder for distribution, or it may attempt to control the retail rates either by undertaking distribution itself or by writing a contract stipulating the rates to be charged. Here again is great latitude. In some cases the energy could all be sold to a few large electrochemical or electrometallurgical plants in the immediate neighborhood of the power site, and the resulting benefit might or might not be passed on to the whole country in the form of lower costs for the resulting chemical or metal products. Alternatively, the electricity may be largely reserved for small-scale industries or for a program of farm electrification in the distribution area.

15·7 Control of Prices and Pricing Practices

Since prices are primary determinants of production and trade, it is natural that control of prices should affect location. A familiar example is governmental support of the prices of farm products by public purchase and storage schemes or by organization or enforcement of output restrictions. The purpose here is to increase the incomes of the producers; in so far as the policy works, the incomes and market potentials of areas specializing in those commodities are likewise increased.

Other types of price control are aimed at keeping down the prices charged by large and well-organized producers with monopoly powers. Not only the incomes of the producing areas but also the terms of supply of the commodity to possible areas of further processing are affected. Thus, a reduction in the price of ingot aluminum may increase or decrease the income of aluminum-producing communities, but it is certain to give a locational advantage to areas specially fitted for aluminum fabrication as against areas making competing products.

Government pressure on discriminatory price systems likewise alters the pattern of locational advantage; *e.g.*, the enforced liberalization of basing-point systems of delivered price quotation has opened up new locations as advantageous steel-fabrication centers. Discouragement of crosshauling practices, on the other hand, may work to the disadvantage of an area hemmed in by competitors and accustomed to sharing their market areas. Obviously these patterns of delivered price are closely related to the structure of freight rates, which is also under public supervision.

15·8 Aids to Technological Advance

In addition to influencing the use of production factors in the ways indicated, governments play a large part in fostering new processes and industries. Systems of patent registration are intended to encourage invention; publicly supported schools, libraries, and laboratories lend further encouragement. The direction of emphasis in these aids can shape the destinies of particular industries and areas. Thus the development of drought-resistant wheat strains made possible the extension of wheat raising to climates previously regarded as impossibly arid; research in new uses for cotton fiber and seeds has already benefited the cotton-producing areas.

Such aids, especially when extended by state or local authorities, are usually for the benefit of industries already established as specialties of the area, but sometimes there is a deliberate effort to mitigate the intensity of specialization by promoting research on the possibilities of new and different types of production suited to the area. A zealous program of crop diversification in south central Brazil, for example, has made cotton, oranges, bananas, and rice important export items.

Public authorities also have an important part to play in publicizing what has been discovered about production and distribution methods and the potentialities of various locations. The publications and field services of the Departments of Agriculture and Commerce, for example, help farmers and other businessmen to exploit the advantages of the locations they have and to choose new locations or market territories more scientifically.

SUMMARY

National, state, and local government authorities can exert a large degree of influence over the amount, kind, and location of industries within their areas of jurisdiction and over the way in which locational selections and adjustments are carried out.

In the process of collecting and spending their funds and locating their own establishments, governments control a substantial share of the geographic allocation of incomes. Public subsidy and location of transfer agencies and control of their rate levels and structures have shaped the whole pattern of transfer costs, while deliberately imposed trade barriers at frontiers have had effects already described in an earlier chapter. Government coordination and support of financial and statistical functions have increased the mobility of capital and enterprise, and various types of subsidy have been used to attract private business investment to specific areas.

In the labor market government action in this country has generally furthered geographic equalization of labor standards and labor costs. Internationally, however, government action is usually invoked to restrict migration.

Negative land-use controls are used to protect related users, to reduce congestion, and in the interests of public-service economy, resources conservation, and military security. Governments have also had to make decisions, with wide latitude for policy, on the allocation of costs and benefits in multiple-use resources developments.

Government control of prices and price practices influences the patterns of incomes and locational advantage.

Publicly supported aids to technological development make new locations possible and improve the utilization and selection of locations.

CHAPTER 16

Policies for Locational Flexibility

THE LAST TWO CHAPTERS showed the extent of public responsibility for locational patterns and adjustments and the principal means by which public policies in regard to location can be implemented. The remainder of this book will be devoted to a consideration of objectives.

The ultimate goals outlined in Chap. 14 [1] can be approached in a number of ways, depending on what we regard as the crucial difficulties to be overcome. If we are concerned mainly with the individual insecurity and social waste involved in locational adjustment and with the danger of the locational pattern's getting out of line with current technical requirements, we may concentrate on easing adjustments by making the economy as flexible as possible. An alternative approach is to foster the kind of pattern that has more inherent balance and stability and requires less violent adjustment of specialized areas and persons. Finally, if we regard the main problem as that of war, locational policies should be keyed into plans for national and world security.

Each of these three main approaches will be taken up in one of the remaining chapters. The present chapter deals with the pursuit of locational flexibility. Two aims are involved: minimizing the wastes and discomforts of transition itself and keeping the locational pattern developing along the lines of maximum productive efficiency.

16·1 Obstacles to "Automatic" Adjustment

In its philosophy this line of policy comes closest to the doctrine of *laissez faire,* or the minimizing of public interference, though in practice considerable public effort may be needed to make it

---

[1] "Full and continuous use of production factors; good all-round living and working conditions; individual economic security; variety of individual economic opportunity; national solidarity, security, and power; and rapid economic progress."

work. Its basis is a large degree of faith in the self-regulating character of economic adjustments in a competitive price economy, with the corollary that the state should merely ease these adjustments rather than deflecting them. The term "lubrication" is best descriptive of the principle of action here envisaged.

Evidences of self-equilibrating location tendencies in the competitive economy are abundant. The bulk of Chaps. 4 to 10 was concerned with the evolution of orderly locational patterns from the self-seeking actions of individual producers. Such automatic responses include, for example, the placing of the production centers of an industry in close relation to points of consumption when distribution costs are important, the migration of enterprises and people to places promising greater rates of return, the allocation of land to the use that can yield the greatest net returns per acre, and the attainment of a compromise between the economies of concentration and those of dispersion in the pattern of an individual industry.

It is equally evident that the adjustment toward equilibrium is halting and imperfect, on account of many kinds of obstacles to perfect competition among individuals and enterprises. The doctrine behind the policy of maximum flexibility holds that the desirable direction in which to exert policy is toward the goal that perfect competition would attain—that the observed defects in the pattern are due either to eradicable elements of monopoly power or to frictional obstacles which are essentially temporary and can be still further reduced by judicious lubrication.

16·2 Improved Information as a Guide for Private Locational Decisions

Among the measures appropriate to such a policy are the compiling and dissemination of information relevant to choice of locations. It was noted in Sections 1·4, 1·6, and 6·6 that individual producers are far from possessing enough knowledge to choose their individual ideal locations or land uses scientifically. Each makes a rough stab at it, in the light of such facts and impressions as he has, and may prosper if he is lucky. Competitive struggle for survival tends to eliminate those who in their ignorance choose poor locations, and in a sense this furnishes a substitute for individual wisdom.

It is, however, a poor substitute. "Nature's method" is wasteful of natural and human resources alike. Imperfections of competition permit some ill-advised locations to persist indefinitely, since only under perfect competition must the individual select the one best location or go bankrupt as the penalty. In any case, trial and error is wasteful because it increases the number of liquidations, adjustments, and new starts in business and involves chronic underutilization of productive capacity throughout the economic system. A larger measure of informed business planning and a smaller turnover of enterprises would be in the interests of economic and social efficiency.

There are many types of locational information that can helpfully be compiled by public authorities or with their assistance and guidance and are helpful particularly to small business. Such data include the locations and specifications of available factory sites; prevailing wage rates and labor supply by localities; potential markets in different areas; relative prices for utility services, fuel, and transportation; and comparative data on the business laws and taxes prevailing in different local jurisdictions. In particular industries such factors as construction cost, climate, quality of water, or various cultural indices of the local population are important to the firm choosing a location.[2]

A great deal of such information is now made available by trade associations, railroads, development companies, and local promotional groups. Such agencies naturally have at heart, however, their own interest rather than that of the general public; their presentations, even if not deliberately distorted, are necessarily incomplete. Biased information may easily be worse than none at all; so there is much to be said for the policy of comprehensive and objective reporting by some branch of the national government itself. The outlay may be many times compensated

---

[2] For an enumeration of the principal types of data relevant to location which are now made available through private and public agencies in this country, see National Resources Planning Board, "Industrial Location and National Resources," Government Printing Office, Washington, 1943, p. 334.

by the increased over-all efficiency resulting from a more logical and more stable locational pattern and a fuller use of resources.[3]

16·3 Encouragement of Labor Mobility

Since one of the principal hindrances to the geographical adjustment of labor supply to demand is ignorance of comparative employment prospects and job requirements, the most direct way of speeding the adjustment is by compiling and making available current information on these questions. Many countries now have well-organized national systems of employment offices which bring men and jobs together. Usually there is a procedure for progressive clearance, whereby an available job is first publicized locally and then in wider and wider areas as necessary until a man is found to fill it.

Even without subsidy, public employment-exchange systems could pay their way and make some contribution to the efficient utilization of man power. It is now almost universally agreed, however, that they merit further development at public expense.[4] Certain other measures that increase labor mobility work less directly and may require relatively greater subsidy.

Public support of education—particularly vocational education —is one important means of subsidizing labor mobility. The trained man has a wider latitude of adaptation to employment opportunities in different areas and thus a greater geographic mobility. Moreover, interoccupational mobility is often a substitute for migration: Labor left unemployed by the closing of one type of plant may be employed by a new industry in the old

[3] Cf. PEP, "Report on the Location of Industry in Great Britain," pp. 219, 221–224, London, 1939. The PEP report suggests three kinds of public informational service relative to location: (a) positive publicity emphasizing the advantages of particular regions for industry or recreation, (b) negative measures in the form of publicity on the undesirability of further development in certain areas, and (c) regular information and advisory services for manufacturers, supplemented by specific publicity on important new factors, such as expected labor shortages, in specific areas.

[4] It is difficult to measure the amount of subsidy actually involved in the operation of public employment offices, since a large part of their operating expenses are incurred in related functions such as unemployment compensation administration.

location rather than by the old type of industry in a new location. The need for migration is greatly lessened if local labor supplies are made more versatile, and this can be accomplished by training. Another important aid to the rapid adjustment of labor to locational change is the discouragement of restrictive residence and seniority requirements for relief assistance or work. When migration automatically involves loss of claim to relief and seniority status, potential migrants may well hang back, even with better jobs in sight elsewhere. A sound encouragement of mobility involves removing such hindrances whenever they result from the selfish pressure of local interests reluctant to share with newcomers.

Finally, migration can be encouraged by direct subsidy. Railroad companies have often encouraged settlers to come to their territory by granting them very low rates, in the expectation that additional traffic would ultimately provide a compensating profit, and governments have on many occasions taken a hand in transferring populations to specific locations. The results in the latter case have not ordinarily been impressive, considering the high cost involved.[5] Resettlement projects, in which public authorities assume responsibility for the initial selection and the continued success of a new location, must be regarded as much more controversial in nature than any of the other measures so far discussed.

16·4   Removal of Trade Barriers

A logical complement to the policy of fostering mobility of labor and capital is that of clearing away artificial barriers to trade. The fullest measure of competition and cooperation among areas, with allocation of activities according to relative efficiency, calls for the reduction of transfer costs to a minimum. This is not to say that transport or communication as such should be sub-

---

[5] *Cf.* Carter Goodrich and others, "Migration and Economic Opportunity," Chap. XI, University of Pennsylvania Press, Philadelphia, 1936, for a critique of resettlement policies in the United States. *Ibid.*, Chap. X, discusses the experience of Great Britain, Germany and Russia in migration control.

sidized, though some have argued that this is desirable for passenger transport at least.[6] The policy here in question involves removing barriers that *unnecessarily* increase the costs or difficulties of transfer and thus deprive us of the full benefits of geographic specialization.

Much can be done toward removing hindrances to trade by encouraging the standardization of goods, the standardization of local requirements that transport agencies must meet, and the integration of transport and communication systems. More positive actions include intervention by the central government to prevent local authorities from imposing discriminatory taxes, requirements, purchase preferences, etc., the real purpose of which is to protect influential local business interests from competition.[7]

Finally, the policy of maximum flexibility may logically seek to maintain competition by outlawing certain monopolistic restraints that tend to freeze the locational pattern. It was mentioned in Chap. 4 that basing-point systems of pricing can retard shifts in an industry if the creation of new basing points is restrained. Other systems of discriminatory pricing also may threaten the prompt competitive adjustment that the policy of maximum flexibility assumes to be the most wholesome regulator of locations. Considerable active intervention is thus indicated, and in some cases, *e.g.*, electric power, the entry of government into actual production is defended on the principle that the industry needs

[6] The structure of postal rates gives in effect a subsidy to long-distance communication, apart from any over-all subsidy involved in operating the postal system at a deficit. Schemes for the "postalization" of freight and passenger rates on common carriers are advanced from time to time.

[7] *Cf.* Section 12·1. The Constitution of the United States, as thus far interpreted by the Supreme Court, does not appear to give the Federal government enough authority to preserve free interstate commerce in practice. During the recent war, the prevailing state of full employment and the obvious national need for unimpeded production brought a voluntary suspension of many such restrictions; with the return of peace, however, they promptly began to return.

On Federal powers and the extent to which they have been exercised, see F. E. Melder, "State and Local Barriers to Interstate Commerce in the United States: A Study in Economic Sectionalism," University of Maine Studies, Second Series, No. 43, Orono, Maine, November, 1937; Board of Investigation and Research, "Interstate Trade Barriers Affecting Motor-vehicle Transportation," 79th Congress, 1st Session, Senate Document No. 81.

a competitive "yardstick" of costs to prevent extortionate rates and consequent restriction of regional development.[8]

16·5   Limitations of the Policy of Flexibility

The policy of promoting flexibility of adjustment is by no means always so simple to apply or even to visualize as its basic premises would seem to indicate. The remainder of this chapter will consider some of the practical problems it must meet in certain situations.

Flexibility, it might be said, is secured by the removal of obstacles to mobility. In many cases, however, the obstacles can be "removed" only in the sense that the costs of an adjustment are transferred to other parties. For instance, if there is an interregional difference in real wages but migration fails to take place because the costs of moving outweigh the prospective gain to the individual, the government can defray part of those costs and thus induce people to move. The taxpayers have to foot the bill; they may argue that the total social benefits of the migration did not really justify its costs. Clearly, the encouragement of mobility should not go so far as to provide all potential migrants with free transportation for themselves and their families and possessions. A judicious policy of "lubrication" cannot disregard the cost of the grease.

The same difficulty arises when the cost involved is not expressed in money. A migration toward higher real-wage areas may fail to occur merely because of the attachment people feel toward their old homes and associations. The real cost of the migration is the breaking of those ties, which can hardly be evaluated in money terms. However, the government might compensate individuals to their satisfaction by some kind of subsidy. This, again, would merely transfer the costs to the taxpayers rather than eliminating the costs.

---

[8] The multiple-purpose feature of many hydroelectric power developments also presents a case for public construction and operation, but unfortunately this same multiplicity of uses makes it extremely difficult to determine the costs of the electricity alone for "yardstick" purposes. This difficulty was mentioned in Section 15·6.

Still another example arises in connection with vocational training. The result of a training program is to increase inter-occupational and perhaps also geographic mobility and thus to bring about a more efficient and flexible adjustment of labor supply. Individual workers gain in increased earning power and opportunity, while society gains collectively from the greater over-all productivity of the better trained and more adaptable labor force. But against these gains must be set the costs of the training program itself. It is clear that some subsidy is good policy here—there is a public interest in a trained and mobile labor supply that cannot well be gauged in private accountings. But there is also clearly a limit. If the training program were indefinitely expanded in scope, a conflict would arise between the aim of maximum individual opportunity and adjustability on the one hand and the aim of maximum net total product (after deduction of the costs of the scheme) on the other. Probably it is justifiable to carry such schemes beyond the point of maximum net total product for the sake of increasing individual opportunity. The precise relative weight to be attached to the interests of the individual as against those of the public as a whole, however, is something that will vary according to the basic social philosophy of the government.

16·6 Should Population Pressure Be Relieved by Moving People Out or by Moving Jobs In?

An important type of practical problem in which the judicious application of a policy of flexibility is highly controversial is that of the relief of areas of population pressure.

The origin and characteristics of such problem areas have been discussed in Chap. 11. In all cases they offer poorer employment opportunities for their populations than surrounding areas do. The obvious "natural" adjustment of these differentials by emigration of the surplus population, it seems, cannot be relied upon. Population pressure is a persistent phenomenon and may easily go from bad to worse if poverty leads to rapid population increase and deterioration of the quality of the labor force. Clearly such situations call for some public action. But what kind?

Here rages a violent controversy, centering on the basic issue of whether it is better to bring "people to jobs" or "jobs to people." That is, either we can try to make people more mobile and facilitate their escape from areas of population pressure, or we can try to divert employment into such areas so as to reduce the need for emigration.

Either policy becomes debatable only when it involves subsidy or discrimination. There can be no legitimate criticism of strictly "lubricative" measures that merely increase the mobility of labor and capital and may result in quicker and better directed emigration as well as a more prompt discovery and exploitation of new uses for the unused or badly used resources of problem areas. It is logical to inform Southern farmers more fully about Northern job opportunities and at the same time to inform industrialists about new uses for Southern native materials and desirable Southern industrial sites.

The case for encouraging migration rests on the argument that low living standards in an area mark it as an uneconomic location for the number of people it has; the fact that better employment is available elsewhere shows that some of those people would be not only better off but more useful elsewhere and should move. Only their imperfect mobility prevents them from doing so.[9]

It is argued, then, that emigration is the sound way to take advantage of the superior productive possibilities of other regions. The only alternative means of relief, according to this view, entails wasteful and demoralizing subsidy and a permanent distortion of the economically desirable pattern of location. Proponents of the emigration policy can point out that the policy of "bringing jobs to people," if carried to its logical extreme, would

---

[9] Conceivably, of course, the imperfect mobility of capital might be at fault, but capital is so much more mobile than labor (particularly within one country) that this is highly improbable. It would be difficult to argue that the lower living standards of the South are due to higher interest rates in that region. Large concerns in particular, with national markets and connections, seem to show very little provincialism where profits are concerned.

eliminate all incentives to migration and allow the whole pattern of employment to be determined by the distribution of population as of the date the policy went into effect, plus subsequent natural increase.[10] It is evident that with the passage of time such a locational pattern would become more and more glaringly out of conformity with current technological requirements and would involve a greater and greater waste of social resources.

The proponents of "bringing jobs to people," on the other hand, can easily show that planned reductions of population through emigration present formidable difficulties. The evacuation of part of the producers of a region has an adverse "locational leverage" on other producers there, so that much more emigration may ultimately be needed in a given case than would appear at first sight.

This application of the "multiplier" principle may be clarified by a highly simplified example. Suppose we have a submarginal farming area populated by 1,000 farm families and 300 families making their livelihood in local trade and services. Let us further suppose that the average farm income in the area is only $900, as compared with $1,200 elsewhere, but that the trade-and-service families are enjoying incomes comparable to those outside.

In this situation it would certainly not be accurate to say that the average receipts of farmers in the area can be raised from $900 to the outside level of $1,200 by simply having a third of the farmers migrate. If that were true, it would imply that the remaining two-thirds could produce just as large an aggregate output as the whole original farm population. It seems more reasonable to suppose that a considerably larger proportion, say half, would have to emigrate in order to enable the rest, by enlarging

[10] "The old competition between districts for industries and population is to be replaced by Planning, and the aim of Planning is to be, not as we might reasonably expect, to redistribute the population on the best scientific principles, but to keep people where they were born. In this it seems to have a close resemblance to the Feudal System, but the uncritical acceptance of the distribution prevailing in 1929 or thereabouts as the ideal, suggests a sort of suddenly truncated belief in the merits of the Competitive System which brought that distribution into existence." Edwin Cannan, Review of Ministry of Labour Reports of Investigations into the Industrial Conditions in Certain Depressed Areas, *Economica*, February, 1935, p. 103.

their farms and perhaps withdrawing the worst land from cultivation altogether, to boost their annual receipts to $1,200 each. That would mean an emigration of 500 out of the original 1,000 farm households.

But the total farm income is now only $600,000 a year instead of the former $900,000. Since the local trade-and-service families are dependent on the farmers and on each other for their market, it is evident that some of them also will have to emigrate. Eventual equalization of incomes with those outside would entail the emigration of 500 of the 1,000 originally submarginal farm families, *plus about* 100 *of the* 300 *trade-and-service families who initially were all making normal returns.*

Nor is this all. The cumulative effect of migration is aggravated by its usual selectivity. If the most productive and enterprising people are the ones to go, the chances for the area to attain a normal level of income are diminished.[11] Finally, the relative rigidity of the costs of local public services has to be taken into account. If the total tax levy cannot be reduced in proportion to population, the per capita tax burden must rise, which makes an equalization of living standards still more difficult. Given time enough, of course, the level of local government expenditures can be scaled down. This proves to be a long-drawn-out process, however, when much of those expenditures goes for amortization and upkeep of fixed facilities; when the population remains scattered so that all the old roads, schools, etc., have to be maintained; and last but not least when there is a strong local vested interest in keeping political jobs in existence.[12]

Some further arguments against the emigration policy rest on social and political grounds. The breaking of local ties entails social and individual costs that are easily overlooked. This view decries any government interference with the right of the individual to live where he pleases.

[11] The validity of this argument against the emigration policy depends on whether a deliberately fostered emigration would be *more selective* or *less selective* than the emigration that occurs without encouragement. To the author it seems quite possible that a system of aids to migration could be worked out that would diminish the selectivity of migration and thus avoid this line of criticism.

[12] All these complications (and others) were illustrated in the cutover counties of the northern Lakes States after the passing of the lumber industry.

The legitimate implication is only that emigration may require substantial incentives but should not be compulsory.[13] The indicated line of argument does not establish any individual's right to remain in a submarginal location and still demand the same level of income that he might earn if he chose to migrate. The fact that some people are willing to make financial sacrifices in order to stay in familiar surroundings does not justify the government in subsidizing them at the expense of others unless we are to believe that provincialism and inertia are desirable qualities needing encouragement.

The real test of the desirability of subsidizing a movement of "jobs to people" is the same as that applied to "infant industry" arguments for a protective tariff: Can the subsidy be temporary? Sometimes there is a reasonable expectation that once certain obstacles are overcome, the region of population pressure can outgrow the need for subsidy and maintain its population at a level and a rate of progress comparable to those of other regions. The discussion of the process of regional industrialization in Chap. 11 indicated the existence of "thresholds" of development over which it may be sound policy to boost a region by temporary aid. In such cases temporary subsidy is justified.[14] None of the other arguments for "bringing jobs to people" that have been reviewed here provide any justification for maintaining population intact in such areas. At most they call for a moderation of the emigration policy.

This controversy has been reviewed at some length because the fumes of emotion and local self-interest pervading it usually obscure the fundamental arguments on both sides. The opponents of emigration, in particular, are often guilty of resting their case

---

[13] The enforced interregional equalization of minimum labor standards is a borderline case, against which this argument may have some relevance. If such equalization proceeds rapidly, it is likely to present many wage earners in the low-wage area with the alternatives of emigration or unemployment, whereas with less rapid equalization they would be faced with the gentler alternatives of emigration or low-wage employment. This point is made by J. V. Van Sickle, Regional Aspects of the Problem of Full Employment at Fair Wages, *Southern Economic Journal*, vol. XIII, No. 1, August, 1946, pp. 36–45.

[14] Strictly speaking, we ought also to require that the region should be able to repay the subsidy with interest once it is "standing on its own feet."

on exaggerated notions of the transplantability of industry [15] or the difficulties of migration [16] or on grounds that are simply not stated at all.[17]

SUMMARY

Individual self-interest and competition provide a basis for rational locational patterns, but the adjustments are not always so flexible as they should be. Public assistance can be justified when it enables firms to make a more knowledgeable selection of locations, when it increases the interoccupational and geographic mobility of labor, and when it removes unnecessary barriers to

[15] It is still a fairly common impression—unsupported by observation—that cheap electric power has made it profitable to establish almost any kind of factory in small towns in farm areas. The conclusion reached by the Study of Population Redistribution, after a careful survey of this question, is relevant here: ". . . it is much easier to move countryfolk to industry than to move industry to countryfolk. Man is a difficult 'baggage to be transported,' as Adam Smith long ago pointed out; his industry—it seems—is still more difficult." Goodrich and others, *op. cit.*, p. 666.

[16] This pessimistic view of migration is founded partly on the lack of success of resettlement programs to specific areas (discussed earlier in this chapter), and partly on the fact that these and other attempts to assist migration have been made largely in depression periods. As Section 14·3 indicated, positive direction of the shift of either industry or people is likely to work only in periods of reasonably high employment.

[17] For example, ". . . Southern poverty is rooted in the exceedingly low rewards going to the agricultural population, and . . . the road to parity must be via a reduction of population pressure on the agricultural resources of the South. This reduction can be realized through a massive migration of Southern rural folk from the South *or* through the provision of greatly increased nonfarm job opportunities within the South, particularly industrial opportunities, since commerce, finance, and the service industries are the handmaidens of industry and grow up parallel with industrial development, or through a combination of migration and industrialization. Planning for a more prosperous South requires that a decision be made as to the relative importance to be given to these two methods of adjustment. We must decide whether the surplus agricultural population of the South should be encouraged to seek nonfarm jobs outside the region or whether outside capital should be encouraged to come South to provide these jobs within the region.

"*To the writer it seems clear that the second alternative should be chosen.* Constructive planning for the South should give precedence to measures that encourage the bringing of jobs to men rather than men to jobs."

J. V. Van Sickle, Regional Aspects of the Problem of Full Employment at Fair Wages, *Southern Economic Journal*, vol. XIII, No. 1, August, 1946, p. 37. Italics in second paragraph supplied.

trade and competition. On these grounds the centralized compilation of market and other locational data for businessmen, the subsidized operation of employment offices and training schools, and action against trade and migration barriers raised by both governments and businessmen can all be defended. Subsidy to transport, communication, and migration, however, is justifiable only when special circumstances warrant. In any case the costs of promoting flexibility must be weighed against benefits secured.

In the relief of population pressure, policy may emphasize either emigration or the encouragement of employment in the affected area. Emigration may require considerable incentives and may have to be larger than would appear at first sight but appears less likely to involve permanent subsidy and the perpetuation of an unsound distribution of population and employment. Much depends on whether or not the selectivity of emigration can be reduced. Only in cases where the "infant industry" argument is valid can the encouragement of emigration be dispensed with and a temporary subsidy to industrial development in the area of population pressure be justified.

CHAPTER 17

Locational Stability and Balance

THIS CHAPTER discusses two concepts hot with controversy. "Locational stability" would appear self-explanatory, though in fact even its definition poses problems. The other concept, "balance," as applied to the economy of an area ordinarily connotes a "well-rounded," *i.e.*, diversified, combination of industries. Balanced local, regional, or national economies in this sense are rightly regarded as a foundation for locational stability, and for this reason the two concepts are discussed together in the present chapter. It will be found, however, that locational stability may be furthered by means other than balance; while balance likewise can serve other purposes in addition to those of locational stabilization.

17·1 The Concept of Locational Stability

The policies examined in the previous chapter seek to alleviate locational maladjustment by easing the processes of adaptation to change. An alternative attack on these same maladjustments is through reduction of the amount of locational change.

The basic thesis underlying policies of locational stabilization is that in the absence of a definite restraint, more locational change takes place than is socially desirable. This implies in turn that some of the real costs of locational change are likely not to be reflected in the accounting of the persons and firms who make the locational decisions. It is argued, for instance, that the movement of an enterprise away from a community (which would be decided on the basis of the costs and earning prospects of the enterprise involved) at the same time imposes burdens on the community as a whole in the form of unemployment, underutilization of public-service facilities, loss of retail trade, and so on. Were all these costs to be borne by the concern that made the shift, the shift might not appear profitable after all. In other words, such a locational change may at times be profitable from a private standpoint (and therefore occur) and yet be wasteful from a social standpoint.[1]

Locational stability can itself be interpreted in various senses. One may have in mind the locational stability of employment, in which case the implied ideal would be a *fixed geographic pattern of jobs.* Pursuit of such an objective would call for active support of employment in any area not keeping pace with the over-all national rate of growth. Such a complete "freezing" of the locational pattern is, of course, impractical, since it ignores the ultimate necessity of adjustment to primary changes in resources, techniques, or population distribution. A less rigid version of the policy would require merely that *no area should experience an absolute decrease in employment;* this would allow some areas to grow faster than others and thus leave some room for necessary alterations in the over-all pattern.

Even this latter policy, however, hardly constitutes locational stabilization in the most relevant sense. It is the need for migration of people, rather than the change in the distribution of jobs, that we are likely to want to minimize. In areas where population is failing to reproduce itself, a steadily declining number of jobs may still provide full employment, whereas in areas with rapid natural increase of population, a correspondingly rapid increase in employment opportunities must occur if all are to find work. Perhaps the most significant and useful sense of the concept of locational stability, then, is the *minimization of the need for migration*—which means minimizing spatial differentials in the percentage of unemployment and the rate of real wages by continuously adjusting the distribution of new jobs to the different rates of natural increase of population in different areas. One

---

[1] Sir William Beveridge states the point in no uncertain terms: "When, through decline of industry in a particular place, a third or two-thirds of its working population becomes simultaneously unemployed, to say that they must move in order to find employment is equivalent to destroying the community and wasting the social capital that it represents. To say that this must happen because, though demand for new industrial products is arising, businessmen prefer to place their works elsewhere, is to lose sense of proportion." "Full Employment in a Free Society," p. 169, W. W. Norton & Company, New York, 1945.

may note that full stability in this sense would generally call for a progressive shift of industry from urban to rural locations and from advanced to backward areas.

17·2 Stability and the Conservation of Resources

An important application of this policy has to do with the exploitation of natural resources, since resource development and exhaustion are among the principal types of change calling for fundamental locational adjustment. The rapid exploitation and exhaustion of a resource usually calls for a large initial movement of population into the area of exploitation, followed by a large reverse movement when exhaustion sets in.[2] Both of these adjustments, and particularly the latter, cause difficulties and great social wastes. Neither boom towns nor ghost towns are desirable.

Some exhaustible resources are irrecoverable, *i.e.*, unavoidably exhausted in the course of time, as, for example, minerals are; others are "sustainable" and can be made to yield indefinitely under proper management or rapidly exhausted by overuse. In this latter category come soils, forests, grass cover, and animal life. The pursuit of a policy of locational stabilization would call for the maintenance of the productive powers of sustainable resources and not too rapid an exploitation of the irrecoverables.

It will readily be seen that such a policy is merely the locational aspect of a general policy of conservation of resources. In fact, bringing locational considerations into the picture simply adds another argument for a policy of conservation: the avoidance of some of the locational maladjustments, stranded populations, and migrations that are likely to occur if the rate of exploitation of resources is left entirely in private hands.

17·3 Compensatory Stabilization

Another approach to stabilization is through the application of public controls to location in such a way as to counterbalance

---

[2] The discussion of problem areas in the United States in Chap. 11 and the accompanying maps (Figs. 11·1, 11·2, 11·3, and 11·4) brought out the importance of depletion of minerals, soils, and forests in this connection.

other forces that threaten change. For example, a producing area that is beginning to lose out in competition with other areas can be helped by subsidies, tax concessions, special transportation rates, preferences in allocation of government supply contracts, or government support in refinancing. All these methods have been used in various countries at one time or another. An earlier chapter has indicated how powerful are the tools with which governments can mold the locational pattern, and it is evidently conceivable that a thoroughgoing policy of compensatory stabilization could be carried so far as to eliminate all private incentive for migration.

Few would recommend such an extreme application. It would mean that the locational pattern would become less and less economically efficient in the light of inevitable changes in such basic locational factors as resource discovery and depletion, the natural increase of population, technological improvements, and economic relations with areas other than the one in which this remarkable policy was being applied. Moreover, the complete absence of migration would foster a provincialism ultimately dangerous to national progress.

However, if it be thought desirable to lessen the amount and frequency of the necessary adjustments, a systematic policy of partial or temporary compensation can be used and very generally is. Something can be said for temporary aid to stricken areas in order to cushion the shock and perhaps encourage a more orderly adjustment, but care has to be taken not to prolong such palliation into permanent subsidy, which removes the incentive for any adjustment at all. There is no virtue in the indefinite preservation of locational anachronisms.

17·4 Stability through Diversification

A third and more fundamental approach to locational stability involves the creation of "balanced" area economies in which necessary adjustments to change are relatively small and easy. Such economies have a kind of "built-in" over-all stability. This is such an important field of policy, involving so many other considerations in addition to stabilization, that its consideration will occupy the remainder of this chapter.

Diversification is the opposite of specialization and involves the presence of contrasting types of economic activity in the same general vicinity. The terms "specialization" and "diversification" pose a problem of definition, since there is no agreed measure of how "similar" or how "different" any two industries or occupations are. Only in some arbitrarily selected sense, then, are we able to say that one area shows a greater degree of diversification than another. There are as many possible measures of diversification as there are grounds for distinction among industries or definitions of an "area." [3]

One relatively precise and useful definition makes diversity identical with extent of self-sufficiency, i.e., the relation of the volume of an area's internal economic transactions to its total internal and external transactions. The corresponding measure of specialization is the ratio of external to total transactions for any area.[4] The discussion that follows will deal with diversifica-

[3] The same holds good for the opposite term specialization. One common way of measuring the degree of specialization of a city is to see what percentage of its total wage earners are employed in the largest single industry. Thus a city with 65 per cent of its wage earners in the cotton-textile industry would be called more specialized than a city with 55 per cent of its wage earners in the steel industry. However, the figures cited depend on the demarcation of industries. If we were to consider each branch of cotton textiles, e.g., spinning, as a separate industry and similarly to divide the steel industry, the percentages might be much lower. On the other hand, if we called "textiles" or "metals" a single industry, the percentages might be much higher. Moreover, the city proper may be strongly specialized in one industry but its suburbs devoted mainly to different industries, so that the metropolitan area as a whole would be relatively diversified. Thus this (or any other) measure of specialization varies with the delineation of the area.

[4] For some purposes it might be more convenient or desirable to relate external transactions to total income rather than total transactions. Still another applicable measure of specialization relates the production pattern of an area not to its consumption pattern but to the production pattern of some larger area of which it is a part. In this sense the degree of "specialization" of the state of Michigan, for example, could be measured by constructing percentage breakdowns of output (or employment) by industry for Michigan and for the United States and adding up the various differences between Michigan percentages and corresponding United States percentages, disregarding positive or negative signs. The size of the resulting coefficient depends, of course, on the arbitrary classification of industries used. This type of measure has been applied by P. Sargant Florence to British and American data; see, for example, National Resources Planning Board, "Industrial

tion in several different senses, which will be clear from the context.

Policies of diversification can operate on at least three distinguishable "area levels":

a. *National self-sufficiency*, or autarky, *i.e.*, making a national economy less dependent on international trade
b. *Regional self-sufficiency*, or "balanced regional development," *i.e.*, reducing the degree of economic specialization of the separate regions of a country
c. *Community diversification*, *i.e.*, reducing the degree of economic specialization of individual towns, cities, or metropolitan areas

A closely allied kind of policy is that of *moderation of the urban-rural contrast*, *i.e.*, suburbanizing the cities or the countryside or both so as to reduce the contrast between rural and urban areas as such.

Much of what has to be said about policies of diversification applies to more than one of the area levels of policy just indicated. For this reason, the discussion will not attempt to take up each level separately in detail. It will be clear that some points apply primarily to individual cities or labor markets, others primarily to regions or whole countries, and others to urban as against rural territory in general.

17·5 Should Diversification Be Subsidized?

Justification for an active promotion of diversification must be based on the thesis that in the absence of policy there would be a bias toward excessive specialization; *i.e.*, there are benefits from diversification that are not fully reflected in the costs and incomes of those who make the controlling locational decisions in private business. There is, indeed, much evidence of advantages of diversi-

Location and National Resources," Chap. 5, Government Printing Office, Washington, 1943. On the basis of the coefficient just described, the most specialized states in the United States are Arkansas and Mississippi (agriculture) and the District of Columbia (government). The most specialized manufacturing state is Rhode Island. The least specialized states are Missouri, Indiana, Wisconsin, and Colorado. *Ibid.*, Table 6, p. 123.

fication of this "indirect" and public sort, which have to be safe-guarded by policy, whereas the advantages of specialization, ac-cruing in larger measure directly to the specializers, assert their influence without state encouragement.

As the discussion proceeds, it will appear that in some cases, *e.g.*, in the utilization of complementary labor groups, better dissemination of labor-market information and removal of some artificial barriers to mobility are enough to release private incen-tives to make a desirable adjustment. Such cases clearly call for nothing more than measures of "lubrication," such as those dis-cussed in the previous chapter. Other social advantages of diversi-fication, however, are not so easily translated into private costs and profits, and public authorities must be guided by their own evaluations in applying positive controls.

The aforementioned benefits of diversification, which will be taken up separately, are

- *a.* Stability of employment and income
  1. Through compensating seasonal fluctuations
  2. Through diminution of the probability of a general local collapse of employment
  3. Through easier replacement of declining industries by new ones
- *b.* Fuller use of complementary labor groups
- *c.* Fostering of more healthy political and social relations within and between areas of diversification

The grounds for active public encouragement of diversification will be set forth in some detail in this chapter primarily because a systematic statement is needed as a basis for better evaluation of specific policies. A word of warning, however, is in order. The danger is perhaps that public authorities will encourage diversifi-cation too much or for the wrong reasons rather than too little. The economies of geographic specialization, analyzed by econ-omists since the days of Adam Smith, are so much a part of the body of fundamental economic principles that, paradoxically or not, they may be forgotten by public administrators or even cast into disrepute by a supposed association with outmoded notions of perfect competition and the impeccability of private enterprise.

Diversification, on the other hand, enlists the support of a variety of interests, ranging from rural legislators and small-town realtors to a small lunatic fringe among sociologists and planners who idyllize country life and see no valid reason for cities or large-scale industry. In outlining what seem to be the real benefits of diversification, the following discussion seeks only to contribute to a more reasoned level of controversy.

17·6 Seasonal and Cyclical Stability

Diversification of industry in a community often means that the various chief industries reach their seasonal peaks of activity at different times of the year. This raises the possibility of a regular seasonal interchange of labor between occupations. In order for this to work, however, the different jobs must be similar enough to allow the same individual to perform both—which rules out occupations of high skill or with other special requirements. The attitude of employers and labor unions also has considerable effect on the feasibility of interindustry transfer. In view of these limitations it is not surprising that such seasonal labor interchange is of little significance in large industrial communities. It is found chiefly in small towns, where agricultural and small-scale industrial employment may complement each other,[5] and, of course, on a large scale in agriculture itself.

Even without interchange of labor, however, diversity of seasonal fluctuations in a community may offer various minor economies. It is easier for seasonally unemployed workers to piece out with the casual odd jobs sometimes called "disguised unemployment" if they are not all trying to do it at the same time of year. Then again, a diversity of seasonal fluctuations of production is likely to regularize the aggregate demand for local utility services through the year, thus making cheaper service possible.

The reader may recall that both of the selective promotion programs mentioned in Section 14·5 (Worcester, England, and Cincinnati) rated contribution to seasonal stability as an impor-

[5] For examples (nearly all relating to rural handicrafts) see Laurent Dechesne, "La Localisation des diverses productions," p. 132, Les Editions Comptables, Commerciales et Financières, Brussels, 1945.

tant criterion of the value of an industry to the community. Cincinnati, with a fairly stable present seasonal pattern of employment, simply wished to retain that advantage by not attracting seasonal industries; Worcester, with a regular winter letdown in employment, would prefer industries with an offsetting seasonal pattern.

Direct dovetailing of employment fluctuations is hardly applicable to the cyclical ups and down of business, for these changes are less predictable and occur almost simultaneously in most forms of employment. It is difficult indeed to find occupations that can be relied on to provide increased employment during periods of general economic depression. For this reason, diversification as such offers little in the way of cushioning the local impact of depression.

But although nearly all kinds of employment are likely to fall off during depression periods, some are much more sensitive than others. Construction, mining, and the production of durable goods (particularly industrial equipment) are subject to larger cyclical fluctuations than food processing, trade, consumer services, or the manufacture of nondurable consumer goods in general.[6] It follows that a community specializing in one of the more vulnerable lines of production, say machine tools, can hedge against depression by diversification involving the introduction of more stable lines. On the other hand, a community already specializing in a cyclically stable line of production, say breakfast cereals, would lose in stability by diversifying in the direction of durable-goods production. The character of products rather than the degree of diversification determines the impact of depression.

In any event, one community's gain in cyclical stability through a changed distribution of industries is merely some other community's loss. Until the problem of maintaining national full employment is solved, there will be cyclically unstable industries which must find a home somewhere, no matter how unwelcome.

[6] For detailed measures of typical cyclical fluctuations of economic series, see A. F. Burns and W. C. Mitchell, "Measuring Business Cycles," National Bureau of Economic Research, New York, 1946.

17·7   Secular and Structural Changes

Secular and structural shifts of industry come as the result of resource exhaustion or development, population growth, technical progress in production or transportation, or institutional and political changes. Unlike seasonal or cyclical variations, they produce long-standing rather than temporary unemployment in a community. Diversification affords some insurance against total collapse of the economic life of an area, since the long-run changes affecting different types of industry are likely to work in different directions. The greater the variety of industries in the area the more remote is the possibility that all or a major part of the area's industries will hit the skids at the same time.

Not only does diversification lessen the probable impact of long-run change, but in many situations it makes for quicker recovery from such adverse changes as do occur. Diversified communities seem to provide a favorable setting for the development of new industries and for the transference of displaced labor and capital into new types of enterprise. Highly specialized production centers, on the other hand, afford no opportunity for local labor and business people (including the bankers) to see out of their rut. There is the danger of their imaginations becoming atrophied, so that they will be slow to see the possibilities of developing new substitute industries when things begin to go badly for the older industries in the community.[7]

17·8   Employment of Various Groups in the Labor Force

It has already been indicated that in many ways a policy of diversification may stabilize the location of jobs or ease the adjustment of labor supply to demand and thus give a closer approach to full employment.

But the "labor supply" is not homogeneous. It includes various more or less distinct groups of persons, and full employment in any local labor market cannot be realized unless there are jobs

---

[7] This and related points are well brought out in PEP, "Report on the Location of Industry in Great Britain," London, 1939.

appropriate for each of these categories in the right proportions. For example, too high a proportion of industries employing women will leave many of the men unemployed; too high a proportion of industries unable to use the old and the young will leave those age groups only partially employed; and too high a proportion of industries using unskilled labor will fail to utilize to best advantage the skilled and potentially skilled people of the community.[8]

Such maladjustments would be more frequent were it not for strong corrective incentives. If, for example, a community has too low a percentage of jobs for women, their wages will be especially low and those who are able will move away. The presence of the remaining low-wage surplus female labor will be an attraction for light industries which use largely women. So both the labor supply and the labor demand tend to adjust themselves toward a better balance.

Like many other "automatic" results of competition and self-interest, however, this tendency cannot be relied on as adequate. Specialization is often cumulative. As already indicated, one-industry communities may develop "blind spots" toward unfamiliar types of industry and think too exclusively in terms of their own specialized type.

There is room, then, for the systematic encouragement of balanced local labor demand by diversification, which here means specifically the grouping of industries employing different kinds of labor. One simple and direct means to this end is the publicizing of the surplus labor supply through public employment exchanges, which may lead to an influx of new businesses requiring that particular group.

17·9 Social and Political Aspects of Diversification

Diversification of industry has been advocated as a means of avoiding the narrowness of outlook that goes with specialization. Not only does diversification furnish a greater variety of local

---

[8] The two selective promotion programs mentioned in Section 14·5 illustrate this. Cincinnati wants more jobs for women, older workers, and Negroes; Worcester wants more jobs for women but already has plenty of work for young people.

occupational opportunities, but also it indirectly increases population mobility. The geographical adjustment of population to occupational opportunity may thus ultimately be improved in two ways: The need for migration is lessened, and the ease of response to this need, *i.e.*, mobility, is increased.

Three applications of this principle will be discussed: the urban-rural relation, the problems of "one-industry towns," and harmonious relations among the larger areas of regions and nations.

CITY AND COUNTRY. Diversification involving moderation of the urban-rural contrast is particularly significant from a broad social point of view. Many would support the idea that the most wholesome sort of settlement lies between the extremes of metropolis and farm, that a "mixed" environment providing contact with both may offer the individual many of the better features of each while avoiding the evils of urban rootlessness and rural provincialism.

One particularly apparent urban-rural contrast is in the rate of reproduction of population. In most countries, due to a complex of social factors not wholly understood, city populations fail to reproduce themselves, whereas rural areas provide a surplus. Part of this surplus is drained off to replenish the cities, but imperfect mobility prevents a complete equalization of living standards, so rural areas are relatively poor and primitive. A systematic policy of suburbanizing the cities and bringing some industry to the country towns should reduce the need for this migration and equalize living standards in two ways: immediately by providing more rural jobs and gradually by reducing the differential in reproduction rates.[9]

"ONE-INDUSTRY TOWNS." Political and social considerations are important when the single community is specialized to the extent of being mainly dependent on the operations of a single business firm (as are many centers of mining and heavy industry). Local

[9] In France a policy of encouraging the decentralization of industry and population is advocated as a way of stimulating the sagging birth rate, long a matter of national concern. *Cf.* Pierre Coutin, Les Répercussions de la localisation des industries sur la natalité, *Rapports et travaux sur la décongestion des centres industriels,* vol. II, pp. 93–107, Délégation Générale à l'Equipement National, Paris, 1944.

self-government operates under a heavy handicap, if at all, when a town is merely an adjunct of a single business.

In the past, firms thus dominating individual communities generally prized their isolation and strove, with some success, to keep out other enterprises that might challenge their monopoly of local industrial employment and control.[10] The methods available for such exclusion are manifold in a community where a single concern or group controls the desirable industrial sites and the policies of local utilities, financial institutions, and taxing authorities.

The spread of collective bargaining and the bearing of a large share of the onus of local depression distress, however, seem to be bringing a change of attitude, and the role of big frog in small pond is no longer quite so highly esteemed. It is realized that whenever a single organization employs a large proportion of the labor force of a community, it unavoidably assumes some responsibility for the local economic structure.

An additional consideration of importance is that communities heavily specialized in a single industry generally present a relatively restricted field for local initiative. The specialized industries that give rise to one-industry towns distribute to national markets, and the main interests of their managements are in every way national rather than local. Usually the ultimate controlling group is absentee, exercising its control from a major financial center, while even the local plant manager and his executives are "out-of-town people" who think of their futures as bound up with the corporation rather than with the particular community where they happen for the moment to be stationed.

The normal consequence of this absentee interest is a weakening of local civic pride and initiative and often a retarded development of those welfare and cultural activities which depend on this pride and initiative.[11]

[10] Such opposition to new industries is naturally greater when the prospective new industry employs the same sex, race, and skill grade of labor as the established one but offers higher wages, better working conditions, or greater scope to unions.

[11] No really comprehensive study of this point has been made, but the conclusions just stated are suggested by the results of a recent study of three "matched" pairs of cities by C. W. Mills and M. J. Ulmer. The cities in each pair were alike in general geographic location, size, distance from larger metropolitan centers, and

INTERREGIONAL HARMONY.[12] The political aspects of regional diversification are distinctly controversial. One view stresses the importance of economic homogeneity or "balanced regional development"; regional differences in economic outlook and preoccupation are seen as a prime cause of discord. A logical policy based on this viewpoint is regional diversification and, in particular, the interspersing of industry with agriculture, so as to make the interests of various regions more similar on matters of national concern. This policy may involve fostering of home industries by subsidies, trade barriers, and other protective controls.

A different view stresses the unifying influence of interregional trade and holds that close commercial interdependence is the key

percentages of Negro and foreign-born population, but in each pair one city was heavily specialized in a particular branch of production and its industry was mainly in large absentee-owned plants, while the other city in the pair was industrially diversified, with a high proportion of small and locally owned plants. A wide variety of indices of social welfare, cultural activity, and community spirit were worked out for the various cities (covering income distribution, quality of housing, home ownership, health and sanitation, public recreational and cultural facilities, education, and use of telephones and electricity). These statistical indices were supplemented by sample interviews. In practically every case the specialized, "big-business," absentee-ownership city of the pair made a notably worse showing than the diversified, "small-business," home-industry city, despite the fact that the average annual wages of industrial workers were a little higher in the former group. It was also noted that the cyclical stability of employment (as measured by an average of year-to-year percentage changes) was better in the diversified cities.

Some caution, of course, should be used in generalizing from the outcome of such a small sample of communities. One factor that may have biased the results to some extent in favor of the diversified cities is that their population growth had been much more gradual over the past generation or so. All three of the specialized cities had grown much more rapidly than their counterparts (one had multiplied its population fifteen times between 1890 and 1930, another twelve times). It is well known that mushroom growth outruns the development of welfare and cultural activities and sometimes health and utilities services and that it takes some time for a city to "grow up to its size" in these respects. All six of the cities slowed down to small or negative growth rates during the 1930's, however, with no substantial growth rate differences in that decade between the specialized and diversified cities. For further details see "Small Business and Civic Welfare: Report of the Smaller War Plants Corporation to the Special Committee to Study Problems of American Small Business," United States Senate, 79th Congress, 2d Session, Senate Document No. 135.

12 This section applies likewise to international relations. For "region," one may read "nation" throughout.

to political and social cohesion, quite apart from the immediate advantages in productive efficiency. The logical policy from this latter standpoint is the encouragement of a maximum of regional specialization by such means as subsidies to transportation and the removal of trade barriers.

Here are two formulas, then, for the attainment of political harmony and national unity: the formula of homogeneity or balanced regional development and the formula of economic interdependence. It is perhaps not generally appreciated that their implications for action lead in opposite directions and that actual public policy must often steer a compromise course.

One must distinguish, of course, between diversification per se and the process of industrialization of backward areas that was discussed in Chap. 11. Industrialization ordinarily enriches the areas involved and increases the absolute volume of their trade with previously industrialized areas, but it may be associated with either more specialization or more diversification. Thus the industrialization of the United States has been accompanied by a huge increase in the volume of our trade with the older industrial nations of Europe, and the industrialization of China will doubtless increase China's external trade manyfold. In neither case, however, is any change in the over-all degree of specialization (as measured by the ratio of external to total trade) necessarily involved. Diversification per se, as distinguished from industrialization, is not necessarily related to progress.

SUMMARY

Social waste involved in migration and other locational adjustments can be reduced by conservation measures or by using public controls to protect existing locations against rapid change. Diversification of industry generally offers fuller and more regular use of the resources of an area, while keeping its economy flexible for necessary locational adjustments. These and other possible benefits of diversification may justify some sacrifice of the economies of geographic specialization.

CHAPTER 18

National Security and Power

AMONG THE BASIC OBJECTIVES assumed for any national location policy is that of security. In a warlike world, to be sure, it may be difficult to draw a line between purely defensive measures and those involving power politics and aggression. It has been said that the best defense is a good offense. The real difference lies between a policy designed to protect the interests of all the inhabitants of a country and a policy designed to strengthen one ethnic or national group at the expense of other groups within the country and outside. The former can be called a policy of national security; the latter is perhaps best known as imperialistic exploitation.

18·1 *Vulnerable Locations and Location Patterns*

The influence of military considerations on location has shown an interesting historical evolution in response to changing techniques of warfare. When pirates roamed the Mediterranean, towns were built on the highest and rockiest hilltops available and surrounded by walls. Walled cities went out of style with the development of artillery, which made it possible to defend a city from separate forts.

As long as wars were fought almost entirely on land and water, locations near the frontiers were, of course, especially vulnerable, and some countries went to great lengths in the 1930's to establish "safe" industrial centers far away from frontiers.[1] The development of long-range bombing planes and guided missiles dur-

---

[1] "The creation of centers of heavy industry in the Urals and in the Kuznetsk area of Western Siberia are instances of the process of locating industry in accordance with strategy. In Yugoslavia the K.K.K. Triangle was selected as an industrial center, its only particular merit being that of remoteness from Italy. In Poland, also, there is a central industrial quadrilateral, situated with similar strategic factors in mind." PEP, "Report on the Location of Industry in Great Britain," p. 178, London, 1939.

ing the recent war, however, exposed the whole of all but the largest countries to destructive air attack and eliminated "safe areas" in small and medium-sized countries.

Atomic fission and biological warfare provide tools of destruction so compact that we must assume they could be carried to any part of the earth by very long-range aircraft, rockets, or even saboteurs. Since no part of the earth's surface is safe, only two kinds of location offer even partial protection: burial and dispersal. Both are enormously expensive.

Underground locations seem practicable only for a very small class of productive installations; they have already been used to some extent for key munitions plants as well as for storage of explosives, works of art, and other valuable and vulnerable objects. So far, sizable underground installations have utilized mine passages and to a very limited extent natural caverns. For new excavations, hillside terrain offers obvious advantages over flat country.

Unquestionably, certain critical factories and other installations will be put underground for protection in many countries in the near future. Where the space required is considerable, old mining areas are likely to provide the best sites, with secondary possibilities in regions where large caves are found, e.g., in limestone formations.

The dispersal of certain critical installations to reduce the risks of air attack was practiced to a considerable extent in Europe during the recent war.[2] It was limited not only by the costs and disadvantages of moving but by the alternative possibility of giving larger urban communities more comprehensive protection from air attack. There is no corresponding protection, however, against the newer weapons, and dispersal plans of a much more

[2] In addition to manufacturing plants, it has been estimated that at least 200,000 administrative and clerical workers in government and business were evacuated from London during the war. For a discussion of the pros and cons of permanent dispersal measures in England (written prior to the atomic bomb), see National Council of Social Service, "Dispersal," Oxford University Press, New York, 1944. For earlier discussions, including the interesting suggestion that *concentration* of essential facilities might make effective protection more feasible, see PEP, *op. cit.*, Chap. VII, and the "Report of the Royal Commission on the Distribution of the Industrial Population" (the "Barlow Report") Chap. VII, Cmd. 6153, His Majesty's Stationery Office, London, 1940.

far-reaching character have been proposed in this country and abroad.

One early plan of this nature involved the relocation of most urban structures of the United States in "ribbon developments" along the lines of a grid of transport and communication lines. This plan would reduce the maximum density of settlement so that even a bomb with a destruction radius of several miles could not seriously disrupt communications over a large area or destroy any considerable proportion of industrial capacity or housing. The estimated construction cost for this plan was of the order of 300 billion dollars, which is larger than our national debt, equal to one and a half year's current national income or comparable to the estimated total money cost of our participation in the recent war. This cost estimate does not include the permanent drain on our productive resources that would be occasioned by such an uneconomic location of industry and population. No one has even attempted to estimate the latter amount in terms of annual cost, but it might well be even larger than the amortization of the first costs themselves.

A less comprehensive program of dispersal, involving only the relocation of especially important types of industrial installations and provision of substitute foci of transport and administration, lies much more in the realm of possibility for the near future. Even this, of course, will involve considerable initial and permanent extra costs, both of transfer and of processing, and will promise only a diminution of the damage likely to be suffered in the event of attack.[3]

18·2 National and Regional Self-sufficiency for Defense

A second principle of strategic location is that of self-sufficiency in essential materials and branches of production.[4] Nationally,

---

[3] For the uninitiated at any rate, this subject is still almost wholly speculative. Suggestive discussion can be found in A. J. Coale, "The Problem of Reducing Vulnerability to Atomic Bombs," a memorandum prepared for the Social Science Research Council, New York, November, 1946 (processed). A summary appears under the same title in the *American Economic Review*, vol. XXXVII, No. 2, May, 1947, pp. 87–97, with discussion by L. N. Dembitz, pp. 109–110.

[4] A "shooting war" with modern atomic and biological weapons probably would not last long enough to make economic self-sufficiency as important as it has been

this means minimum dependence on any external trade that is subject to interruption and emphasis on the use of domestic or protected sources of materials. Fewer imports mean fewer exports, and the self-sufficient country is thus drawn in upon itself geographically, with port and frontier cities playing a smaller role than they would in the absence of an autarkic policy. Such a pattern is also well suited to the principle of avoiding exposed locations for essential industries, which still has some limited military relevance.

For maximum security the principle of self-sufficiency should be carried beyond the national level to the regional level. Just as ships may be saved from sinking by dividing the hull into watertight compartments, so a country may reduce the risk of a knockout defeat by regionally compartmentalizing the essential industries in such a way that no one region is indispensable to the rest.

Complete regional self-sufficiency would call for such sacrifice of the economies of specialization as to be out of the question in most countries, but a partial regional independence can sometimes be arranged without inordinate loss of efficiency. If the production units installed in some regions to fill out the compartmentalization scheme are at a great competitive handicap and would require continual subsidy, it may be cheaper to hold them in reserve in peacetime while production is concentrated in the lower cost areas.

Regional self-sufficiency reduces at the same time the risks of interruption of the flow of materials, intermediate products, and finished products. Still further insurance against this risk can be provided by locational integration, *i.e.*, by grouping the various related steps of a complex process. Within each region, for instance, the production of airplanes may be carried on in a relatively compact area, with aluminum plants, parts plants, and assembly all close together.

Obviously, this is not always possible, and too extreme a cluster would be undesirable from the strategic point of view as well. Security calls for small detached production units when there is

---

in wars to date. We must, however, reckon with the possibility that these weapons of mass destruction will be effectively outlawed or that there will be periods of economic warfare of various degrees, in which self-sufficiency will count.

danger of air attack. An easier way of ensuring uninterrupted transportation between plants is to locate the plants in such a way that at least two alternative routes of transport are available for each haul.

18·3 *Imperialistic Exploitation and Locational Policy*

The foregoing principles are basic to the policies followed by a nation in its own defense. An aggressive policy of imperialistic exploitation, on the other hand, which seeks not so much the safety of an area as the enrichment of a particular group, rests on somewhat different principles. These are best illustrated by reference to the late unlamented German plans for a "New Order" in Europe, some of which were already in effect when their basis collapsed in 1944 and 1945.

Imperialistic exploitation calls for a much higher degree of centralization of control than mere security does, since the objective is to drain off from the subject territories all they can produce over and above a subsistence minimum. Control of most of continental Europe's important industrial plants and financial institutions passed early to Berlin as a part of the imperialistic scheme for a coordinated economy run by and for the ruling group. The same plan called likewise for a far-reaching standardization of industrial methods and an integrated financial system.

The imperialistic economy likewise follows the principle of minimum dependence upon trade with the outside world and strives to attain a balance of production and consumption through seizure of complementary production areas as new "colonies" or through the utilization of domestic ersatz materials. As early as 1938 German manufacturers were forbidden to import certain materials, not so much because of shortage of foreign exchange as in order to force them to develop substitutes.

When only national security is at stake, the self-sufficiency principle applies, as we have seen, regionally as well as nationally. But imperialistic exploitation logically goes in for extreme regional specialization within its sphere of control. Its essential aim is the protection and enrichment not of the whole area but of just a part—in Germany's case, the Reich proper. Consequently, the subject territories cannot be trusted with the industries essential to the war economy, and the last thing that is wanted is to allow them to attain any semblance of regional balance or self-sufficiency. To as great an extent as is technically possible, the basic industries—including especially the assembly of war equipment—are located in the home area of the ruling group.

The Nazis' ultimate plan contemplated leaving the countries outside Germany and Bohemia-Moravia practically devoid of heavy industry. During the war, of course, while the existing capacity was needed for military purposes, plants outside Germany were kept in operation, but most of them were tied into German control groups so that they could be treated as marginal plants and closed down as soon as the war was won. A considerable amount of machinery and skilled labor was shipped to Germany from the occupied countries, and the program provided for restricting higher education and training opportunities to Germans, leaving the subject peoples relatively devoid of leaders, executives, and skilled labor.

There is thus a far-reaching contrast between the regional industrial pattern dictated by considerations of national defense and that dictated by imperialistic exploitation. The former exhibits a considerable measure of regional independence and industrial self-sufficiency; the latter comprises a central highly industrialized core inhabited by the elect, surrounded by enslaved "colonies" devoted primarily to agriculture and handicrafts, and systematically prevented from developing industrial skill, leadership, or diversity.

The discussion above has been based on the premise of a warlike world in which some nations practice the enslavement of weaker peoples and all nations must plan for defense. It is earnestly to be hoped that the premise will turn out to be wrong and the discussion irrelevant.

A more constructive line of discussion—which, however, would require another book to pursue it—is the relation of locational policy to the improvement of international relations and thus to world security and prosperity. It is possible here only to indicate that this problem is essentially the same as that of domestic locational policy within any one country and is made difficult primarily by the fact that we have not yet developed enough international sovereignty to cope with it. The tools are waiting for the hand to wield them.

SUMMARY

Even partial defense against modern weapons calls for expensive dispersal of industry and population and for burial of critical installations. At the same time, any prolonged war (military or economic) requires maximum self-sufficiency within any area or region subject to isolation.

Imperialistic exploitation of tributary territories entails a deliberate intensification of internal interregional specialization, with advanced industrial development concentrated in the master region. This is illustrated by the Nazi plans for economic administration of Europe.

International harmony and cooperation will require authority to apply some of the same basic locational policies as are appropriate domestically.

Appendix

EXPLANATION OF FIGURE 3·9

This map is designed to illustrate the principal variations of orientation in response to transfer route layout. It represents an imaginary network of routes, comprising all the lines in the figure. Along these routes a plant or plants will be located, to serve markets that may be anywhere on the network. The plant uses two materials: wood, which is obtained from Woodville, and coal, obtained from Coalville. Ignoring long-haul economies in transfer, let us say the relative transfer costs per mile for appropriate amounts of wood, coal, and the product stand in the ratio of 2:3:4. The attractions toward Woodville, Coalville, and the market respectively are therefore in this 2:3:4 ratio.

Under these conditions there is no unique optimum plant location nor even a unique type of orientation. A number of possible orientations can occur, depending on the sequence of the materials sources and market on the route system. Since the sources are here given, it will suffice to see what happens to the point of minimum transfer cost as the market is assumed to be at one point or another on the system.

OPTIMUM PRODUCTION LOCATION AT WOODVILLE. For any or all markets between Woodville and Charleston,[1] including the branch lines from Woodville and Sexton Junction, the best production location is Woodville. If the plant were to be located instead somewhere on the stretch just described, both materials would have to be brought in from Woodville. Under the conditions assumed, it is cheaper to carry the product a given distance than to carry both materials that distance. A net saving in transfer cost would result in that case from moving the plant back to Woodville. To locate east of Woodville, on the other hand, would entail extra ton-mileage on wood and the product, which could be reduced by moving the plant back to Woodville. This saving would more than compensate for the extra ton-mileage on coal.

OPTIMUM PRODUCTION LOCATION AT COALVILLE. On the branch line serving Coalville, markets beyond Coalville can best be served by a plant at Coalville. Putting the plant farther east would entail extra haulage of both materials; putting the plant farther west would entail extra haulage of coal and product.

OPTIMUM PRODUCTION LOCATION AT A JUNCTION POINT. By reasoning analogous to that followed in the two previous cases, it will be seen that

---

[1] Charleston is located just halfway around the loop from Coalville Junction; *i.e.*, the rate from Coalville Junction to Charleston is the same by either route.

301

each of three junctions commands a market territory of its own, *i.e.*, each is the best production point for markets in a certain stretch of line. Avery Junction and Dowd Junction are best for serving markets anywhere on the branch lines that emanate from them. Coalville Junction commands the branch to the west (but not that going to Coalville) and in addition all the main-line and branch-line territory between Coalville Junction and Williamstown.[2]

OPTIMUM PRODUCTION LOCATION AT THE MARKET. On the route between Woodville and Coalville, transfer costs will be minimized if production takes place at the market; if there are several markets in that stretch, there should theoretically be a plant at each. The basis for market orientation here is that the two materials are coming from opposite directions; their locational pulls offset each other sufficiently so that the attraction of market is the decisive factor.

The territory between Charleston and Williamstown presents a more complicated picture, depending on the relations between the three forces of attraction involved and between the distances Woodville–Coalville Junction and Woodville-Charleston. (The distances Charleston-Williamstown and Coalville Junction–Williamstown are respectively equal to these, as noted before.) Under the conditions of the case in hand, both the Woodville and the Coalville Junction market areas will extend some distance into the stretch between Charleston and Williamstown but will not meet; there is a zone of market orientation between, where the two materials come in from opposite directions and are processed at each market. For markets on any branch line in this stretch, the best production point is at the junction where the branch leaves the main line. A plant at Dowd Junction would best serve all markets on the branch lines debouching from there.

It can be shown algebraically that a zone of market orientation on the stretch between Charleston and Williamstown will exist only if the distance Woodville–Coalville Junction is greater than:

$$\frac{2P(W + C - P)}{(W - C + P)(C - W + P)} \times [\text{Distance Woodville-Charleston}]$$

where W, C, and P are the relative locational forces of wood, coal, and product.

If the characteristic economies of long hauls were to be taken into account in the figure, the conclusions here reached would not be substantially modified. There would be some curtailment of the areas tributary to, *i.e.*, best served by, plants at Coalville Junction, Avery Junction, and Dowd Junction, since three hauls are involved when a plant at any of those points serves an out-of-town market, whereas only two hauls are involved when markets are served by local market-oriented plants or by a plant at either material source (Coalville or Woodville). Long-haul economies put a premium on minimizing the number of hauls, as terminal costs are thereby minimized.

[2] Williamstown is located just halfway around the loop from Woodville; *i.e.*, the rate from Woodville to Williamstown is the same by either route.

Select Bibliography

CANOYER, H. G.: "Selecting a Store Location," U. S. Bureau of Foreign and Domestic Commerce, Economic Series No. 56, Washington, 1945.

CLARK, SIR COLIN: "The Conditions of Economic Progress," Macmillan & Co., Ltd., London, 1940.

DEAN, W. H.: "The Theory of the Geographic Location of Economic Activities" (selections from Harvard doctoral dissertation), Edwards Bros., Inc., Ann Arbor, Mich., 1938 (processed).

DECHESNE, LAURENT: "La Localisation des diverses productions," Les Editions Comptables, Commerciales et Financières, Brussels, 1945.

DENNISON, S. R.: "The Location of Industry and the Depressed Areas," Oxford University Press, New York, 1939.

FOGARTY, M. P.: "Prospects of the Industrial Areas of Great Britain," Methuen & Co., Ltd., London, 1945.

GOODRICH, CARTER, and others: "Migration and Economic Opportunity" (Report of the Study of Population Redistribution), University of Pennsylvania Press, Philadelphia, 1936.

Great Britain: "Report of the Committee on Land Utilization in Rural Areas" (the "Scott Report"), Cmd. 6378, His Majesty's Stationery Office, London, 1942.

Great Britain: "Report of the Expert Committee on Compensation and Betterment" (the "Uthwatt Report"), Cmd. 6386, His Majesty's Stationery Office, London, 1942.

Great Britain: "Report of the Royal Commission on the Distribution of the Industrial Population" (the "Barlow Report"), Cmd. 6153, His Majesty's Stationery Office, London, 1940.

HOOVER, E. M.: "Location Theory and the Shoe and Leather Industries," Harvard Economic Studies, vol. LV, Harvard University Press, Cambridge, Mass., 1937.

ISARD, WALTER: Some Economic Implications of Atomic Energy, *Quarterly Journal of Economics,* vol. LXII, No. 2, February, 1948, pp. 202–228.

——: Transportation Development and Building Cycles, *Quarterly Journal of Economics,* vol. LVII, No. 1, November, 1942, pp. 90–112.

—— and CAROLINE ISARD: Economic Implications of Aircraft, *Quarterly Journal of Economics,* vol. LIX, No. 2, February, 1945, pp. 145–169.

League of Nations: "Industrialization and Foreign Trade," 1945.

LÖSCH, AUGUST: "Die räumliche Ordnung der Wirtschaft," Gustav Fischer Verlag, Jena, 1st ed., 1940 (available in microfilm from University Microfilms, Inc., Ann Arbor, Mich.); 2d ed., 1944; English translation published under title "The Economics of Location," Yale University Press, 1954.

MCKENZIE, R. D., and A. H. HAWLEY: "Human Ecology," The Ronald Press Company, New York (in preparation).

MCLAUGHLIN, G. E.: "Growth of American Manufacturing Areas," Bureau of Business Research Monograph No. 7, University of Pittsburgh, Pittsburgh, 1938.

MITCHELL, R. B., ed.: Building the Future City, Annals of the American Academy of Political and Social Science, vol. 242, November, 1945.

OGBURN, W. F.: "The Social Effects of Aviation," Houghton Mifflin Company, Boston, 1945.

OHLIN, BERTIL: "Interregional and International Trade," Harvard Economic Studies, vol. XXXIX, Harvard University Press, Cambridge, Mass., 1933.

PALANDER, TORD: "Beiträge zur Standortstheorie," Almqvist och Wiksells boktryckeri-a.-b., Uppsala, 1935.

Political and Economic Planning: "Report on the Location of Industry in Great Britain," London, 1939.

U. S. Bureau of the Census and U. S. Bureau of Agricultural Economics: "Changes in Distribution of Manufacturing Wage Earners, 1899–1939," Washington, 1942.

U. S. National Resources Committee: "Our Cities: Their Role in the National Economy," Government Printing Office, Washington, 1937.

——: "The Problems of a Changing Population," Government Printing Office, Washington, 1938.

——: "The Structure of the American Economy," Government Printing Office, Washington, 1939.

U. S. National Resources Planning Board: "Industrial Location and National Resources," Government Printing Office, Washington, 1943.

WEBER, ALFRED: "Ueber den Standort der Industrien," Part I, Reine Theorie des Standorts, Tübingen, 1909. Translated by C. J. Friedrich as "Alfred Weber's Theory of the Location of Industries," University of Chicago Press, Chicago, 1928.

Index

Catalog

If you are interested in a list of fine Paperback
books, covering a wide range of subjects
and interests, send your name and address,
requesting your free catalog, to:

McGraw-Hill Paperbacks
330 West 42nd Street
New York, New York 10036